PULL OUT: Men, Modern Life, and Mutiny
by Arvin Vohra

2018

Published and distributed by
Roland Media Distribution
www.RMDGlobal.net

Copyright © 2018 by Arvin Vohra

Edited by Chelsey M. Snyder

Cover Design by Ryan "ryanurz" Biore
Typesetting by Art Biro Network (info@artbiro.ba)

Published in the United States of America. All rights reserved. No part of this book may be reproduced in any manner whatsoever without the written permission of the Author, except in the case of brief quotations embodied in critical articles and reviews.

Library of Congress Control Number: 2018949373

ISBN: 978-1-7325034-0-3

ARVIN VOHRA

PULL OUT

MEN, MODERN LIFE, AND MUTINY

To the Phone.

CONTENTS

THE MYTH AND THE TRUTH 13

1. THE DISEMPOWERMENT OF MEN 21

Chapter 1:
Lessons of our Forefathers.................................. 23

Chapter 2:
Symptoms of Defeat 27

Chapter 3:
Power is the Power to Say No. 33

Chapter 4:
We're All "Cucks"... 39

Chapter 5:
Paternity Uncertainty 51

Chapter 6:
The Paternity Test Threat................................... 55

Chapter 7:
Modern Marriage: The Question of Virginity.............. 61

Chapter 8:
The False "Tradition" of Marriage 73

Chapter 9:
Rejecting False Monogamy 79

Chapter 10:
Classic vs. Romantic:
A Further Study of Denied Male Reality 89

Chapter 11:
The Cultural Rot of Third Wave Feminism. 97

Chapter 12:
Lower Standards for Women. 107

Chapter 13:
More on Safe Spaces. 113

Chapter 14:
The Classical Mindset and Child Support 119

Chapter 15:
The Culture War:
Rape Culture or Theft Culture? 125

Chapter 16:
How Theft Culture Defiles Us 131

Chapter 17:
Example of Pulling Out: Art. 141

Chapter 18:
Capitalism is force 151

Chapter 19:
Financial Slut 157

Chapter 20:
Financial Consent: His Money, His Choice 161

Chapter 21:
Silencing Opposition...165

Chapter 22:
Silencing Part 2:
Marcusian Techniques of Intellectual Debate..................173

2. THE POLITICAL IS PERSONAL............................177

Chapter 23:
Studying Cultures; Building A Subculture 179

Chapter 24:
Getting Started With Life....................................195

Chapter 25:
Pulling Out 201

Chapter 26:
Changing World Politics.....................................209

Chapter 27:
What We Can Learn From
the Gay Rights Movement 217

Chapter 28:
The Personal is the Political................................223

Chapter 29:
The Basics of Social Reality 231

Chapter 30:
Humor 235

Chapter 31:
The Fluidity of Reality......................................241

Chapter 32:
Creator Rights and Preemptive Action.......................255

Chapter 33:
Engineering vs. Behavioral Solutions 265

Chapter 34:
The Unspoken Demons:
Depression and Anxiety among Men 273

3. MEN AND MASCULINITY 283

Chapter 35:
Rites of Passage 285

Chapter 36:
Examples of Pulling Out:
Non College, Non Military Options 291

Chapter 37:
Chivalry and Warrior Culture 297

Chapter 38:
Classical Warrior Culture as
an Alternative to Middle Class Culture 301

Chapter 39:
Lessons from Warrior Culture 313

Chapter 40:
The Two Poles of the Masculine Experience:
Adam and Jesus 323

The Myth and The Truth

Men rule the world. Patriarchal norms control everything from language to romantic relationships. Men hold the reigns of political, economic, and personal power.

At least, that's what we're told.

We're told that men have unfair legal, social, and economic advantages. We're told that laws favor men, men are overpaid while women are underpaid, and relationships and marriages favor men over women.

We are told we need to eliminate our privileged prejudices, and work to accept other views of reality. We're told to find ways to compensate for our privilege and power, especially by feeling guilty and being silent.

The men who question those notions are quickly shouted down, mocked as Mens' Rights Activists, and called sexist bigots.

The men who disagree with any part of the third wave feminism belief system, or its siamese twin "social justice", are just as quickly silenced.

The myth is that men rule the world, that men control all aspects of social reality, that everything is built for men. But during the last several years, working with men and boys from all over the country, I have seen something completely different.

The theoretical, privileged, powerful, patriarchal male should feel free and unshackled, able to do what he wants, even able to command obedience from his significant other. But I've seen the opposite. Men who feel emotionally and psychologically trapped, as if forced into a mold that doesn't quite fit. Men who are henpecked into psychological submission by their wives or girlfriends, cornered into contracts that don't benefit them at all.

The privileged man would know that his home is his castle, that his home is his own dominion. But many men feel that their home is not theirs, that it's just some place they pay for. Objective reality supports this, with women controlling all aspects of the house, relegating men to basement "man caves".

The theoretical, privileged, powerful male should feel entitled to say whatever he wants, and expect to be heard. But the men I've spoken to on college campuses feel that they cannot express or even believe their own political and social views. Many are struggling to try to believe the views that they deeply consider false, just to fit in with the now dominant intellectual and social reality.

The theoretical, privileged male should expect a legal system that at least treats him reasonably, a medical system that cares for his well being, and an education system that at least warns him about likely problems. But the reality is that men are treated like garbage in family court. It's no secret that they rarely get custody of children, often have to fund the lifestyles of the women they are no longer married to, and generally lose the houses they paid for. The man living in some basement apartment while his ex wife lives in the expensive house he is still paying for has become a cliche.

But it gets much worse than that.

One common situation occurs when men divorce unfaithful wives after discovering that a child is not biologically theirs. To their utter shock, they learn that they still have to pay child support for someone else's child! Men in this situation often feel betrayed by the political and legal system that could create a law so outrageous. But they are just as angry at the doctors who never warned them about the importance of early paternity testing, or at the educational institutions that forced them through dozens of redundant safe sex seminars, but never bothered with a single warning about verifying paternity.

Not that long ago, when men were treated fairly by courts, men so defrauded could sue both the wife and the lover for financial damages. But today, they are required to financially support the products of fraud against them for 18 years. It would be like requiring a raped woman to bear the rapist's child, lose custody of that child to the rapist, and then pay child support for that child for 18 years. In our current society, that would never happen to a woman. But men are forced to pay for the products of crimes against them every day.

As boys, privileged young men should expect an education that caters to their natural preferences. But the reality is, as one book and study after another has argued, primary and secondary schools are failing boys. Boys are less able to fit into an educational system created by women and for women, that values diligence and obedience over intelligence and knowledge. Those who refuse to go along with the new, feminized education are drugged into submission with anti-adhd drugs.

This theoretical, privileged man should glory in a world that supposedly caters to his desires. But the reality is that men are feeling trapped and lost. They are seeking escape through alcohol, drugs, video games, pornography, and nihilism.

The myth is that social reality caters to men. The fact is that at personal, social, and political levels, men are being stifled or even attacked. Men are being forced into a reality that does not fit, that denies the validity of their basic perceptions.

Reality does not cater to men.

In 1984, the main character, Winston, boldly proclaims that, "Freedom is the freedom to say that two plus two is four." This freedom is not confined to mathematics, but to all parts of reality. Freedom is the freedom to call a spade a spade, a man a man, a woman a woman, and a bad decision a bad decision.

In most man-silencing college campuses, a person who says that someone with a penis and a Y chromosome is a man, not a woman, will be called a bigot and a transphobe. A man who suggests that women should not have kids that they cannot afford will be called a bigot, a poor-shamer, a sexist, and a racist. A man who indicates any preference for virginity in a spouse or girlfriend will be called a psychopath, a misogynist, and worse.

And yet, these are extremely common opinions among men. While not universal, they are common aspects of male reality, both now and for pretty much all of human history.

Many men will certainly loudly declare their support for laws that demand that male-to-female trans people be legally treated like women in all aspects of social life. They will be particularly vocal about this in the presence of young women of the "social justice" persuasion. They will insist that such a person is a woman, not a man.

But those men won't usually be as sexually interested in a male-to-female transgender as in a biological female. Their level of sexual interest in a transgender female is often around what is it for a man. Heterosexual men, at the level of sexual reality, generally consider any person with a Y chromosome and a penis to be a man, not a woman. Even among LGBT people, who might be more open to an alternate view of gender, only half would date someone who is trans, according to a May 2016 study by Match.com. Clearly, phenotypes matter.

It is also quite common for men to personally oppose welfare for women who keep having kids they cannot afford. The argument isn't terribly complex: it's moronic to have eight kids when you couldn't afford even one, and it's preposterous to expect taxpayers to pay for it. Men are told that as men, they have no right to even have opinions on the issue, although women are certainly allowed to have every kind of opinion about all male behaviors - especially anything that might financially or emotionally affect women.

And of course, many men often prefer and seek out virginity in a sexual partner. Economic analysis quickly shows that virginity has a clear value. In areas in which prostitution is common, the price for a virgin is about 100 times higher than the price for a non-virgin. Just a few decades ago, a non-virgin was considered unmarriageable in most parts of the west; in other words, the marital demand for a virgin was infinity times higher.

These are all real viewpoints, real beliefs that real men have. And these male views are not just being disagreed with; male reality is being attacked. Men are not told, "It is polite to call a man in a dress a woman." We are told that "Gender doesn't exist", or that there are several dozen different genders. Books like *The Purity Myth* insist that virginity significance is make believe; men are told to accept that alternate reality or face extreme social consequences. On college campuses and in many cities, women are not attempting to convince or persuade men. They are just shouting them down and insisting that obvious parts of reality are entirely imagined.

As male reality is silenced and negated, as men are being forced into a dysreality that they can only pretend to believe, they are feeling trapped, restricted, suffocated, and lost. Without a connection to a reality which they can believe to their core, they are untethered and often feel like shadows of themselves.

Emotionally, men are becoming stunted and restricted, to the point where their emotional range includes little more than anger, anxiety, and depression. I've lost count of the number of men who have told me that they no longer feel even romantic emotions, that they are just going through the motions of dating and even sex.

Some even describe subtle physical symptoms. Many have described a kind of tightness of the chest that they cannot explain the source of.

These are not men in prison or living on the streets. They are generally men considered quite successful. In fact, it's often those who are financially successful, or young men who are high academic achievers, that feel this most acutely.

This book is about freeing yourself from that dysreality with new tools and perspectives. Some of them come from ruthless applications of economics and psychology. Some come from close studies of techniques used by effective organizations and cultures. Some are methods I have developed or modified. Many are borrowed from movements that successfully changed social reality, including the gay rights and womens' rights movements.

I'm tempted to say something like, "This book isn't for the faint of heart." After all, the content is, by current standards, unsettling, cutthroat, and "inappropriate". The techniques demand work, and the perspectives require you to look at things in socially forbidden ways. But the fact is, those of us who need these ideas the most are those who have been psychologically beaten down into believing we are faint of heart, when the reality is that we are not.

This book is for every man.

THE DISEMPOWERMENT OF MEN

CHAPTER 1:

Lessons of our Forefathers

It has become common in the men's movement to seek to turn back the clock, to attempt to recreate the past. Some men believe that if we act the way men did in the past, we'll regain some lost greatness. That idea is insanely stupid.

During the revolutionary war, the British soldiers dressed in bright red and lined up in nice, orderly, parade style ranks. They got slaughtered by the guerilla tactics of the American revolutionaries. An empire at the height of its power got defeated by a randomly trained, ragtag group that could barely be classified as an army.

Can you imagine an army today using the tactics the British used back then? Can you imagine a modern general saying, "This is what the British did at the height of their empire; let's do that now!"

Obviously not. It's a tactic that everyone knows doesn't work, and everyone knows how to defeat.

What men did in the past didn't work. It was a strategy that failed then, against an inexperienced, restricted opponent. In the past, women faced every kind of obstacle, including lack of voting rights, social and legal barriers to working, and cultural barriers to speaking out. Despite all that, they overwhelmed the male culture at the time. Our current situation, of being silenced on campuses, of being forced to pay for the products of paternity fraud, of being denied access to our own children, of being psychologically beaten down in marriages, is the proof.

Part of that comes from the effectiveness of the strategies used against men. But most of it comes from the sheer ineffectiveness of the strategies used by men. The men of the past had a monopoly on voting, business, family power, and law. Despite those huge advantages, they still lost. That's how bad their strategy was. With every advantage imaginable, they still lost.

The men of the past are not role models. They are incompetent failures. They are historical laughingstocks from whom we can only learn what not to do.

Their failures did not come from bad luck. They came from bad thinking.

Instead of trying to adapt and innovate quickly, they clung to their decaying institutions. When they should have been innovating faster than their opponents, they instead sought to maintain increasingly meaningless legal and social systems.

The men of the past insisted on every kind of ignorance and every kind of dependency. Some decided that it was masculine to literally be dependent on others for food, and refused to learn how to survive on their own. Obviously, a man who can't prepare his own food is dependent, and in a relative position of negotiating weakness.

Even when they tried to rebel, they did so with laughable ineffectualness. For example, various rebellions against marriage have been going on for decades. The men who played with the ideas of those rebellions figured everything out...except any effective way to have and raise kids outside of marriage. Their rebellions never amounted to anything, because they didn't think them through. Sure, men found ways to enjoy some freedom in their 20s. But they never knew how they would have kids. So, when they did have kids, they had them on someone else's terms. To see what that looks like, feel free to visit family court, or talk to men whose ex wives use their kids as financial weapons against them. Or talk to men whose ex wives use other people's kids, products of paternity fraud, against them.

We do not need to repeat the mistakes of the men of the past, or use their failed strategies. We don't need to do what they did, because what they did failed, even when they had every possible advantage. If we use that now, we will just fail faster.

Instead, we need to do what they failed to do. We need to replace their blind acceptance of cultural norms with a brutal analysis and questioning. We need to replace their total lack of awareness with vigilance. We need to replace their constant desire for cultural approval with an indifference to the approval of others.

The "strategy" used by men of the past combined blind acceptance of social norms and a willful ignorance of economics and psychology with a dependency on social approval. They adopted a mentality of, at most, weak willed resistance to change. They clung desperately and blindly to the past, like people who haven't figured out their jobs have been made obsolete by technology.

Instead of clinging to the past, they should have fought for a better future. Instead of standing still, they should have forged ahead. Instead of looking backwards, they should have imagined a better future for us.

They were unwilling, or more likely unable, to challenge the institutions they clung to. (Just to be clear, they were unable because they were too small minded and stupid). While the movements that succeeded re-imagined every part of society from economics to sex, men clung to a fading past of disintegrating institutions.

We need to be better than they were. When they lost, they had every possible advantage. We don't have that now. Our strategy, our mindset, needs to be a thousand times more effective than anything they could have considered. We need to act with incisive intelligence and unshakeable discipline. Our weapons are our minds and our awareness, and those weapons must be sharpened. We need to think more deeply than they were willing to, challenge everything men of the past held sacred, and devise new strategies, rather than reminiscing about obsolete ones.

The next section looks at economics, one of the many areas in which men of the past failed, and how it shapes our culture. Men of the past supported every kind of ill-considered economic view, from mercantilism to New Deal welfarism. Of course, there were great economists in the past. Adam Smith was certainly one. But those men were the exceptions. Today, thanks to the incompetence, timidity, and myopia of men of the past, we now face cultural and economic defeat.

CHAPTER 2:

Symptoms of Defeat

The rising occurrences of men being silenced on college campuses, robbed in court, forced into small corners of houses they pay for, and stripped of their realities are not unrelated coincidences. They are symptoms of defeat.

They are not even particularly unusual symptoms of defeat. They are the most standard symptoms of defeat that exist.

Native Americans, after being defeated, were robbed of their land, forced onto small reservations, and stripped of their social reality. Their religion and language were gradually erased, and their kids were forced into school systems that didn't fit. They were subjected to wave after wave of missionary attempts to "fix" their culture, "fix" their religion, "fix" them. Their ways of being and thinking were almost entirely eliminated, and they were forced into molds that they believed were foreign, uncomfortable, and false.

Thousands of years ago, when the Aryan tribes conquered the Dravidian tribes in what we now call India, the same thing happened. The Dravidians were forced into a religion and caste system that treated them worse than dogs, denied their entire understanding of reality, and separated them from their prior way of life.

In these cases, and many like them, an initial military victory paved the way for cultural conquest. But in the case of men, there was no major military defeat. Instead, it began with a fundamental economic change: the loss of male ability to withhold economic resources. Men lost their economic right to say no.

Male power comes from economic power. That power is the power to either give or withhold economic resources. A man can provide for the mother of his offspring, and not provide for the mother of someone else's offspring. He can choose to whom he gives his resources, and whom he denies.

Let's look at how that has worked in marriage. If we strip away sentimentalism to reveal the underlying economic truth, for most of the last centuries, marriage has been an exchange of resources for sex and reproduction. To put it in the bluntest way possible, women have provided sex and reproduction, and men have provided resources.

Traditionally in the west, this was a total exchange. The man gave all of his resources to one woman and the offspring she produced, and the woman gave all of her sex and reproduction to one man. Women were expected to be virgins at marriage, and men were expected to provide for one woman, and the offspring they produced. A non-virgin was considered ruined and unmarriageable, and a man who couldn't provide was also considered unmarriageable. Men provided total resource fidelity, and women provided total sexual fidelity.

Note that this was an exchange of male resource fidelity for female sexual fidelity. It was not an exchange of sexual fidelity for sexual fidelity. For example, a man's having an affair was not considered grounds for divorce. However, if the wife had extramarital sex, it was definitely considered grounds for a divorce.

Most Christian cultures followed this type of monogamy. Other cultures found other methods that worked for them. Islam allowed a man to have up to four wives, as long as he could provide. If the man was not a fornicator (meaning, if he was a virgin, or had only had sex inside of a marriage), then it was only appropriate for him to marry virgins. He also had to provide for them equally. Again, it was an exchange of resources for sex and procreation.

In most cultures, though not all, the exchange was of resources for sex and procreation. Many men and women have attempted to argue that this is because men are inherently better at providing. In the modern era, this isn't really true, and I honestly doubt it was ever as true as many men would argue. It also doesn't really matter whether men are better at providing or not. What matters is that they are really bad at producing children.

In economics, we talk about absolute advantage and relative advantage. Suppose a lawyer can type 100 words a minute, and he also knows how to practice law. Suppose there is also a secretary who can type 40 words per minute.

The lawyer has an absolute advantage in typing and practicing law. He is better at both. However, he still might hire the secretary. While the secretary types slower than the lawyer, the lawyer's time is better spent on the more in-demand process of practicing law. He might make $1000/hour doing that. Even though the secretary types slower, it makes sense for the lawyer to pay the secretary $10/hour to do the typing.

In this situation, we say that the secretary has a relative advantage in typing. Even though he is slower at typing than the lawyer is, he is so much worse at law that it makes sense for him to dedicate his limited skills to typing.

He's a slower typer, but even so, he still spends his time typing.

Now let's consider that in the male-female marriage example. Suppose the woman is better at making money and also better at producing offspring. What should the man do?

Obviously, he should still focus on providing resources. It would make zero sense for him to focus on producing offspring. He can't do that.

Can he raise kids while the woman is the breadwinner? Sure. But that's just a different type of resource being provided. He's providing time, care, and effort. All the man can do is provide resources - money, time, skills, etc. The magic of procreation is out of his reach.

I know that the men of the past insisted that a man who raised kids was not a real man, but given that those men were defeated by a restricted opponent, I'm going to go ahead and ignore their views.

Because men can only provide resources, their only source of power is economic. Women have reproductive power, sexual power, and economic power. Men have only economic power.

Even if women made 100 times as much as men do on average, universally eliminating economic power would hurt men more. It would mean that they have no power sources at all left. Using the lawyer and secretary example, it would be as if typing robots were invented. They would replace the only skill the secretary had. The lawyer would still have other abilities; the secretary would be powerless.

Only women can bear children. In a market sense, the sexual demand for women is greater than the sexual demand for men. An average woman could find 100 willing male sex partners a day. An average man probably could not find 100 willing female sex partners a day.

Let's take a moment to define what power actually is, in the sense of economic, reproductive, or sexual power. As used here, power means:

- Having something that people want

- Having the ability to decide who gets it and doesn't get it.

Suppose that the second criteria, the ability to say yes or no, was removed. It would, at the very least, neutralize the power. More likely, it would turn it into a liability.

Look at the parallel for womens' sexual power. Suppose that women could not turn men down for sex. Then the last thing you would want to be is an attractive or fertile woman. You'd spend all day either evading rape or getting raped.

If economic power were similarly neutralized, having resources would be meaningless. The ability to create or provide resources would not give you any advantage if everyone could immediately take them from you. You'd spend all day either avoiding robbery, or just getting robbed.

The ability to say "yes" or "no" is fundamental to power. If you cannot say no, then you have been disempowered. Power is the power to say "no".

What would happen if only economic power was neutralized? Would it affect men and women equally? After all, in the modern world, both men and women have economic power.

The problem is that men have only economic power. If economic power is taken from everyone, then it leaves men with no power, and women with some power. The only scarce resources that men can possibly have power over are economic ones.

Some people have argued that men have reproductive power as well, since a woman can't really get pregnant without a man's sperm. But this ignores basic arithmetic. A woman can get pregnant and produce a child, at most, once every nine months. A man can theoretically impregnate several women a day. Sperm is nowhere near as scarce as entire pregnancy cycles. Women control the scarce resource.

Some have similarly argued that men can have sexual power as well. To some extent that's true. Very attractive men are often in demand. But let's look at the actual numbers.

Online dating has given us plenty of data on the subject. According to an October 2016 article from CNET, men on Tinder swipe right 46 percent of the time, while women swipe right only 14 percent of the time. Women's sexuality is over 3 times more in demand than men's.

Male power comes from economic power. Our current disempowerment comes from economic disempowerment. We have lost our economic ability to say "no".

CHAPTER 3:

Power is the Power to Say No.

Let me ask you this: can a man today choose to withhold or deny resources?

A divorced man cannot. Unless he has a strong prenuptial agreement, he will be forced to pay alimony. No matter what, he will be forced to pay child support. In fact, in many states, he will be forced to pay child support even if he has been cuckolded, and the child is not biologically his.

In recent years, men in Texas, Oklahoma, Michigan, and other states have been forced to pay tens of thousands in child support - after having DNA evidence prove that they weren't the father.

Some of these cases are truly bizarre. Gabriel Cornejo was accused by a long past ex girlfriend of being the father of her child. The DNA test showed that he wasn't. The state of Texas still declared that he owed $65,000 in back payment. Why? The law stated that he had to pay child support from the time of birth up to the point that the paternity test proved that he was not the father!

Carnell Alexander was ordered to pay $30,000 for a child that wasn't his, and that he didn't know about. Why? The mother put his name on a hospital form. He never knew about that, or about the child, until he was pulled over for some minor traffic stop. Suddenly, he was being arrested for failure to pay child support for a kid he had never known, and did not father. Even after DNA tests proved his innocence, he was still ordered to pay. Why? He didn't challenge the paternity within 3 years of the child's birth. Given that he had no reason to know about the child, that was an insane requirement.

In a 2015 issue of the Akron Law Review, Vanessa S. Browne-Barber listed her findings about legally disestablishing paternity in the U.S. The results are shocking. She writes:

"The majority of jurisdictions require disestablishment actions to be brought within a stipulated period of time. These statutory limitations range from a requirement to file a petition within three years of the birth of the child or, alternatively, within three years of the time that the presumptive or legal father knew or reasonably should have known that another man is the father of the child."

In other words, in many states, men only have 3 years from the birth of the child to sue for disestablishment. If you wait longer than that, you have to pay child support until age 18, even if you can prove that the child is not yours.

Remember all the times your teachers, counselors, doctors, and college advisors warned you about that? Neither do I. This rampant abuse of men's natural rights is ignored by the institutions that are supposed to protect you. Most men don't know that they have a limited time window.

Note that if a woman waits more than 3 years to tell you about the existence of a child, as happened with Carnell Alexander, then you might be totally screwed. You might literally be forced, by the state, to pay child support for a child that has nothing to do with you. If she writes your name on the hospital form, you might become financially responsible for a kid that has nothing to do with you.

According to Denver family law attorney Ron Litvak, who was interviewed by ABC news after a colorado father was also forced to pay for a child he discovered wasn't his, "It's very rare that a court will ever allow someone to terminate their parental rights unless someone else is willing to step into that role."

This isn't just the millions of men who are unknowingly paying for a child that is not theirs. These are situations in which the courts know that the child isn't the man's, and are forcing him to pay anyway. In state after state, cuckolded men are being forced to pay for the products of paternity fraud, even after that fraud has been determined. Instead of punishing the women who committed the fraud, they are punishing the men who are the victims. The men who were the victims of the crime are being punished by the state.

In the most backwards parts of the world, women are punished for being raped. Instead of punishing the rapists, those countries punish the victims.

Despite America's supposed enlightenment, our supposed civilized state, our role as the country that other countries should look to as an example, we are doing something disturbingly similar to men. The men who are getting defrauded are then being punished by the state. The state is punishing the victim, and then rewarding the fraud! The women who commit the fraud get monetarily rewarded. As far as I know, in backwards parts of the world that punish rape victims, the rapists don't then get a monetary reward from the victims.

But the fact is, even men that have absolutely nothing to do with a particular woman or child can still no longer choose to withhold resources. You have no choice in the matter. Through taxation, your money is going to pay for the care of children you had nothing to do with. It's not just food stamps and welfare. It's public schools. It's college subsidies.

As a man, your economic power has become increasingly meaningless. This is not because women can now work, and thus don't need a man. It's because even women who do not work can get your resources with ease.

In the current situation, the cuckolded man isn't really the one who has it the worst. He at least got some value from the adulteress. Maybe he got some sexual enjoyment or some companionship. Everyone else is far worse off than he is. The rest of us have to pay for her childcare, but get absolutely nothing in exchange. We're all getting tricked into paying for every woman. We cannot choose to withhold resources. The woman doesn't even need to bother sexually deceiving anyone. She doesn't have to date you and lie to you about her other men on the side. She just needs to have kids, and she gets your money.

In the current situation, you are being cuckolded by every woman with kids in America (excluding those that homeschool or use private school). You are being tricked into paying for her kids; she is cuckolding you effortlessly. She doesn't need to lift a finger to make it happen. She's getting your resources, and providing you with nothing.

One may argue that eliminating that ability to withhold resources affects women as well. And that's true. Economically productive women are losing the leverage that comes from the ability to grant or withhold resources. But they are still maintaining control over their sexual and reproductive value. They've lost some of their power, since they can no longer withhold resources. But they've kept some of their power, since they can still produce offspring. They still at least have some leverage.

Men, on the other hand, have lost the only kind of power they had: the ability to withhold or grant resources. Thus disarmed, men have been conquered in one area after another. In culture, in colleges, in schools, men have been beaten down, all negotiating power stripped away.

Today, quite a few men realize what has happened, but they feel fundamentally trapped, not just by law and culture, but by limited possibilities. They feel that the only possible arrangements are the exchange of resources for sex and reproduction, or the current situation, in which men give up resources in exchange for nothing.

But that's nowhere close to true. A casual glance at history and nature easily shows us alternatives. For example, you can have situations in which men provide zero resource fidelity, and women provide zero sexual fidelity. The bonobos monkeys are a classic example. These highly sexual monkeys have absolutely no concept of sexual fidelity. No male monkey has any reason to believe any particular child is his. Thus, male bonobos provide nothing for children at all; the females take care of that on their own. The male bonobos pursue casual sex, forage enough to feed themselves, and then just laze around all day.

You can have a proportional solution. Men differ vastly in their ability to provide resources. Some men are billionaires. Others barely make enough to get by. Women, on the other hand, don't differ as hugely in their ability to provide sexual fidelity.

Recognizing this, in many human cultures men could have as many women as they could support. For example, wealthy merchants might have a few wives; kings might have hundreds. This was described in the Bible, in various Eastern histories, and continues to this day in many parts of the world.

In this situation, each woman's sexual fidelity captures a certain amount of resources. Instead of all of a woman's sexual fidelity being exchanged for all of a man's resource fidelity, a woman's sexual fidelity has a market value. Men buy as many sexual fidelities as they can afford.

The worst situations are sex slavery, in which a women provides sexual fidelity in exchange for nothing, and manual slavery, in which a man provides resources in exchange for nothing.

The latter is what we have now. You're working several months of the year just to pay for other people's offspring. Half of your earnings are used to pay for every kind of childcare program for kids who are not yours. You've become accustomed to it. But it's obviously not the only way things can be.

Many of the above solutions have obvious issues. The current culture is highly indoctrinated against paternity testing, parents who live separately, and polygamy. Furthermore, men often prefer to know that a child is theirs, and to care for it, so a bonobos arrangement might not be ideal. But the fact is, there are many alternatives that could be fought for and won. Refusing to fight so we can continue to be slaves is the only definitively idiotic option.

CHAPTER 4:

We're All "Cucks"

Recently, many political conservatives have been using the word "cuck" to describe basically any male they don't like. Cuck is short for "cuckold", but in current slang it has completely lost its meaning. It reminds me of when "gay" was a common slang term for anything that the speaker disliked, even if that thing had nothing at all to do with homosexuality (e.g. "It's so gay that we have a math test right before spring break.")

The word "cuckold" comes from the behavior of the cuckoo bird. This bird lays its eggs in the nests of other birds. Those birds go through the effort of looking after the eggs, and even the cuckoo's offspring. They put in their labor to care for someone else's offspring. Interestingly, in the bird kingdom, female birds are the ones most often "cuckolded"!

Thus, cuckold refers to a man whose wife had been impregnated by someone else, who was then tricked into raising that man's offspring. Like the bird sitting on the cuckoo's eggs, the man is pouring in his labor to support someone else's genetic offspring.

Etymologically, this isn't about sex. The cuckoo bird does not have sex with the defrauded bird or its mate. Instead, the cuckoo tricks the bird into wasting resources on the cuckoo's offspring, rather than on its own offspring. Cuckoldry is about misdirecting your resources to support someone else's offspring rather than your own.

Today, anyone who unwillingly pays massive taxes to support the offspring of others is functionally being cuckolded.

The fact that he is aware that he is being cuckolded doesn't make it better. If anything, an aware cuckold is more pathetic than an unwitting one. The unwitting cuckold has been tricked, but hasn't accepted some perverse value system that makes him work long hours to support someone else's offspring. The knowing cuckold has not just been defrauded, but has also been forced to accept a value system that treats him like garbage.

Q: Wait, doesn't everyone benefit if we all support all children?

A: Not really. First, forcing you to pay for other people's children doesn't really benefit society economically. Instead, it encourages people who are neither financially nor psychologically ready to raise children to have them. Subsidizing bad decision making is bad public policy. If you subsidize corn, you'll get more corn. If you subsidize irresponsibility, you'll get more irresponsibility.

Past the public policy perspective, there is also the simple, blunt genetic fact. The more your kids have, and the less other people's kids have, the better it is for your genes. That's not public policy; that's not a political opinion; it's just basic genetics.

Earlier, I described the behavior of one of our genetic relatives, the bonobos monkeys. Since bonobos don't know if a child is theirs, they put zero effort into supporting any children. But we have other relatives that approach things differently. When a new gorilla defeats a previous alpha male, his first order of business is to kill the infants fathered by the previous alpha male. His goal is to focus resources on his offspring, not someone else's.

I certainly don't think we need to go that far! But we absolutely must understand that our genetic imperative is to provide for our own offspring, not for the offspring of others.

Breaking Free

How do men begin to break free? The process begins by understanding and accepting one critical fact: all public goods and services weaken economic power. If food, education, housing, and entertainment are available to everyone, why exchange sexual fidelity for resource fidelity? Why exchange anything at all for resource fidelity?

At a political level, economic power is increased by working to dismantle any and all welfare and public service programs. Today, half of your money (or more) is taken as taxes. Income taxes, property taxes, sales taxes are the blatant ones. But there are also excise and hidden taxes that only show up as higher prices for finished goods. You work half the year to pay for the welfare programs, ranging from food stamps to public schools, that diminish your own power.

Roosh Vazalideh, a writer who discusses methods of seducing women in various countries, crudely illustrates the way that welfarism diminishes male power even in terms of seduction. In his book *Don't Bang Denmark*, he writes "A Danish person has no idea what it feels like to not have medical care or free access to university education. They have no fear of becoming homeless or permanently jobless. The government's soothing hand will catch everyone as they fall," and that women don't need to attract men "because the government will take care of her and her cats, whether she is successful at dating or not."

Katie Baker, in an article entitled "Cockblocked By Redistribution: A Pick-up Artist in Denmark," responds to Roosh by essentially agreeing with his view that welfarism disempowers men. The only difference is that she considers that a good thing. She writes, "His gripes focus on benefits that ensure single women (and men) aren't in dire need and that coupling is decoupled from dependency...and that Danish women are less likely to be financially dependent on men and therefore feel less pressure to 'settle' or change their behavior."

It's not exactly true that Danish women aren't dependent on men. Their welfare state would crumble if men stopped playing along with it. It's that no individual woman gets any significant economic or survival advantage from any particular man. No individual man can withhold his resources from her. She has guaranteed access to any man's resources, with or without his consent.

Of course, this redistribution doesn't apply to procreation, so women in Denmark maintain plenty of negotiating power. Women's reproductive capacity is certainly not socially redistributed. Women maintain a major portion of their power. The men are left with none.

Male power has an inverse relationship with welfarism. More welfare means less male power. Less welfare means more male power.

As America drifts more and more towards welfarism, our power decreases. If we can shut down welfarism, our power returns to its natural level.

Instead of treating men as slaves for 6 months out of the year by stealing half their income, eliminating this welfarism restores dignity and increases negotiating power. If you can choose to withhold resources, you have more power than if you cannot.

At a personal level, men must recognize that the strategies of the past will no longer work. Male behavior in the past was based on control of, at the very least, the fruits of your own labor. Men no longer have that control. That means that any strategy developed during the time when men did have control over the fruits of their labor are now obsolete. All marriage and relationship approaches developed during that time are obsolete. All household management approaches developed during that time are now obsolete. All cultural approaches developed during that time are obsolete. We're operating with less power than what men of the past had when they were defeated. That means we need to fundamentally rethink how we approach life. The timid, genteel ways of the past won't work.

What Happens to Disempowered Men

Don't fall into the trap of thinking that male economic disempowerment is good for women. It does almost as much damage to women as it does to men.

A man who can withhold or give economic resources is saving the best part of himself for his partner(s). Yes, he is denying his resources to women with whom he is not involved, but he is also providing and caring for those with whom he is involved.

To make himself more desirable, he makes himself economically more effective. He becomes more industrious and innovative. He creates and provides.

That process doesn't just produce children that are cared for. It doesn't just produce men who embody creative excellence and ability. It produces buildings and bridges, farms and technology. It produces small innovations that accumulate, or huge paradigm shifts that reshape economies.

What happens to disempowered men, who can no longer choose to withhold resources?

A large portion of them turn to other methods of attracting mates, often through psychological viciousness and manipulation. This approach was seen in the pickup artist movement that has grown into the Red Pill movement.

The pickup artist movement focuses on using psychological tactics to seduce women. The movement produces constant innovations. Instead of men figuring out the best way to build skyscrapers or microchips, they pour their focus, time, and energy into techniques for seducing women. This is often done by sabotaging the confidence of the woman in question, having her seek approval, manipulating her trust, etc.

This has grown into the Red Pill movement, which takes its name from a scene in *The Matrix* in which the main character takes a red colored pill in order to leave a pretty illusion and face true reality.

Parts of the Red Pill movement seem to espouse psychological viciousness for its own sake. A generation of potential innovators and creators, people with clever minds and solid discipline, people who are willing to innovate and work hard, is pouring its energy into psychologically manipulating and abusing women. That is a direct consequence of disempowerment through welfarism. Those men cannot withhold resources; ability to provide no longer helps with their genetic imperative. They have turned to the only tool left to them: psychological abusiveness. Today, you literally have men taking courses on how to become sociopaths.

On the far opposite end of the spectrum, you have Incels. Incels stands for "Involuntary Celibacy." Incels are men in their late 20s, 30s, or 40s who have never had sex, although they certainly want to. When I first learned of this group, I expected to see what most people would expect. People without jobs or skills, undisciplined and lazy.

Instead, what I've seen is basically a trove of what most people would have considered husband material for most of human history. People with good jobs or businesses, strong work ethic, who want a woman to care for and dote on. On a purely aesthetic level, many are physically attractive, and, not surprisingly given their pent up drives, spend a decent amount of time working out. Many have become frustrated, obviously, turning to anger and dark humor.

Many of these men had single moms, and had third wave feminism hammered into their brains from an early age. They are often sweet but hapless. They lack the killer instinct to compete with Red Pillers.

These are men who chose a path of hard work, respect, and kindness. The result has been involuntary celibacy.

Young men today look at the two paths, one of becoming a psychological abuser who gets sex, and the other of being a compassionate provider who does not. Is it any surprise that millions are turning to psychological viciousness?

Welfarism disempowers men, and in doing so is turning more of them into increasingly vicious psychopaths. Explore the red pill groups on reddit and facebook to get a taste of what the movement is like - and to see its size.

What we have now is essentially a brain drain. Clever and creative men are being drained from useful fields, and are pouring their energy into psychological viciousness. Millions who could be designing better industry, tech, or agriculture, are instead designing better ways to manipulate and subvert women.

Women, ask yourself what kind of men do you want our society to create? Where do you want men to put their efforts? Do you want men to put their effort into creating and providing, or into abusing, manipulating, and subverting? Do you want men to innovate new ways to build cars and computers, or to innovate new ways to psychologically manipulate women?

Dismantling the entire welfare state, returning to men their natural right to give or withhold the resources they earn, will reverse this disease that has spread through this country.

The Nanny State and the Welfare State

Over the last decades, there has been an increasing political and cultural rejection of the "Nanny State." The "Nanny State" is government that protects us from ourselves. Laws against victimless crimes are generally considered Nanny State laws.

For decades, they were an accepted and unchallenged part of American Public Policy. But today, the Nanny State is losing popularity. More and more Americans have started to agree that if you do something to yourself, whether it's riding a motorcycle without a helmet, smoking marijuana, or snorting cocaine, it's no one's business but your own. Even though those are arguably foolish things to do, more and more of us are agreeing that it's not a place for government to step in.

This change has represented a major cultural shift. The transition from acceptance of a Nanny State to rejection of it has been a monumental achievement. It was, not too long ago, seen as a quixotic and impossible goal. But persistence is starting to pay off.

The opponents of the Nanny State spoke out, even when no one was willing to listen, or even when they were actively hated. In the 1980s, congressman Ron Paul spoke against the War on Drugs, and mostly got shouted down. But his willingness to speak out at that time allowed the anti Nanny State movement to grow and change laws.

Today, the Welfare State is as popular as the Nanny State was. Even among opponents of the Welfare State, it's common to see implicit acceptance of the Welfare State. I have seen the same people oppose generational welfare, and shortly thereafter talk about how they, their parents, and their grandparents all went to public schools! I have seen people oppose socialism with one breath, and oppose ending public schools in the next. American public schools are probably the largest welfare program in history. They have become so deeply ingrained in American culture that most middle class people use them. America today literally has middle class, and even upper class, Americans using welfare - often generationally.

Fighting the Welfare State isn't easy. But if we expect to regain the power that comes naturally from our work, it's the only option. The existence of the Welfare State is the single biggest enemy of men's natural rights and power. Ending it, especially ending its most popular parts, is the most important goal of our movement.

Historical Male Rejection of Marriage

In *The Hearts of Men*, Barbara Ehrenreich discusses the historical flight from marriage that took place during the 20th century. She indicates that even feminist writers like Charlotte Perkins Gilman, admitted that men who got married were paying "a high price for dubious and often inept domestic services". On the other hand, the maverick and legendary H.L. Menken indicated that a married man "views it as a great testimony to his prowess at amour to yield up his liberty, his property and his soul to the first woman who...turns her appraising eye on him."

Ehrenreich mentions a famous Playboy mock advertisement, that further comments on this situation:

―――・●・―――

TIRED OF THE RAT RACE?
FED UP WITH THE JOB ROUTINE?
Well then...how would you like to make...as much as
$50,000 working at Home in Your Spare Time?
No selling!
No commuting!
No time clocks to punch!

Yes, an Assured Lifetime Income can be yours now, in an easy, low-pressure, part time job that will permit you to spend most of each and every day as you please! - relaxing, watching TV playing cards, socializing with friends!

―――・●・―――

The advertisement is, of course, describing the role of housewife, and the men stupid enough to provide for it.

Now compare these mocked men to those of us forced to pay into the welfare state, paying for women we've never met, for kids we didn't father. If the married man is a dupe, what does that make us? They at least got the inept domestic servant in exchange for their economic productivity. We just pay into the welfare state, and get nothing other than disempowerment. If marriage is foolish, accepting the welfare state is downright insane. The married man mocked in the 20th century was paying too much for something. We're paying too much for nothing.

Hugh Hefner, founder of playboy, was a classic example of someone who simply refused to let social norms dictate to him what he was going to do. He lived in open and flagrant violation of them for most of his life. He showed us that it just didn't matter if society didn't like something. Just one man, refusing to play along, proved that there was more than one way to live life. His life itself was a profound act of social mutiny. His magazine, his clubs, his very existence mocked and de-legitimized the hegemony of monogamous marriage. He boldly spoke and argued for what was, at that time, essentially unthinkable.

Hef attacked not so much marriage itself, but rather the ideas underlying it. Today, we need to do the same to the welfare state. We need to say that if I'm not intimate with her, then I will not pay a cent for her. If it's not my kid, I will not pay a cent for it. We need to say, "The fruits of my labor are mine, to keep or give to those who have earned it by doing something for me, specifically. I may not make a lot of money, but what I make is mine. It should not be used to support women I don't know, and kids I didn't father."

Right now, that may feel scary even to think, and terrifying to say aloud. The first hundred times I said it, I was more than a little nervous. But I got used to it. You can too. And if enough of us get used to it, the value system that supports the welfare state will be called into question, and it will fall. And without that support, the welfare state itself will be a thing of the past, and you will have full and fair access to the economic value you create. You will regain the economic power to say no, and the natural rights, powers, and benefits that derive from it.

CHAPTER 5:

Paternity Uncertainty

For most of human existence, a man could never be 100% certain that a child was genetically his. The woman always knew, but the man didn't. (Genetic paternity testing is relatively recent, and is insufficiently used even now.)

This created "paternity uncertainty". Men face uncertainty about whether or not the kid they are pouring resources and labor into is actually theirs. Men don't want to waste their labor and economic resources on someone else's genetic material. They also don't want to fail to provide for their own genetic offspring.

Many theories that apply genetics to human social interactions have based major parts of their analyses on paternity uncertainty. They have argued, with good cause, that this uncertainty has shaped major parts of culture, including social norms and religion. For example, in most cultures and religions, women were severely punished for adultery (not men, just women). Virginity was strictly enforced, and a non-virgin woman was considered completely unmarriageable. Proof of virginity was expected on a wedding night. Furthermore, women were often kept completely isolated from all men for most of their lives to ensure that they couldn't even flirt with other men. And women were usually kept financially dependent on their fathers and then husbands, to ensure that the consequences of straying would be severe.

All of this attempts to mitigate the risk of a man caring for offspring that isn't his, and the marital structures that were created over the centuries reflected this.

Even today, our behavior is heavily influenced by paternity uncertainty. Romantic love helps reduce paternity risks. Living in the same house does too, for that matter. A relationship style of constant contact also reduces that risk. A man who rarely sees or talks to his wife has a higher risk of paternity fraud.

Embracing the new reality

When the fundamental assumption on which a strategy is based is no longer true, the strategy may need to be thrown out entirely and replaced with something radically different. Today, men need strategies that are radically different from those used by our great grandparents.

And the changes are not all bad for men. They are just different. It's true that men no longer can derive power from choosing to withhold or provide resources. But modern technology has erased the need for paternity uncertainty. Paternity testing is easy and affordable. That's a huge change. The fundamental challenge that males have faced for the entire history of the animal kingdom has been defeated.

In the past, all men faced paternity uncertainty. But today, we just have paternity stupidity instead. A man who fails to do a paternity test at birth has only himself to blame. Men who talk about the probability that their woman will cheat on them being nonexistent are missing the point. You wear a seatbelt every day. And yet, you probably have a car accident less than 0.01% of the time. Medical checkups routinely test you for many of unlikely diseases…just in case.

The actual probability of being cuckolded, is somewhere between 1 and 30 percent (different studies use vastly different methodologies). The risk is high enough. Many of those men were confident that the woman would never stray. They were all wrong.

Paternity testing is just as basic as having a prenup. Those who are about to be married all fundamentally believe that they will never get divorced. But then they look at the odds of divorce among people who never thought they would get divorced. Anyone with even a basic amount of sense gets a prenup. The same applies to a paternity test.

But the implications of eliminating paternity uncertainty go far, far beyond that. In the past, marriage, nuclear families, resource dependency, and even religion were used to ensure female sexual fidelity and reduce paternity uncertainty. But today, science now allows us to entirely eliminate paternity uncertainty. Men don't need to provide homes, depend on religious rules, or really do anything at all to handle paternity issues. We just need to get a cheap paternity test.

The implications are staggering. In the past, having kids with someone living in a different home was a risky proposition. Living together decreased the risk of paternity fraud. Living apart increased that risk.

But today, an intelligent male faces a zero percent risk of being defrauded. Science has saved us.

And it has started to open up new options for us. Men can have kids with women living in different houses without any paternity risk. Men can hire surrogates to have kids, thus procreating without traditional relationships. All of the old traditions are no longer necessary, we just have to have the courage to make new possibilities happen.

CHAPTER 6:

The Paternity Test Threat

Widespread paternity testing could change huge parts of reality. It eliminates a concern held since the invention of sexual reproduction in the animal kingdom, and certainly for all of human history. In the past, no man could know for certain that a child was genetically his. Men could, at most, try to increase the odds by being physically present, engaging in long-term relationships and support, etc. Men couldn't just wander the world freely, since that would make it far more likely that their supposed kids were not actually theirs.

Today, that is no longer the case. A simple, affordable, non-invasive test can prove whether a child is genetically yours or not. You no longer need to live with a shred of doubt.

This allows us to start rethinking the sexual relationships, financial support systems, and child-rearing systems we have, and what systems we actually want. We're not locked into the systems our forefathers created in order to reduce their own risk of paternity fraud.

Thanks to electricity, we don't need to hire lamplighters any more. We certainly can hire them, if we really want to. Gas lamps are still possible today. But they aren't necessary.

And thanks to paternity testing, we don't need to rely on the methods used in the past. We certainly can attempt to recreate what men did in the past. But we don't have to. We can make new rules, based on new science.

Highly welfarist countries have correctly recognized this as a threat to their way of life. At the most basic level, ubiquitous paternity testing would probably increase the rate of divorce by approximately the rate of cuckoldry. If 20 percent of kids are the result of paternity fraud, for example, we can expect that those marriages would end in immediate divorces.

As of this writing, France has banned at-will paternity testing. Men cannot simply get a paternity test whenever they want. Instead they either need consent from the mother, or a nearly impossible-to-get court order. In 2013, France issued only 1500 such court orders! According to International Biosciences, a DNA testing firm, French men who use foreign DNA laboratories to do paternity testing without French government approval could face a year in prison and a 15,000 Euro fine. Men who seek the truth can be fined and imprisoned.

One major justification for this pro-fraud law is that ubiquitous paternity testing would increase the rate of divorce. Yeah, no kidding. Heaven forbid that those who are defrauded get justice.

I believe that the proponents of this pro-fraud legislation, and similar ones being proposed in Germany, also realize the further implications of ubiquitous paternity testing. With ubiquitous paternity testing, many men won't need to bother with marriage at all. There's no reason to hang around to make sure that a given kid is yours. You can literally just check. Pay for and emotionally support your genetic offspring; don't bother with the others.

If nothing else, this pro-fraud legislation lets us know that welfarists understand the potential impact of ubiquitous paternity testing. Their rejection of basic science in favor of invented reality (French law states that the father is whoever the mother says it is, not, you know, the person who is scientifically the father) shows how seriously they take this threat. Their brazen attempt to destroy this core part of male reality, to violate basic male rights, lets us know that they don't care about us at all. They know they're operating against our best interests, and they're okay with it. In fact, they think it's better this way.

They are willing to attempt to deny not only male cultural reality, but also basic scientific, biological reality. They are willing to violate the natural right to the truth, in a pathetic attempt to try to preserve their false reality.

They have revealed two things. First, their social structures are houses of cards that will fall apart at a single touch from scientific truth. Second, they need us to play along. They need men to be willing to pretend that a non-biologically related child is somehow their own child. They need us to be willing to pay for kids that are not our own. They need us to continue to vote for their political representatives, vote for their welfarist laws that trap men in cycles of insane, unwarranted debt to the products of adultery. And they are willing to block access to the truth in order to keep us playing along with their nonsense.

Could it be that we hold more cards than they pretend we do?

The Abandonment of Institutions

Men of the past, for the most part, were unwilling or unable to stop trusting and respecting institutions. They maintained a dogged trust of political, scientific, legal, and medical systems, even as those systems gradually turned against them. The political institutions they trusted gradually erased their economic power by taking away the ability to say "no". Today, those political institutions make it impossible for us to deny anyone access to our resources. They disempower us - and charge us for the "service."

Medical, educational, and scientific institutions have been almost as bad. Men have trusted those institutions to provide guidance. They have sought protection and good advice, but gotten neither.

Women are encouraged to get pap smears every year, in order to decrease the risk of cervical cancer. They are reminded to do self tests and get mammograms. Many public awareness campaigns are funded by robbing you through taxation.

If you went to college, you probably got an earful about what is and is not date rape. But among those repetitive speeches, did anyone ever think to even point out the importance of a paternity test? Did your biology teacher? Did your genetics teacher?

They haven't let you down out of stupidity or forgetfulness. They are hiding that information on purpose. They think it's better for men to be defrauded than for mothers to accept the financial risks of their own unfaithful decisions.

In fact, the scientific community is currently wrestling with this issue. Large scale genetic mapping would be extremely beneficial for all people. It would help us predict genetic issues, and let us adjust accordingly. Genetic diseases can often be moderated if they are predicted in advance. If we know we have some risk factors for a particular disease, we can adjust behavior to reduce other risk factors. This process could literally save millions of lives.

But...doing so would reveal paternity. That would be really inconvenient for dishonest women. According to the Atlantic:

"The law of unintended consequences is about to catch up with the genetic-testing industry. Geneticists and physicians would like us all to have our DNA sequenced. That way we'll know about our genetic flaws, and this knowledge could let us take steps to prevent future health problems. But genetic tests can also identify the individuals from whom we got our DNA...The problem would not loom so large if non-paternity were rare."

They don't see paternity awareness as a benefit. They see it as a negative unintended consequence!

They don't see preventing men from being defrauded as good. They would rather see the defrauding continue.

The medical community does not care about men. Please don't give me the "Well, this is about money, not health" argument. Doctors constantly talk about how particular problems can make you lose wages, or cost a lot to handle, so take care of them early. But in the vital area of paternity, doctors are not your allies.

The scientific community has equally been beaten into submission by the interests of dishonest women. Since it might accidentally protect men financially, they are concerned about using testing that would literally save lives and protect health.

Doctors encourage STD testing, and rightly so. But their failure to encourage paternity testing is inexcusable.

If you are a doctor, scientist, or opinion leader, encourage men to get paternity testing. The specific time frame varies based on the local laws, but remind them that it must be done shortly after birth. Encourage them to do it while the mother is pregnant.

If you are planning to be a father, get a paternity test. Don't wait. The sooner you do it, the stronger your legal position. In most states, you only have a short window to challenge paternity. After that, you pay child support until the child is 18 (unless you intelligently signed away your rights beforehand, by signing a sperm donor contract after having sought legal advice).

If you are a man, understand that the social, medical, and scientific hierarchy has abandoned you. They see you as a problem or an afterthought. You cannot rely on them at all. They will sooner let millions of people die needlessly from genetic diseases than let you know if you've been defrauded. They will never remind you to protect yourself.

That means you must take responsibility into your own hands. You must accept that no one but you will help yourself. Schools, doctors, hospitals, The Ad Council - no one is here for you. They do not care about your values or your reality. To them, if you get cuckolded and defrauded, it's because you were asking for it, and the woman needed it.

If they will do that to you in something as clearly obvious as paternity fraud, what else will they do to you? Are these people you want to trust? Do you want to trust their institutions, or follow their expectations?

CHAPTER 7:

Modern Marriage: The Question of Virginity

What does it mean to have your reality erased? It means no longer being allowed to think what you actually think. It means no longer being able to feel what you actually feel. In the realm of politics, sex, and marriage, that's where many men find themselves.

As we've already seen, the viciousness that has become somewhat popular among many men's movement writers is not an indication of power; it is the desperation of a caged animal.

But what exactly is the cage? When I speak to men around the country, the cage seems to be not so much around their behavior, as around their mindset. Men actually have more behavioral freedom today than in the past. It's the mental cage that is so crushing. Many men have found that the second they express any thoughts, they are screamed into submission. Others feel as if, even internally, they are not allowed to think the thoughts that they actually believe.

One common complaint I've heard is something like, "You can't even make a dirty joke at the office anymore." That complaint, though common, is weird. I don't know of any office at any point in history in which dirty jokes were at all tolerated, with the possible exception of docks and lower end brothels. I believe "You can't tell a joke in the office anymore" is really a euphemism for, "You can't say what you think anymore."

This mental cage is a social one, assisted by legal force. Socially, male reality is denied and shouted down. At the same time, social, educational, and medical institutions are working to keep men uninformed, hapless, and entirely unprepared for the reality they will face. As if that weren't enough, laws and governments are also actively treating men like dogs.

In order to build a counter-strategy, men must first familiarize themselves with what is going on and how to handle it.

Let's start with the most taboo of modern sexual subjects: virginity. Today, a man who indicates any distaste for promiscuous women is shrieked at for being a "slut shamer". A man who indicates a preference for a partner with less sexual experience is seen as a sociopathic predator. A man who indicates a desire for a virginal wife is likely to make a third wave feminist's head explode.

Today, it is considered sociopathic to even indicate a preference for what was an absolute requirement for literally millenia. Virginity is discussed everywhere from the Old Testament to Downton Abbey. But today, it cannot even be considered.

If you want to understand what it looks like to have your reality erased: that's what it looks like.

The true preferences of men have not changed. For most of human history, most men cared about virginity; a few did not. It's no different today.

Today, however, most men are not able to admit their preferences publicly. Some cannot even admit their preferences to themselves.

And yet, in parts of the world in which the masks forced on us by social pressure fall away, the huge preference for virgins reasserts itself. In parts of the world in which prostitution is common, the price for virgins is about one hundred times higher than the price for non-virgins. In parts of Southeast Asia in which virginity is available for sale, it may cost a thousand dollars. A normal prostitute might cost ten dollars.

In the open market, the price is even more different. In 2016, an 18 year old model sold her virginity for 2 million pounds sterling through Cinderella Escorts. Since then, others have followed suit, often commanding similar prices.

Compare that to normal prostitutes. Even a very high end prostitute rarely costs more than a thousand dollars a night. In this case, virginity costs a thousand times more than sex.

In western societies of the past, the relative value differences were even larger. A woman who had had sex before marriage was considered entirely unmarriageable. In other words, the economic value of a virgin was essentially infinity times higher than that of a non-virgin. In many Eastern societies today, the same holds true. It would be either blind to economic reality, or incredibly dishonest, to pretend that virginity does not, in an authentic marketplace, command a higher value than non-virginity.

Even the most welfarist of the third wave feminists will agree to the importance and value of virginity, if you ask the right questions. They will agree that the first time is important, transformative, both in how the woman interacts with her partner and how she interacts with herself. They will readily admit that the first time affects how you interact sexually with the world, and how you see yourself sexually. Just as some baby birds will imprint on and follow whoever they see first, the first man a woman has sex with creates a powerful effect on her. This imprinting is not insignificant; it is major and impactful.

Why else do so many feminists oppose companies like Cinderella Escorts? If virginity doesn't matter, then what difference does it make? If virginity is unimportant, then women who can get men to pay $100k-$3M for their virginity are only gaining; they're losing nothing. But whether you look at it economically or psychologically, from the male perspective or from the female perspective, from a religious or atheistic perspective, it is impossible to deny one basic fact: virginity matters.

Many religious people believe that premarital sex is cheating on your future spouse. From that perspective, past sexual partners are significant for the same reasons that current sexual partners are. No matter how much you give up, you will never have all of her. You can be as faithful, dedicated, and monogamous as she wants, but she will never be able to be fully yours - no matter how much she might want to be.

Comedians often joke about this, since it is a common and universal issue. Chris Rock says:

"Guys, never ask a woman how many men she's slept with. 'Cause you don't wanna know. Just be happy you're fucking her now…. First of all, no matter what she say, it's too much for you! No matter what she say, she can go, 'Two,' you be like, "Two?! Two?! Two?! No, no, no, two?! Two?! I guess that's how you was raised!'"

Most men lack the verbal skills or social courage to say anything. They are told that they are afraid of experienced women, that any virginity preference is a sign of weakness. Obviously that only works if we pretend that "repulsed" and "afraid" are the same. Plenty of men are repulsed by a woman's sexual past. Afraid? Not so much.

Now let's objectively look at the current marital situation. Men are expected to give up more than men have ever given up. In addition to committing resources, they are now also providing sexual monogamy, time, and a much higher level of emotional support.

But what are they getting in exchange? Economically, they are getting 1/100th (or less) of what men got in the past.

Men who get married today are paying champagne prices for spoiled beer.

Opening the Rest of the Box

In my conversations with men around the country, I've heard the same phrase repeated: "Pandora's box has been opened."

In these conversations, men are referring to modern female sexual behavior. Women today, these men argue, face no economic or social repercussions from sexual promiscuity.

At a young age, women are more sexually in demand than men are. Young women have the option of a constant stream of sex with as many partners as they can handle. Some research suggests that she is literally incorporating some of the DNA from the semen of those sexual partners, soaking up the DNA like a sponge. It's a part of her, and some of it may be passed onto her offspring. As of this writing, the research is in the very early stages. The basic principle has been shown with fruit flies[1], and other research suggests it may hold true with humans[2].

The scientific jury is still out, as of this writing. But, most men aren't super excited about the potential mothers of their children having performed various combinations of oral, anal, and vaginal sex with large numbers of men.

For many women, Plan A is to engage in those sexual behaviors during their "high demand" years, and then, when they are no longer in high sexual demand (in their 30s), to settle down and get married. The market demand for a heavily used woman in her 30s is not really the same as the demand for a sexually unused woman in her late teens or early twenties. And so, at that point, she's ready to settle down, and expects some poor simp to give her complete sexual mo-

---

1) Time: *How Previous Sexual Partners Affect Offspring*

2) NIH: *Male microchimerism in women without sons: quantitative assessment and correlation with pregnancy history*

nogamy, financial support, and emotional support. Some men who want to have kids view this as their only option.

Many men's groups are futilely attempting to close Pandora's box, to somehow reverse the cultural trend. I say the opposite: let's open Pandora's box the rest of the way.

Right now it's half open. Women have realized they can engage in every kind of promiscuity, and that after all that, they'll still find someone to marry them once they are ready to "settle down". Many men aren't terribly thrilled at the concept, but they feel stuck. Men who want to have kids feel like they have no other option.

That is false, and is essentially making the same mistakes that men of the past did: clinging to the illusion of an institution, when the reality of that institution has entirely vanished. The reality of traditional marriage is gone. Traditional marriage is not about being 200th in line to have sex with someone who has quite possibly incorporated the DNA of dozens of men, and may well pass some of that to your offspring. What we have now is not traditional marriage.

So let's drop our preconceptions, let's stop clinging to institutions that have vanished in everything but name, and look at this situation economically and objectively.

In the open market, virginity matters. Virginity is valuable. Virginity costs a hundred times as much as sex.

In the open market, procreation also matters. Surrogates cost almost as much as virginity, albeit for different reasons. Virginity is expensive because of scarcity. Each woman can give the gift of virginity exactly one time.

Surrogacy is expensive because it takes a lot of work. Even though a person can be a surrogate many times, it takes a lot of work. It's 9 months of carrying a child, and then a challenging birthing process.

But sex, by itself, is just not that valuable. Sexual fidelity has some value, but if a woman has already been with a few dozen men, how valuable is her faithfulness now? If it's already been 100, are you really willing to sacrifice your freedom to prevent it from getting to 102? Really, what difference does it make? Are you willing to commit to sexual monogamy, put your finances at risk of divorce, child support, and legal fees, all for that?

Your genetic imperative is to survive and reproduce, not survive and have sex. Sure, sex is pleasurable, but so are massages with happy endings, pornography, masturbation, music, good food, and video games. If it's just the physical pleasure, you're dealing with a minor addiction.

More likely, it's not a purely physical pursuit, but a psychological and spiritual one. I get the excitement of the psychological pursuit. But that pursuit should end before it turns into the marital tedium of redundant sex with a woman whose sex no longer holds any market value, and who demands, in exchange, your sexual monogamy.

Spiritually - how spiritual can it be to be 90th in line? Or even 10th? Study the major religions of the world, and see how often they discuss virginal wives as opposed to the extreme opposite.

Guys will do all kinds of things out of desperation. In jail, they'll even have sex with each other. But you're not in a prison, other than the one you create for yourself through inertia and clinging to vanished institutions.

Virginity and procreation matter. Both can be had. Virginity can be purchased, sought in non-urban communities, sought in traditional countries, etc.

How about procreation?

That can be purchased too, via surrogacy. But it doesn't have to be.

If you're in your 20s, interacting with women around the same age, understand this: right now, women your age have only experienced extreme sexual power. From the time they were teenagers, they've been in high sexual demand. They assume they'll always have that position of power. They've never been in their 30s. That's why they are shortsightedly planning to function with all the chastity of a public gas station toilet, assuming that in their 30s, once they are done "having fun", there will be plenty of men waiting to marry them.

But when they get to their 30s, things are quite different. Now they are running out of time to have kids. There isn't a line of suitors around the block any more. Many of the guys who are interested in marriage are only really interested in marrying women in their teens or twenties. The number of women in their 30s who want to get married is far greater than the number who actually will get married.

Some of the unmarried women end up as childless spinsters. The bold ones may go to a sperm bank. The rest? That's where you come in.

You can start discussing procreation options. Not a single one of those options needs to involve even a hint at sexual monogamy for you. And it shouldn't. If you can manage to stay in decent shape, keep improving your social skills and education, and improve your economic level, you'll be more in demand in your 30s than you were in your 20s.

Procreation should either give you or her complete custody, and no child support. Either you get the child, or she does. The other can be invited to see the child, but it should not be assumed. That means you need to talk to a lawyer about using the right surrogacy contracts (where you get the child) or sperm donor contracts (where she gets the child). Get professional legal advice on the safest way to do this.

The nice thing about women in their 30s: they tend to be more responsible, earning more, and more competent. They often have the wherewithal to raise kids without emotionally damaging them the way a 17 or 18 year old single mother might.

You can do this process with as many women as are willing. And as their options dwindle, willingness tends to increase.

In fact, some women go so far as to steal sperm and impregnate themselves! According to a February 2014 article on rollingout.com, Dr. Sharon Irons, performed oral sex on Dr. Richard Phillips, and then used the sperm to impregnate herself. He unsuccessfully tried to sue her. She literally violated his trust and went through truly bizarre measures to have a child. And this was a highly educated woman.

This shows the lengths to which women will go to get pregnant when they are running out of time. Women want to have kids, and they have a very limited time window.

Other women have gone even farther. According to a January 27, 2017 report in ABC News, a houston man's ex girlfriend literally stole his sperm from a sperm bank to impregnate herself!

Many men's groups see semen theft as a problem, as it violates men's rights. It certainly does, but it also highlights a major opportunity. If women are willing to steal sperm to secretly impregnate themselves, and not even tell the father, clearly men have more child production options than we think. We don't need to give up freedom to have kids. We don't need to shackle ourselves to some kind of fake "monogamy", in which the woman has been ransacked by a line of previous sexual partners, and we can't say anything. We don't need to give up anything. We just need to be willing to give our sperm, and to get the right legal advice to protect our finances.

Women are willing to steal to get pregnant, to help you fulfill your genetic destiny. Why would you possibly sacrifice your freedom?

Why would you even consider modern marriages, the worst deal offered to men in the history of the human race?

Even if the women keep the kids, that doesn't stop you from giving money to them. Even if you have no legal requirement, you still arguably may have a moral obligation. At the very least you have self interest; you want your genetic offspring to be ahead of others, to have more opportunities and advantages.

In the past, having kids with a woman who didn't live with you was risky. How would you know if the kid was yours? But today, it's easy to tell. You can verify with a paternity test, and provide only for your own genetic offspring, and no one else's.

Trying to close Pandora's box or to cling to vanished institutions is idiotic. Instead, open it the rest of the way. Women are adapting. We can adapt too.

Bullshit Tolerance

If you want people to accept a nonsense reality, you need to increase their bullshit tolerance. To bring yourself back to actual reality, try lowering your bullshit tolerance.

What's the difference between a lie and bullshit? A lie is something possible, that just didn't happen. "I ate a turkey sandwich today," is a lie, since I didn't, but theoretically could have. "A person with a penis and a y chromosome can be a girl" is bullshit. "A politician's marital lifestyle matters more than his policies," is bullshit. "Gay marriage will destroy straight marriage," is also bullshit, as is, "They hate us for our freedom."

If a girl who has had sexual intercourse says, "I am a virgin," she's lying. If she says, "I am a born-again virgin," that's bullshit, since it suggests that such a thing is possible.

"You got cuckolded. Genetic testing proves that it's not your kid, but it's still somehow your kid and your financial responsibility," is also bullshit.

Bullshit is worse than lying, since it attempts to rewrite your fundamental understanding of reality. If I just lie to you about what I ate, how much money I make, or where I live, I'm not altering your fundamental understanding of reality. I'm just giving you incorrect facts. But bullshit attempts to distort your understanding of the nature of reality.

I think Tony Montana said it well in Scarface: "I always tell the truth, even when I lie." He was happy to lie. But he wasn't bullshitting anyone.

Increasing bullshit tolerance is just preparing you to have your natural rights violated.

It's considered impolite to call bullshit bullshit. Even when people "call bullshit," they are usually just calling out a normal lie.

I recommend doing it anyway. Everyone around you knows it's bullshit. The person bullshitting you may be furious when you call them out on it, but everyone else will be grateful.

What if you can't? What if you can't work up the nerve? Then just say it to yourself, internally. Tell yourself that the person is spewing fantasy world bullshit.

To start reducing your bullshit tolerance, I recommend blunt comedy. The more politically incorrect, the better. While political correctness and bullshit tolerance are not the same, they are fundamentally correlated.

If believing the latest politically correct thing requires huge mental gymnastics, you're dealing with bullshit. Learn to spot it, mock it, and refuse to tolerate it.

Sex as Intimacy Rather Than Value

This chapter presented sex as a thing a man gets from a woman. That's one perspective on sex, albeit not a complete one. Sex can also be an expression of physical intimacy. Both people desire it; it's not a one way street.

That is a perfectly reasonable way to look at sex. But does close friendship, intimacy, or even love necessitate giving up all other women for a girl whose private parts were essentially public parts for a decade?

The simple fact is that men and woman go through their peaks of demand at very different times. Women are most economically desirable somewhere between 16 and 19. For men, it's around 35. A man who gives up his peak era to bind himself to a woman who is far past her peak era is either very kind, or very foolish.

CHAPTER 8:

The False "Tradition" of Marriage

Men who agree to the marriages common today are not agreeing to "traditional marriages." They are agreeing to an ersatz marriage, with a higher price tag. They are paying more and getting less.

There is nothing "traditional" about monogamously marrying a woman who has had 100 previous sexual partners. That "tradition" has existed for maybe 30 years. The actual tradition of marriage fundamentally involves virginity.

That's why brides wore white on their wedding days. White was a symbol of purity. Furthermore, after the wedding was consummated, in some cultures the couple would display the wedding sheet, reddened by hymen blood.

That is the real tradition. The current thing is not a tradition at all. It's just an agreement pretending to be a tradition.

Out of some desire for social approval, family approval, or female approval, men routinely follow this new "tradition" of marrying promiscuous women.

But other men are pulling out. They know a scam when they see it. They know that when you change the fundamental details of a deal, it's not the same deal.

Some are pulling out of marriage because they see that the price is too high. They don't want to be relegated to a "man cave" in their own house. They don't want to be nagged and browbeaten.

They don't want sexual monogamy. They want peace, autonomy, and self-determination.

Others are pulling out of marriage because they see that they are getting second rate goods. They know that the original marriage agreement was an exchange of resource fidelity for sexual fidelity. Virginity was the primary part of that sexual fidelity.

More and more men are simply opting out of marriage. Even from 2000 to 2014, marriage rates dropped 13 percentage points, according to sociologist Mark Regnerus. That's almost an entire percentage point a year!

Men realize that the new agreement, which is exchanging resource fidelity AND sexual monogamy for a woman's highly compromised sexual fidelity is not the same agreement. It's a worse agreement. Many men are rejecting that agreement entirely.

It is vital to recognize that sexual monogamy is a new part of the price tag. It was not part of the original agreement. Men were expected to have mistresses in the recent past, or concubines in the farther past. The wife got resources, and her kids became the heirs, but there was no expectation of monogamy.

Women correctly point out that because women can work now, they don't "need" to agree to that kind of arrangement any more. That's true.

But men don't "need" to agree to the new arrangement either. We'll talk about many more alternatives in this book, but the current point is that there is no "force of tradition" behind current marital agreements. American men who get married under this new system are not following a tradition. They are just agreeing to something.

A completely different agreement that you may make will be just as "traditional". Any form of sexual agreement, procreation agreement, or child-raising agreement is just as "traditional" as the new marriages.

Over the last decades, women got creative and revised the old marital agreements. Now men can do the same.

When someone argues that "Traditional marriages are better for kids," that may be true. But the new marriages are not traditional at all. They are entirely nontraditional agreements. Your nontraditional agreement may be better for your kids than these other nontraditional agreements.

Marriage Vows change

On September 12, 1922, the Episcopal Church voted to remove the word "obey" from bridal wedding vows. "Love, cherish, and obey" became "love and cherish." The idea was that the wife was not expected to obey her husband. This change happened during one of the most important time periods in Women's rights. Women had just gotten the right to vote 2 years earlier, through a hard won constitutional amendment.

Like the feminists of that era, I agree with the sentiment. I don't believe that a woman should be expected to unquestioningly obey her husband. Frankly, I don't think that such an arrangement is good for the man either, no matter how dominant he is. CEOs who surround themselves with yes men often end up making stupid decisions. A good CEO has a good CFO, COO, and CTO who are not yes men, not blindly obedient, who will challenge him when he makes a questionable decision, and refuse to obey when he makes a truly stupid one. A good president has a good Chief of Staff, Vice President, and group of advisors who play the same role.

But this change matters precisely because it was a big and significant change to the expected structure of marriage. Marriage meant one thing. Then there was debate and a vote, and then it meant a different thing. The second thing was better, but it was also extremely different. A fundamental part of marriage can change, and it did change. As culture changed, marriage changed with it.

And as the nature of marriage can change, the cost of marriage can also change. What you would be willing to give up for a virginal obedient woman may be different from what you would be willing to give up for a sexually used up, bossy nag. It's not necessarily less. It could, theoretically, be more. But it's something you need to deeply and correctly think about.

For the last two hundred years, women have been learning to change social and political reality. During that same time period, men have been learning pretty much nothing. We are behind the curve right now. We are leaving things unquestioned, taking deals that make no sense, getting tricked into believing that institutions that have historically changed many, many times are somehow infinite and permanent. We are accepting all the changes that are bad for us, and failing to fight for the changes that are good for us.

Today, marriage has become imbalanced, and no longer reflects cultural reality or personal expectations. Will we reject that, just as feminists rejected the word "obey"? Will we demand changes, propose alternatives? Will we create something that makes sense for us, or will we keep on living in these lopsided, nonsensical cages?

At the time, by the way, women's rights activists were often attacked and hated. Many even avoided the title women's rights activist. Today, many of us are derided and insulted as men's rights activists. Afraid of being socially attacked, we meekly deny it.

But it's time for us to pick that title up. It's time for us to be proud that we will fight for our rights and freedoms. More than that, we need to actually fight for our rights and freedoms by refusing to comply with one-sided, immoral deals because they are supposedly "traditional." First, they are not. Second, if they were, they would need to be changed.

Feminists realized that "obey," while traditional, was wrong. They fought it until it changed.

Will we do the same? Will we fight these idiotic arrangements? Will men show the same strength and determination that early feminists did?

We can shape and create our relationships, marriages, family laws, social mores, and personal expectations far more easily than early feminists did. We don't face the same challenges. We're allowed to vote, own property, and work. There's no excuse to let the current system stand.

CHAPTER 9:

Rejecting False Monogamy

Revisiting Reality: The "Serial Monogamy" Myth

Psychotherapist Esther Perel said, "Monogamy used to mean one partner for life. Now it means one partner at a time".

Monogamy, actual monogamy, does not mean have 100 sexual partners, just one at a time. That's serial polyandry, not monogamy.

Today, women are calling this type of serial polyandry "monogamy". Then, they are insisting that men engage in sexual isolation with them, long after the women have engaged in long-term serial polyandry.

Monogamy actually means one partner for life. It means virginity at marriage. It may not be for you. That's fine. But then monogamy is not for you.

"Serial monogamy" is an oxymoron. If you are willing to consider "serial monogamy", which is really just serial polygamy, consider every other option as well - including simultaneous polygamy. Don't let someone browbeat you into believing that serial polygamy is a type of "monogamy" Mono means one, not fifty. Serial "monogamy" is a type of polygamy.

In fact, scientists and lexicographers agree. Dictionary.com includes the following definition for polygamy:

> "*In Zoology*: the habit or system of mating with more than one individual, either simultaneously or successively."

What people today call "serial monogamy", biologists would correctly call "successive polygamy".

An Organized Attack?

The new pre-marital promiscuity is not just a case of young women being taken advantage of, or being unable to control themselves. It is a very active assault on male reality. This shift towards promiscuity is actually encouraged by important women leaders. Sheryl Sandberg, COO of Facebook and author of *Lean In: Women, Work, and the Will to Lead* (cool title, right?) gives this advice:

"When looking for a life partner, my advice to women is date all of them: the bad boys, the cool boys, the commitment-phobic boys, the crazy boys. But do not marry them. The things that make the bad boys sexy do not make them good husbands."

Other women leaders have decided to go on a full scale reality assault and deny that virginity exists. In *The Purity Myth*, Jessica Valenti derides "the lie of virginity - the idea that such a thing even exists". In other words: male reality is just some imaginary delusion that needs to be erased.

The New Female Sexual Cycle

The original female sexual cycle basically involved getting married young and virginal. The woman had sex usually with only one person in her entire life. She dedicated her entire sexuality to her husband.

In exchange, the man gave her full resource fidelity. Given that she was giving him all her sexuality, it seemed reasonable.

Today, the female sexual cycle is very different. It usually looks something like this:

- Have sex for the first time relatively young, often in a "serious" relationship.
- While getting comfortable, have sex with a handful of men.
- Go through a few years of intensive sexual experimentation. I've heard women describe this as the "slut phase", "trampage", and "anyone and everyone." Those who want to give this a prettified political justification will refer to it as "a right to date."
- Once tired of having sex with a long line of men, find some sap to marry.
- Most of the time, the marriage ends in divorce, and the woman keeps half of the man's assets.

Guess what? It's not a bad plan for women. They get to do whatever they want, without consequences. And if you interact with women primarily in phases 1-3, it's pretty good for men too.

But phase 4 and 5 seem a bit stupid for men to engage in. Why trade full resource fidelity for a small fraction of a woman's sexual fidelity?

Unfortunately, men often want to have kids, and most 16-year-old women (in their pre-slut phase) aren't really ready for that. It seems to men, then, that the only viable option is to marry a woman who is post-slut phase.

But that doesn't make any sense of any kind. First, while in America "slut shaming" is now a social crime, in much of the rest of the world, slutting is the social crime. There are plenty of countries in which you don't have to be the 50th guy in line, or even the second.

Given that you can provide a green card, you are a desirable person indeed!

Don't make the mistake of confusing dating with marriage. When you're dating, you're just seen as some guy trying to get laid. The market demand for you is low. There is no shortage of guys trying to have sex.

If you're trying to get married, the market demand for you is high. There is a shortage of men who want to get married. A massive shortage. According to John Birger's *Date-onomics: How Dating Became A Lopsided Numbers Game*, this is particularly pronounced among college educated men and women. Between ages 25 and 29, there are 5.5 million college educated women and only 4.1 million college educated men. Research from Brookings suggests that among those with college educations between the ages of 25 and 34, the ratio of employed men to childless women is 88 to 100. Generally speaking, for a man to be marriageable, he needs to have a job, and for a woman, she needs to be childless and of child-bearing age. These numbers show a clear advantage for men who are looking to get married, and a clear disadvantage for women.

As people get older, things get even more dire for women. According to sociologist Mark Regnerus, for every 82 men under 40 that want to get married, 100 women under 40 want to get married.

Compared to the 3:1 demand for dating favoring women (as evidenced by Tinder data), that is quite a difference indeed!

Your marriage league is, almost certainly, higher than your dating league. When it comes to sex, the Tinder research mentioned earlier in this book suggests that men swipe right more than three times as often as women do. The sex and dating market highly favors women. But, the marriage market favors men.

And there is the other option of kids without marriage.

The fact is that women who are finished with that slut phase are usually older, earning more, and able to raise children just fine on their own. Men can sign away all rights (that they don't have anyway) and responsibilities and let the woman handle it, providing support as agreed to. The especially beneficial aspect of this method is that men actually end up more likely to see their own kids. The mother isn't guaranteed your money, and so she has to let you see the kids if she wants your support. This gives men far more negotiating power than the current non-existent power the courts give us. This whole process involves using a donor contract (not just a normal prenuptial agreement). So, get legal advice in your state before embarking on this.

Instead of trading all resource fidelity for a tiny fraction of the woman's sexual fidelity, just provide a sufficient amount to supplement resources needed for child raising.

Men who want to raise their own children can hire a surrogate, or just sign a surrogacy contract with someone whom they are dating. With the right legal advice, they can potentially get full legal custody.

Even though surrogacy can be expensive, it's cheaper than divorce. It's also cheaper than raising children, which is becoming increasingly expensive. If you can't afford surrogacy, you probably can't afford childcare either. Wait until you can.

Some men dream of finding chaste wives and forming a partnership. It can be done, but in America the numbers are against you. If that's what you're looking for, look in other countries. Given that you earn U.S. dollars and can provide a green card, you're in a pretty high league in many other countries.

Further Consideration of Incels

As mentioned earlier, Incel stands for "Involuntary Celibate." Incels are men who have never had sex, despite wanting to. Analyst F.

Roger Devlin describes the change in what information women are exposed to, and the beginning of what today has led to this growing incel movement.

"Formerly, most people lived parochial lives in a world where even photography did not exist. Their notions of sexual attractiveness were limited by their experience. Back in my own family tree, for example, there was a family with three daughters who grew up on a farm adjoining three others. As each girl came of age, she married a boy from one of the neighboring farms. They did not expect much in a husband. It is probable all three went through life without ever seeing a man who looked like Cary Grant."

With mass media, things have, of course, changed. Women see more very handsome men on a regular basis. The men are both physically attractive and, thanks to screenwriters, verbally dexterous.

But the process doesn't stop there. As monogamy vanishes (and, to restate the obvious, serial monogamy is a type of polygamy, not a type of monogamy), women are approaching sex differently. They aren't looking for a provider. The welfare state is their provider. Even women who earn money generally plan to use public schools, the largest aspect of the male-disempowering welfare state. Women are instead looking for excitement and romance.

That is, of course, their right. Anyone has the right to pursue whatever they want. However, they don't have the right to force others to pay for it. Why should an incel be forced to subsidize the lifestyles of women he doesn't interact with, or kids he obviously didn't father?

According to Helen Smith, author of *Men on Strike*, data suggest that 20 percent of the men are having 75 percent of the sexual encounters. The remaining 80 percent of men are left to fight over the remaining 25 percent. Of course people are going to be left out.

Most of these women simply never meet or interact with the 80 percent of men who are less lucky. To them, those men simply don't exist. They've never met them. It's not that they are unsympathetic. It's that those men are simply outside of their awareness.

Obviously, this isn't great for incels, many of whom would be good providers. Being a provider is not valuable when women can simply use government force to force those men to pay for their lifestyle anyway.

But it's not great for women either. Women expect their romantic fantasy to go to the storybook conclusion, in which the heavily polygamous man gives up all women just to be with her alone. This tends not to happen as often as many women would like. More and more are ending up alone and childless while they wait for something that will not happen.

There are many cultural ways to address this issue. First, the current laws and social taboo against simultaneous polygamy need to go. Let adults make their own decisions, unrestricted by nonsense. Second, the welfare state needs to end. The only people who should pay for any woman or child are the woman herself and her actual partner(s).

Forcing an incel to provide financially for women who don't know or care about his existence is a larger psychological attack than many can bear. There has already been at least one act of violence caused by this. If we keep ignoring the degradation of our brothers, there will be more.

If you are in incel, stop playing along with this idiocy. Remove from your mind the obviously outdated ideas of romantic love, or providing for worthwhile women in America. This is about economic warfare and strategic ruthlessness. It's about looking abroad for real opportunities. Why settle to be 20th in line for an American woman, when there are women all over the world waiting for green cards, or who would be overwhelmed to be provided for by someone who earns a salary in dollars? If someone writes unfair rules against you, why keep playing by them? Don't resort to violence. Use your brain to find opportunities.

And use your voice to fight against what has put you in this position. If you have a decent job, and yet that job seems to be getting you absolutely nothing, ask yourself why. Why doesn't your ability to provide matter any more? It's because the welfare state is taking your money without your consent, forcing you to provide for women who don't know or care that you exist. Fight that. If someone wants something from you, they should earn it from you. They have no right to force you to pay for their "lifestyle". If you aren't having sex with someone, you shouldn't pay for her birth control pills, or her food, or her shelter, or her anything. If a kid is not yours, and you didn't adopt it, you shouldn't pay a single cent to support it. Let there be an actual benefit to being your partner. Those who are not your actual partners should get nothing from you.

And stop using the word incel. Your celibacy is not involuntary. It's based on the voluntary, and stupid, decision to keep playing by someone else's rules. You keep living in America, or a welfarist western nation. That's your voluntary decision. Visit a poorer country, and see how long your celibacy actually lasts. Go abroad, and find one, two, or fifty women worth providing for, and who will actually earn it from you.

Sexual Pressure: The Last Ditch Effort of Those Whose Reality is Being Rejected

Your power to leave is far greater than welfarists want you to believe. Their cultural power is much weaker than they want you to believe. The desperation of their tactics shows how uncertain they are, how deeply they understand that their illusions are on the verge of collapse.

When your social reality is being threatened, you use rhetoric, debate, and logic to fight back. If that doesn't work, you use visual propaganda, art, and clever slogans. If that doesn't work, and you are a woman, you can use sex.

A fascinating trend has emerged in recent months: young women declaring that they will only have sex with men who share, or will pretend to share, their political views. I have seen dozens of screenshots of online dating profiles that say, essentially, "If you voted for anyone but Hillary, swipe left."

I wouldn't put it past political strategists to use fake profiles to accomplish that, but many of them do seem genuine. Recognizing that men have finally started rejecting welfarism, these young women are becoming desperate. Their way of life is being threatened.

Sometimes, the sexual pressure is not that blatant. I've met many men who have pretended to support "feminist" welfarism in order to get sex. I have also met many men who have been turned aside entirely for their political views.

I've experienced it directly, more than once. The first time I heard, "We can't date because of your political views," I was pretty taken aback. Now I just find it funny. Note that this is not from women who have read this incendiary book, but from those who know that I don't support taxation funded birth control or tax funded schooling. (By the way, for those who are looking for strategy rather than principles: people who claim to reject you because of your political views generally change their mind when you refuse to capitulate. Refusing to bend to pressure makes you seem more confident, attractive, and charismatic. Many politicians intentionally set up engagements with groups with whom they disagree. Then, they publicly disagree, and hold firm, refusing to pander. This makes them look strong and resolute. Bill Clinton's team called this process "counter-scheduling".)

Do not compromise your principles just to get access to someone else's genitals. Do not let someone else's genitalia tell you how to speak, what to say, what to think, or what political views to have.

Those in the trans movement are fond of saying, "My genitals don't define my gender." I think we need to start saying, "Your genitals can't change my principles."

Someone who will offer her genitals as some kind of Pavlovian reward to those who support her welfarist politics is part political prostitute, and part regular prostitute. She is expecting political agreement in exchange for sex. But, that political agreement also just so happens to give her money. Would you compromise your principles to get a chance at the public-access genitals of a woman who is trading sex for your support of welfare?

CHAPTER 10:

Classic vs. Romantic: A Further Study of Denied Male Reality

In *Zen and the Art of Motorcycle Maintenance*, Robert Pirsig delineates between the Classical and Romantic mindset. The classical mindset looks at the underlying reality. Engineers and physicists epitomize the classical mindset.

The Romantic mindset focuses on initial impressions and surface level aesthetics. Fashion designers and art history majors may epitomize the Romantic mindset.

It would be a gross oversimplification to suggest that the male mindset is exclusively classical. Romantic, feelings-first, initial-impression approaches to reality can heavily impact men. Don't men like foods that taste good, but lack any nutritional value? Don't men prefer the sounds of a soothing and enticing voice to a shrill and grating one? Don't men prefer attractive women to unattractive ones?

And yet, despite all that, the classical mindset is a core, fundamental part of male culture. The search for underlying truth, for the scientific facts often hidden from immediate view, has shaped male culture as surely as almost any other force. The classically oriented fields - math, physics, engineering - attract a much larger percentage of men than the romantically oriented fields like art history. While male culture is not exclusively classical by any means, the driving principles of male culture are predominantly classical.

We've discussed paternity already. A man isn't content with a child that appears to be his (unless he has intentionally adopted a child). He doesn't want a clever facsimile, a convincing forgery. He wants the real thing. He's not content to be cuckolded.

The same is true in the case of virginity. Women are sometimes bewildered by the few men who indicate a strong preference for virginity. Of course, many women just shout these men down, but quite a few are actually curious. Their questions, though, come from a romantic mindset. They may ask what the difference is. Does it feel different? Is the physical sensation itself somehow more pleasurable?

But it has nothing to do with the immediate perception. It's not about pleasure or pain. It's about truth and falsehood.

A fake Picasso may look identical to the real thing, but be worth only a tiny fraction of the amount. What's the difference? They look the same? They contain identical imagery. And yet, they are not the same thing at all.

From a purely romantic perspective, there is no real difference between a convincing forgery and an authentic, between a virgin and a nonvirgin, between a child that is genetically yours and one that is not. And yet the classical mindset sees the chasm between truth and falsehood that separates them.

To the romantic perspective, a real sapphire has more in common with a fake sapphire than it does with an authentic Picasso painting. After all, the real and fake sapphire look pretty much the same, and neither look at all like a Picasso painting. But to the classical mind, the real sapphire and the real Picasso painting are both in the category of truth. The fake sapphire is on the opposite end of the spectrum, and belongs in the category of forgery.

The classical mindset, which has shaped so much of male reality, is not content to classify forgeries and authentic things in the same group. To attack the classical mindset is to attack male reality itself.

But in the realm of sexuality, paternity, virginity, and gender, the classical mindset is itself coming under attack. Consider, for example, the growing transgender movement. Some parts of the movement argue simply that people own their bodies, and can alter them however they choose. Others demand to be treated, in terms of social politeness, as the gender of their choosing.

But a very large part of the trans movement demands not just politeness, but that others believe that they are their chosen gender, not the gender normally associated with their DNA.

It brings up an interesting question. How is a trans person who identifies as a woman, who acts like a woman, who has had surgeries to look like a woman, wears makeup, dresses like a woman, any different from a biological female woman? The trans woman and the biological woman have different DNA, but no one brings an electron microscope to the bedroom. The trans woman cannot produce offspring, but most men aren't planning to procreate with every person they sleep with. So, why does it matter?

For many men, it's the difference between the real Picasso and the forgery. It's the difference between the natural ruby and the lab created one. From a romantic perspective, there's not much difference at all. From a classical perspective, there's all the difference in the world.

Any person has the right to self identify however they like. But anyone else has the right to see reality from a classical perspective if they choose. A person with a Y chromosome and male genitals has every right to identify as a woman. But that person has no right to force anyone else to agree with that assessment.

That's not to say that trans people aren't found attractive. Many men find them quite attractive. But to say that they are no different from genetic women is just false.

The classical mindset is a powerful part of masculinity, and shapes male reality. Attempts to denigrate it or erase it entirely must be recognized, and strongly resisted.

Beware of the common slogans of the romantic mindset. The most common is "Perception is Reality". It is not. If it were, optical illusions would be truths, racism would be science, and physics would not exist. Seeing past immediate perception and into true reality is one of the most powerful parts of human culture in general, and male culture specifically.

By the way, the assault on classical reality is not confined to sex, DNA, and procreation. The original definition of racism involved judging people by the color of their skin, rather than by the content of their character. It's easy for the classical mind to oppose this type of racism. The classical mind, in its very nature, seeks the underlying truth of a person. It is inherently not content to judge a person by the color of his skin, just as it is not content to judge anything at all by its surface appearance. You can't reliably predict someone's intelligence, work ethic, or knowledge just by looking at their skin color. Original racism was illogical, and classically minded people rejected it on the grounds that it was stupid.

The problem with classical anti-racism was that it only really welcomed the elite. When you get right down to it, most people, of any race, if judged by the content of their character, are mostly lazy and useless. Most black people, just like most white people, were not ready to be judged by their ability. They wanted to be judged as worthy and good, whether they were or not.

This is not a unique quality of any race of people. All people on earth would prefer to be judged as excellent, even if they don't deserve it.

First wave anti-racism involved seeking civil rights, fair treatment by the government, property rights, etc. Second wave anti-racism involves Affirmative Action and other programs that insist that minorities are excellent, even when they are not. Instead of judging by ability, Affirmative Action gives people the rewards that come from merit – even if they don't have any merit.

The romantic mind often appreciates this, as it creates a harmonious appearance. It puts more shades of skin color into offices and colleges.

The classical mind finds Affirmative Action absurd. Sure, if viewed from the sky, Affirmative Action creates a pretty result. But it enables and encourages laziness, insults rationality, and pretends that ability comes primarily from cultural baggage rather than discipline and work ethic.

Just as an assault on Kosher diets would be a de facto assault on Judaism, the assault on the classical mindset is a de-facto assault on masculine culture. It is an assault on the culture that stretches from the Ancient Greek Philosophers to the Enlightenment visionaries, and continues in the present.

We must calmly but uncompromisingly fight the assault on the classical mindset, a major linchpin of male reality.

Parallels Between Affirmative Action and Third Wave Feminism; The Classical Mindset and Feminism

Like first wave anti-racism, first wave feminism made classical sense. Women are people, with the same rights as anyone. A woman who worked had the rights to the fruits of her labor. If she's going to be taxed, she has the same rights to vote against those taxes as any man does. If she's able to get a job, she has the right to keep the salary she earns.

She has the same rights to compete in the free market as a man does.

Much of first wave feminism was about the rights of women to keep their wages and property. As Susan B. Anthony declared:

"There is an old saying that 'a rose by any other name would smell as sweet,' and I submit it the deprivation by law of the ownership of one's own person, wages, property, children, the denial of the right as an individual, to sue and be sued, and to testify in the courts, is not a condition of servitude most bitter and absolute, though under the sacred name of marriage?"

That's first wave feminism. That's the feminism that makes sense, with respect to the classical mindset. That's the feminism that says a woman should keep what she earns, unless she voluntarily exchanges it for a good or service. That's the feminism that demands that women have the right to do with their earnings and property what they choose.

But the problem the first wave feminism faces is the same as the one that first wave anti-racism faced. Most people, when judged by their abilities or by the content of their character, fall short.

Modern anti-racism has turned into a special interest group for minorities that serves to weaken them. Instead of focusing on self improvement in a competitive environment, today's minority groups look for made up excuses for underachievement, while ignoring their obvious causes. Blaming incidences from hundreds of years in the past that cannot be changed, ignoring the behaviors of the present that can be changed, and demanding special favors have all become their norms of behavior. Now that Jim Crow laws are gone, now that any legitimate external reason for failure is gone, these groups are essentially using imaginary phantasms as excuses. Their approaches do not fit within the classical mindset because they don't make logical sense.

Instead of demanding equal opportunities, they are demanding equal results. They are turning to various forms of welfarist approaches.

Modern feminism has become the same. Any legitimate, external barriers to the economic success of women are gone. Women can keep their wages, vote, etc. Brilliant, hard working women with useful skills can make plenty of money.

The problem is that weak, undisciplined women want to be feminists too. Real feminism, first wave feminism, the kind that judges people by their abilities and work ethic, is great for people with abilities and work ethic. But it doesn't let the stupid and lazy be part of feminism.

Third wave feminism fixes that with its focus on welfarism. Anyone can whine for welfare. You don't need to have the discipline of the early feminists who only wanted to work and keep the fruits of their labor. You just need to be willing to screech and complain.

In fact, today you don't even need to be able to debate. The tactics of third wave feminism, which basically involve declaring every area a safe space and shrieking all opponents into silence, takes no real rhetorical skill. Even a child can have a tantrum.

Real feminists wanted to keep their earnings, and spend them according to their own choices. Modern "feminists" just want someone else to pay for their birth control.

The men who reject this kind of false feminism are often inspired by the real feminism of the past. I'm often inspired by the great early feminists who fought against the dominant culture of the time. I think we should be more like them, willing to challenge the dominant culture. We should fight for our natural rights, and against the blatant abuses of them, no matter how badly society reacts. I doubt the dominant culture was particularly kind to early feminists. They fought anyway. That's what we need to do now.

CHAPTER 11:

The Cultural Rot of Third Wave Feminism

When we look at the early women's movement and compare it to today's women's movement, we intuitively sense some important, critical difference. It's something deeper than the fact that the early women's movement was fighting for fairness, and today's women's movement is just fighting for more stuff for women, regardless of fairness.

The early movement seemed more dignified. Early feminist freedom fighters sought the freedom to pursue greatness, while today's feminist movement seeks freedom to pursue degeneracy. Early feminists sought the right to earn money through work. Today's feminists seek the "right" to get paid to do nothing.

There are, roughly speaking, two general categories of freedom. One category of freedom enables us to pursue excellence, to become more than we were. The other category of freedom allows us to pursue degeneracy, and become less than we were. The first category includes the freedom of speech, the freedom to start a business, the freedom to build on your own property, etc. The latter category includes the right to smoke marijuana, dress like a buffoon, and not read. Both categories of rights are natural rights. You have every right to be a high, illiterate moron. But it may not be a right you want to exercise.

In his *Oration on the Dignity of Man*, Pico De Mirandola says, "To you is granted the power of degrading yourself into the lower forms of life, the beasts, and to you is granted the power, contained in your intellect and judgment, to be reborn into the higher forms, the divine."

The earlier feminist movement fought for the rights to work, own property, vote, speak freely, etc. The modern feminist movement is fighting for the "rights" to have others buy them birth control pills, to dress like prostitutes without being judged as prostitutes, and to get blackout drunk in public but still be safe.

From a purely political perspective, women have the natural right to be moronic drunks who dress like third world prostitutes. I 100% consider this a natural and fundamental right. But if I were giving life advice to any particular woman, I doubt that, "Get drunk and dress like a buffoon" would be included.

While both the early and recent feminist movements fought for freedom, the former was fighting for power and greatness, and the latter are fighting for freedom to do whatever you want and not suffer the consequences. Early feminists seem fearless, responsible, powerful, and inspiring. Today's third wave feminists come across as entitled, whiny, and annoying. Many male readers may admire feminists like Susan B. Anthony, Elizabeth Cady Stanton, and Rosa Parks. Far fewer readers admire those who fixate on having others pay for their birth control pills and defend the right to dress like an idiot.

That's not to say that all modern feminists do that. Sheryl Sandberg encourages women to "lean in" and be ambitious, succeed in their careers, etc. She discourages women from falling into submissive gender roles, and instead encourages them to strive. Many men (including me) look up to her as a business leader and personal visionary. After all, I wouldn't go through the trouble of satirizing a title of a book that I didn't respect.

But the fact is, *Lean In* has been attacked by many women for teaching women to be overly independent, to ignore the "needs" of disadvantaged women, and to encourage a level of competition that women cannot adapt to. (The "needs" are the need to have a bunch of children other people pay for, through taxes.)

For example, Rosa Brooks writes in the Washington Post:

"We need to fight for our right to lean back and put our feet up. Here's the thing: We've created a world in which ubiquity is valued above all. If you're not at your desk every night until nine, your commitment to the job is questioned. If you're not checking email 24/7, you're not a reliable colleague. But in a world in which leaning in at work has come to mean doing more work, more often, for longer hours, women will disproportionately drop out or be eased out."

Brooks rejects the "women should be allowed to compete on equal terms with men", instead favoring the rhetoric of, "we need to change things to make life easier for women."

Elizabeth Bruenig writes in the New Republic:

"The idea of feminism rests on the notion that all women can be united on the axis of their womanhood, and that our collective lot can be improved by boosting the place of that axis in the matrix of society. What will make things easier for women, therefore, will make things easier for an individual woman. But the reverse, moving from the individual to the general, is not true: What makes life easier for an individual woman will not necessarily make life easier for women at large. In the case of Sandberg's corporate feminism, what makes life easier for any given woman high on the corporate ladder might actually make life harder for women toiling near the bottom rungs."

In other words, she rejects the "feminism as female excellence" in favor of "feminism as a type of socialism." Individualistic, powerful, feminism has no place in this collectivist feminism aimed squarely at the bottom.

Vanessa Garcia, in the Huffington Post, argues:

"Sandberg asks women to "sit at the table," to "lean in." Which sounds good on the surface, but what she's asking is for women to lean into a corporate culture created by men... Sorry, a women's bathroom and a parking spot just isn't enough and, for me, it's not even a good enough place to start. I want more, and I won't become a submissive to get it."

Her definition of "becoming a submissive" is essentially to do something of economic value that you might not just do as a hobby, in order to get rewards. Instead of becoming more skilled, getting more privileges in concordance with economic value, she wants to get more privileges just because. Nor does she suggest that women start their own businesses where they can make their own rules, as male tech entrepreneurs did in the 90s, freeing themselves of suits and ties – or as Ariana Huffington did with the paper that Garcia writes for. For her, it's not about earning advantages, but rather about hammering social and legal codes to have those advantages given to women.

The feminism of excellence is struggling right now against the feminism of laziness. The feminism that tells women to work hard, take risks, and be unafraid – lessons that men have been taught for centuries – is fighting the feminism that tells women they should be entitled to everything on earth, paid for by someone else. Sandberg tells women to start companies, take business risks, be determined, not fall apart in the face of defeat. Lazy feminism tells women to shriek and scream until someone they aren't screwing buys them birth control pills, or someone who's never shared their bed pays for their childcare needs.

It's easy for men to see this in the women's movement. It's much harder for us to notice this in our own culture. Right now, the masculinity of excellence is fighting for its existence against the masculinity of laziness and entitlement.

Take, for example, the hiring difficulties in Colorado and Georgia. According to the New York Times, construction companies are finding it impossible to find enough workers who can pass a drug test. Young men are facing a choice between marijuana and employment...and choosing marijuana. In other words, men are being more lazy and entitled than the laziest of the Entitlement Feminists. Just like Entitlement Feminists, men are choosing the freedom to be a lazy degenerate over the freedom to pursue excellence, or even basic employment.[1]

At a deeper level, the individual power orientation of early male principles has given way to a freedom that says simply, "I can do whatever I want." That type of childish freedom, while technically still freedom, gives a man all the power of a child.

I get why men today slack. What the hell is the point of working? A man's life is random sex in your 20s, followed by marriage to an angry, used up nag, followed by expensive divorce, followed by having your children stolen, followed by expensive child support. That's not rare: more than half of marriages end in divorce. Why put effort into any of that?

Many books on seduction teach us how to get laid while being total slackers. Our direct experience show us that our sex lives are easier and more fun when we are lazy slackers. After all, when you are a lazy slacker, women won't try to psychologically browbeat you into a marriage; there's no point. You're just some guy to have fun with in the short term – the ideal situation for a young man. We see

---

1) The New York Times: *Hiring Hurdle: Finding Workers Who Can Pass a Drug Test*

no shortage of rich and successful men that have fewer sexual options than deadbeats.

In fact, as men move to higher positions of power and respect, their options become socially limited. It's socially fine for a gas station attendant to have three kids with three different women at the same time. It's less fine for the CEO of a major company, a Senator, or an Ambassador to do the same thing. If anything, being more successful as a man just means being more restricted. Why give up getting high and drunk for that? What is the use of success if it comes at the cost of your freedom?

But the true fact is, a high level of success, combined with psychological skill and discipline, can give you more options than what are available to slacking deadbeats. You need to learn to develop economically useful skills, and then wield them unapologetically. Don't seek social respect, which will only confine your behavior. Just develop economically valuable skills, and then pursue whatever you actually want. Unless, of course, you want social approval. In that case, start wanting something different, and then pursue that.

The glorious thing about economic value is that people need whatever you have. Men of the past knew this well. Einstein was notorious for his constant womanizing. No one cared. They had a choice between a womanizing genius who could help make the U.S. military unstoppable, and some monogamous, humble guy who could not. The choice was obvious.

A Hollywood actress may oppose homosexuality on religious grounds. But that actress would be limited to only heterosexual makeup, hair, and wardrobe staff. That moral stance would come at a significant economic inconvenience, to say the least.

If you can provide sufficient economic value, then you can live by your own code and value system. Others will have to adapt.

Look at how short-lived and ineffective most commercial boycotts are. People boycotted Chick-fil-a because the owners had an anti-gay political stance. But at the end of the day, the desire for chicken won. The economic power of an organization that can deliver tasty food in a friendly, organized setting was enough to allow the owners to have whatever political views they wanted.

People often talk about the difference between being liked and being respected. The idea is people will like you if you agree with them, or buy them things, or flatter them. But they will respect you for your integrity, etc.

There is definitely some truth to that. But that kind of respect is actually mostly just a different flavor of being liked.

But, when you have economically valuable skills, you don't really need to be liked or respected. If you know how to perform a life saving surgery, and the patient hates your religion and clothing, the patient just has to deal with it or die. If you can make awesome web pages, but people disapprove of your personal life, they can either just stomach their disapproval or do without.

But you don't even need something that unique. If you can show up to work on time, sober, and work hard, that makes you valuable. If your employer disapproves of your personal life, he's welcome to choose someone else whose personal life he likes better. But chances are, that person won't be as timely, reliable, and hardworking.

They say, "Money talks, bullshit walks." In other words, if you have money, you get things. Money has a voice. If you just have showmanship, you don't.

The same is true of any economically valuable skill. "Economic value talks, bullshit walks." Economic value has a powerful voice.

Economic value isn't just money. It's possessing skills that other people need. It's having anything that businesses and customers don't have an infinite supply of. Timeliness, reliability, math skills, computer skills, cooking skills, customer service politeness, physical strength, and patience are just a few examples.

Your economic skills give you freedom to live your personal life as you see fit. The more economic skills you have, the more freedom you can command.

Even if your sole goal is the freedom to be high all the time, more economic power helps there as well. Sure, for a low level beginning carpenter, employers can demand that they pass drug tests. But a highly skilled master carpenter can simply build expensive furniture in his own workshop and sell it - while being high the entire time.

As you work to build your economic skills in pursuit of total social freedom, you must remember that there are two categories of economic skill. You must build both in order to have the economic power that leads to personal freedom.

The first category is specialized skill. For example, being good at carpentry, economics, music software, engineering, law, investing, medicine, design, public speaking, writing, singing, playing soccer, etc.

The second category includes reliability, responsibility, and timeliness. In America, especially, these are rarer skills. Be the type of person who is always on time, gets things done right, etc.

Build both of those skill categories, and you'll never have to beg society's permission for living however you want to live.

Economic power, in the form of economically valuable skills, brings freedom. Improve your economic ability, and you won't need to compromise who you are.

Don't be like Tiger Woods. As an athletic superstar, he had every opportunity to unapologetically be who he wanted to be. He could have said, "Listen, if I want 27 girlfriends, then that's my business. If you don't want to be part of my life, or be one of my sponsors, fine. Go have the second best golfer in the world endorse your sunglasses."

Instead, he thought that at such a high profile, he had to at least pretend to live a "traditional" life (note: Kings and emperors from eastern and western cultures routinely had several dozen wives and concubines, so the word traditional is still a laughable concept).

Then, when he got caught cheating, he came across as a weak liar. He also lost a ton of money in his divorce.

Don't let people control you based on how much they like or respect you. Don't seek that approval like a dog. Build your economic value, recognize your own economic value, and then use your economic value to unapologetically increase your personal freedom to live how you actually want.

CHAPTER 12:

Lower Standards for Women

Affirmative action makes people weaker. Holding people to a lower standards hurts them.

Today, in many parts of the country, women are holding themselves to a totally different standard. In the past, women were looking for husbands. When it comes to a wife, men usually have pretty high standards. That meant women had to meet higher standards.

But now, loosely speaking, the goal of many women is not to find a husband, but rather to find a person, or people, to have sex with. Since many men will have sex with basically any woman, women don't have to reach a particularly high standard to achieve that.

In the past, women worked to make themselves attractive - not just physically, but in terms of their personalities. When looking for wives, men demand high levels of physical and personal attractiveness.

But when looking for sexual flings, men don't really care that much. The result is that women don't have to try that hard. In fact, they can try to make their personalities unattractive. Flip through any online dating site, and you'll see pictures of women with bizarre expressions, flicking off the camera, and adopting every kind of unattractive behavior imaginable. Young men looking for sex don't particularly care. Those women still get hundreds of men looking to sleep with them.

One common quote on those dating sites: "If you can't handle me at my worst, you don't deserve me at my best." Women are literally advertising their psychological problems, and indicating that men should be prepared for lunatic behavior.

But when women in their late 20s and early 30s decide they are ready for marriage, they are often brutally shocked by the reality they face. Sure, men will put up with social justice nonsense for a quick lay or even a short fling. But they won't tolerate that when looking for wives. No man one wants his kids raised by a welfarist idiot. No man is saying, "One day, I hope she teaches my daughter how to scrunch up her face at the camera and make obscene gestures."

It has created an economically interesting situation. There is no shortage of women, but there is a shortage of wives. In the reverse, there is no shortage of men, but there is a major shortage of husbands. A woman may enjoy shrieking a man into submission. But she doesn't respect him as a role model for her sons.

Example: Women with Only Male Friends

It's not uncommon to meet women who only have male friends. They'll often brag about being one of the guys, and therefore cooler than average women. They'll also explain that women are flaky, unreliable, whiny, etc., and thus they don't like making friends with them.

Over the last decade, I've found that this approach is no longer the exception for women. It has become the rule. Even here in D.C., a dense, crowded city with all kinds of people from all parts of the world, with every political and cultural background, I meet plenty of women with literally zero female friends. This is much less common among men. While I do occasionally meet men with only female friends, they are not exactly what you'd call "socially normal". Usually, they are very handsome and have personality disorders; women overlook their personality deficiencies for sexual reasons, but men obviously don't.

One of the sillier statistics I've heard is that 90 percent of people consider themselves better drivers than most other people. The truth of those opinions is mathematically...unlikely. It is also unlikely that such a large number of young women have personalities so far superior to the personalities of all other young women that they simply cannot be friends with other women.

It's more likely that men tolerate their personalities for sexual reasons, and other women do not. With the endless patience that comes from sexual desire, men can tolerate personality deficiencies. Women who don't have equally strong sexual desires for other women won't.

In other words, many women have found ways to make themselves so unlikable that no one who doesn't want to sleep with them can tolerate their personalities. They literally cannot stand each other.

In my book *Why Hillary Lost*, I discussed the shock that many young women felt when Hillary Clinton lost the 2016 presidential election, despite every possible advantage. They could not see how unlikable she was. To many young women, her personality, arguably one of the least likable personalities in the history of politics, was just a normal way for a woman to act. Those that attributed her unlikability to sexism were surprised when research showed that she was often even more unlikable as a man. Maria Guadalupe, associate professor of economics and political science at INSEAD created an interesting bit of research. She had a female actor use Trump's lines and mannerisms, and a male actor use Hillary's words and mannerisms, copied exactly from their debates. She then had audiences watch these performances and gauge their reactions.

The reactions suggested that Hillary was even more hated as a man. As one liberal audience member said, "In the real debates I thought Hillary won hands down, [but] this has totally made me question my judgment."

Compared to many young women, though, Hillary Clinton's personality was downright charming. She was insincere, petty, and arrogant. But, at least she was willing to debate. When a political opponent disagreed with her, she argued back. She did it without an ounce of grace, but she at least did it.

Today's young women don't even reach that level. On college campuses, those who disagree with their welfarism are shrieked and shouted into submission, not debated with. As abrasive as she was, Hillary didn't insist on safe spaces where no one was allowed to disagree with her, or get triggered and start crying or #LiterallyShaking if someone suggested that women should pay for their own birth control. Compared to today's average college shrieker, Hillary Clinton, notorious for her abrasive personality, would be one of the most charming women on campus!

This is a result of the kind of sexual affirmative action that comes from considering sex, not marriage, an achievement. Women say, "If my personality is good enough that people want to have sex with me, it's good enough." Most men will put up with plenty of shrieking to have sex with a reasonably okay looking woman.

Young women today are surrounded by "White Knights" who constantly praise their intolerable personalities in hopes of getting sex. They are surrounded by normal men who will tolerate or ignore their personalities for sex. They have convinced themselves that the fact that no woman can tolerate their personalities is proof of their awesomeness. And, because of all this, America's women are becoming more and more unlikable. Having learned in college that shrieking is the way to get what they want, since men tolerate basically anything to get sex, they continue that strategy through relationships and marriage.

Young men should realize that that behavior is not normal or reasonable. Do not let your home be turned into someone else's safe space, where only their way is allowed, and anyone who disagrees will get shrieked into submission. Stay single. Find a foreign wife or wives. Find someone from some other kind of background. These behaviors that you've grown up with from women are not normal or reasonable. The fact that so many women cannot tolerate each other's unlikable personalities is all the proof you need.

An adult human should not be a larger drain on time and mental energy than an infant dog. It's true that all human relationships require work. But the result should still be a net positive. Businesses require investment and effort, but they should eventually yield profit. Relationships in which the input is 100 and the benefit is 2 are just not worth your effort.

Example: Emotional Labor

A common buzzword in feminist circles is "emotional labor." The idea is that many service industries require workers to be polite and pleasant. This takes emotional effort. This "emotional labor", some argue, is underpaid or underappreciated. Labor that requires hard to develop skills, like surgery, is paid more than labor that requires only politeness, like being a host or hostess.

Many men find it difficult to understand the difference between normal business politeness, which has been part of all business at all times in human history, and "emotional labor" which seems to be a new phenomenon. That's because there is no difference. "Emotional labor" just means being polite to customers. (By the way, surgeons and lawyers also have to be polite to customers.)

Why then, is this suddenly such an issue? As women lower their standards of personality from "pleasant enough to marry" to "not too annoying to have sex with", they have lost the normal politeness that all businesses on earth assume any reasonable person can have.

On college campuses, you can shriek at anyone who disagrees with your crackpot ideas. In business, that tends to go over...less well. In college, sex is pretty much the most powerful currency. But, in business, skills, politeness, timeliness, reliability, and sobriety matter. You can be intoxicated, tattooed, and angry all the time in college, and people will still want to have sex with you. For that matter, you can be intoxicated, tattooed, and angry in the business world and people will want to have sex with you. They just won't want to hire you.

"Emotional labor" hasn't been a particular challenge for heterosexual men, since we're pretty used to it. It takes emotional labor for a heterosexual man to keep smiling through some insane welfarist rant long enough to have sex with someone. We have plenty of practice. Compared to dating or seducing women, the "emotional labor" required for business politeness is minimal. Compared to tolerating the shrieking and browbeating that has become common in marriages, the "emotional labor" of business is nothing.

But for those who have gotten used to making their personalities as unbearable as possible, normal business interaction must require quite an unfamiliar amount of emotional labor indeed!

CHAPTER 13:

More on Safe Spaces

Safe spaces were once private areas where people could discuss shared vulnerabilities. Like Alcoholics Anonymous meetings, they were small, enclosed areas where people could share secrets.

Since then, the Safe Space movement has gotten out of hand, seeking to conquer greater and greater physical and social areas. The movement is trying to turn the entire planet into a Safe Space.

Perhaps unexpectedly, Alcoholics Anonymous and Narcotics Anonymous are the more sensible ones here. AA members don't expect to be applauded outside of AA meetings just because they mention that they haven't had a drink in 5 hours. They get that there are areas in which the rules cater to their vulnerabilities, and that in the rest of the world they need to act sane.

The Safe Space movement doesn't get that. To them, the entire world should be their safe space.

You'll notice that while safe space culture pretends to be about respecting views, it basically only allows the views in line with welfarism. Wearing Republican or Libertarian clothing can be more than enough to violate a safe space. In December of 2017, Michael Esposito, Sebastian Balaslova, and Aaron Spring were kicked out of a Fordham University Bronx campus coffee shop for wearing MAGA hats supporting Trump. They were told that their hats violated the safe space policy at Rodrigues Coffee Shop. The video was released on the CampusReform website, and reported by FOX, the New York Post, and other major media.

True safe space policy is simple. If you support the welfarism that disempowers men, you can speak. If not, shut up.

This culture has come with an even more dystopian dark side, as it has extended into many common social venues.

The intention behind the rampant adoption of safe space policies makes sense: women should not be afraid of being assaulted when at a social venue. If someone poses some kind of a threat, refuses to respect another person's boundaries, etc., then it makes sense for the venue to protect its clients.

However, it can go too far. The policy of providing immediate protection to someone in danger has turned into a kind of McCarthy-era, no-evidence-required culture in which any woman can target any man with made up accusations.

In many venues, no evidence of any kind is required to get a man kicked out. In fact, the man doesn't even need to be accused of anything noteworthy! I've heard from men who were banned or put on probation for things as nebulous as "intense conversations." My guess: those conversations probably weren't about welfarist ideas like tax funded birth control, or why women should empower themselves by having nine hundred sexual partners. They were, quite possibly, in some way against that.

Or they could have been about nothing. Men who are politically outspoken are often targeted by these attacks. All a woman has to do is say that a man had an "intense conversation" with her, or near her, or within her hearing, and he's gone. Women can lie with complete impunity, since there is no open court testimony, no cross examination, no rights of the accused.

Could those men get any clarification? Of course not. In safe spaces, men have no rights (unless they are welfarist white knights, of course).

The most basic principle in western law is the right to cross examine your accuser. The plaintiff gets to present an argument, and the defendant gets to defend. That's why we call them "defendants" not "The Silent". The defendant gets to hear the charges and evidence against him, and then defend himself. The charges must be for something that makes sense, and the evidence has to exist.

In the United States, this is expressed in the Sixth Amendment to the Constitution, which indicates that the accused has the right "to be informed of the nature and cause of the accusation; to be confronted with the witnesses against him...." The accused must know exactly what he is being accused of, told what the evidence is, and presented with witnesses that he or his legal counsel can cross examine.

But safe space culture doesn't allow that. Just an accusation of "intense conversations" can be enough. They have become just another tool of welfarist culture and male silencing.

Of course, many of these safe spaces are private organizations, although many do receive tax funding. Private organizations have no requirement to follow the kind of due process expected in public courts.

But what kind of precedent is this setting? How long before due process is suspended in courts based on some safe-space nonsense?

Remember, we're living in a time when a man can be forced to pay for the products of his wife's infidelity. Sanity and decency are no longer parts of our court system. The old law, in which the man could sue his wife and her lover for damages, has been replaced by a new law, in which the man has to pay for the lover's genetic offspring.

Is it so impossible to imagine that other basic human rights will be suspended from our courts? The right to confront your accuser is a fundamental right, but it's nowhere near as fundamental as your right to not be forced to pay for someone else's genetic offspring.

If a more fundamental right can be so thoroughly trampled, why not a less fundamental right?

But, in these stories that I have heard from so many silenced men, I see a powerful hope. If our words weren't dangerous, they wouldn't try to silence them. If our intense conversations couldn't destroy their welfarist culture, they wouldn't care if we had them. If our ideas weren't spreading and powerful, they wouldn't try to squash them.

In their efforts to silence us, they have revealed where they are weak. They have told us the strategies we should use.

The words that trigger them, that leave them #LiterallyShaking, the "intense conversations" that get people banned - those are the right ones. That's where their weaknesses are. Those are the words that will destroy their welfarist, male disempowering culture.

Those trying to silence us may seem strong. They are not. These are people who can't afford $30 a month for birth control, and don't have the discipline for abstinence or condoms. Their only abilities are shrieking or banning other people into silence.

Refuse to be silenced.

Stop using social media to share pictures of puppies. Start using it to oppose welfarist culture and "social justice". If people shriek and cry at you, that's a sign that you're doing it right.

It's also a way to embolden others who think like you. When you first speak out, either in person or online, you will be the only one. Others who think like you will stay silent, until they know you won't back down. No one wants to be the only one speaking up. But if they know you'll be with them, they'll find the courage to speak.

You'll probably get a few friend requests and followers. Those are the people who agree with you, but don't have the courage to speak out yet. Give them time. Think of how long it took you to speak out.

If you can't find the words, don't worry. Share from other sources. If you like parts of this book, copy whatever parts you like, and post them on social media; just don't tell the publisher.

The pen is mightier than the sword, and your voice is more powerful than your silence.

CHAPTER 14:

The Classical Mindset and Child Support

When I hear that something is "for the children", I get nervous. Most assaults on natural rights, on logic, on justice are given that justification. Today, using children as a facile justification, the assault on male reality and culture has reached unbelievable levels.

We've already discussed one extreme case, in which a cuckolded man is legally forced to pay for a child that is not biologically his. This lunacy violates and assaults male reality and basic common sense in obvious ways, and does not draw on any historical precedent.

The justification used is, not surprisingly, "the interests of the child." But obviously any child will benefit from more money. This facile excuse just uses shallow emotional appeal to entirely deny the reality of the man. In more blatant words, they're saying: "Don't worry, we'll viciously violate your natural rights, but it's okay, because it's For the Children."

But the abuses of common sense and natural rights don't stop there.

A male below the age of consent cannot legally give consent to sex. While I personally believe that anyone who has reached puberty has the natural right to consent to sex, the law does not. In the eyes of the law, a woman over the age of consent who has sex with a man under the age of consent is guilty of statutory rape. Legally, the man cannot consent to sex.

However, apparently he can consent to 18 years of child support. That's right. Boys who cannot consent to sex, who are "coerced" into illegal, "non-consensual" sex, often have to pay child support. According to a 2014 article by Alia Beard Rau in USA Today, Nick Olivas had sex with a 20 year old woman when he was 14. According to the law, that's statutory rape. She got pregnant. He had to pay child support.

This is not a new phenomenon. The same article mentions a 13 year old boy in Kansas who impregnated his 17 year old babysitter. He also had to pay child support. So did a 15 year old California boy who had sex with a 34 year old neighbor. The neighbor was convicted of statutory rape, but the young boy still had to pay child support.

And still it gets worse. Women have secretly used a man's sperm to get pregnant without the consent of the man at all, and then successfully sued for child support. I mentioned the case of Dr. Richard Phillips before. Dr. Sharon Irons saved his semen, used it to impregnate herself without his consent, and then used the courts to force him to pay child support. This was a doctor who lost this legal battle. With far more discretionary income to spend on legal fees than most of us have, Dr. Phillips still lost.

Men with lower economic power are even further stomped on by the legal system. They have to get used to unbelievably low paychecks (child support is taken out before the check is received). In a 2016 Splinter News article, "How Our Racist Child Support Laws Hurt Poor, Black Fathers the Most", Collier Meyerson described the experience of Orenthius Perkins. Perkins says, "I remember I got a job working at the interstate Ford dealership at the time and I got a check for zero dollars."

And if the mother is on welfare, the money doesn't even go to the kids, but rather to the government!

I'm opposed to welfare in all forms. But note that the welfare rules are specifically designed to harm the man. Even if the woman doesn't care about child support, the man's wages are still taken. They just go to the government.

Men who can't pay child support are often jailed. In other words, mothers who are poor are subsidized. Fathers who are poor are stripped of their rights and thrown in prisons.

But it's not just these unusual types of child support cases that are absurd. The standard agreement that most family courts come up with is that the mother gets custody, and the father pays child support.

What kind of division is that? One parent gets the kid, and the other one pays? That would be like dividing a cow as follows: I get the milk, and you get to provide food for the cow.

If anything, the person paying the child support should be the one with custody. The person paying should get the benefits.

If we keep fighting, we'll probably be able to change some of these laws. Already, men's rights groups have successfully changed laws in several states so that cuckolded men no longer have to pay child support. Laws that make young male statutory rape victims still have to pay child support will probably also be changed. Over time, the general structure of child support may change to be less ridiculous (if we fight for it).

But even in the short term, there are changes that men can experience. Begin by understanding the current situation: in America, men have no real paternal rights at all. Men get less custody, but pay more in child support. According to attorney Jasmine Hernandez in a 2015 New York Post article entitled "Stop Stacking the Legal Deck Against Dads", only 17 percent of men become the primary custodial parent. The rest of the time is the usual nonsense: women get the kids, and men pay.

Those paternal "rights" are worthless and meaningless. So, throw them out. While you cannot negotiate child support before having kids, you can, in many cases and in consultation with a lawyer, just sign away all of your paternity rights…and financial responsibilities. These are similar to the contracts that sperm donors use, and are referred to as Known Sperm Donor contracts. On the downside, you no longer have any guaranteed custody rights. But the fact is, as a man, you never had them in the first place.

On the upside, you no longer have to pay state mandated child support, ever. No woman will be able to use your children as weapons of financial extortion against you.

But you can still choose to pay child support…and negotiate custody in exchange for that support. It might not be called child support, but you can come to a custody agreement with the child's mother. Instead of relying on the courts that treat you like a dog, you can work outside the courts, and come to a financial agreement that works for you.

If you want primary custody, you just do the reverse. Instead of a sperm donor contract, you use a surrogacy contract. Be warned: these are much harder to enforce. Some jurisdictions do not allow surrogacy, or recognize its legal validity. That shouldn't surprise you: family courts are all about protecting women, and ignoring the rights of men. However, enough states recognize surrogacy that it's a very realistic option.

Intentional singleness has another major advantage. When the child is applying for college, he will probably pay a much lower tuition. As a donor, the law does not recognize you as the father. Thus, your assets are not counted when colleges calculate his tuition. He will be the child of some single mom (or if you have custody, a single dad). He will get a lower tuition, since he will be given more "financial aid". (If you're concerned about the moral issues, don't be. Colleges intentionally charge inflated rates, and then reduce them for around 70 percent of students. It's just their way of promoting socialism by charging successful people more.)

Marriage has a 60 percent chance of divorce. Divorce during formative years has a 100% chance of creating academic and emotional problems for the child, and a 200% chance of creating bratty behavior. Marriage does not help kids. It just puts them at risk.

Intentional singleness leads to stability, eliminates the risk of the emotional chaos of divorce, and prepares kids for success. As an added bonus, it protects your finances.

The most common result in American procreation is this: a man and a woman living separately, the kids living with the mom. The path to that destination includes emotional trauma for all parties, including, and especially, the kids. The man is often robbed through alimony if he doesn't have a prenup, and robbed through child support no matter what. And yet, men still go through this lunatic process and consider it Plan A.

It's time to look at things differently. If the end result is your children living with their mom, and your having custody only by her permission, what is the most direct and painless way to get there? How can you leverage her for more permission to see your kids?

The courts won't help you, but you can help yourself, even if you don't have overly abundant financial resources.

One way is to skip the marriage and divorce, and make living apart Plan A. When you're ready to have kids, sign away all rights and responsibilities. If the girl you're dating isn't ready for that, just wait a couple years. Once a woman reaches 30 or 35, she's usually much more amenable.

Consider it a preemptive divorce. If the ending state is going to be living apart anyway, find the most direct, least disruptive way to get there.

Come to some custody and payment agreement beforehand. It may not be legally enforceable, but clear expectations always help.

Then remember this: if she denies custody, you can withhold payment. You aren't legally required to do anything.

Obviously, when you do something like this, for the love of god talk to a lawyer. Spend a couple thousand now. If you do not have a couple thousand for a lawyer, you cannot possibly have the resources for children.

If you are going with this type of approach, you will also need to adjust your conscious and unconscious mindset towards different types of women. Often, men have a slightly higher level of attraction to women who are much less financially powerful than they are. I believe this comes from our old instincts that tell us that a weaker woman is less likely to stray and get impregnated by someone else. But remember, paternity uncertainty is no longer relevant, since you can get a paternity test for cheap. Don't base your modern behavior on prehistoric principles.

And don't fall into the trap that men of the past did. They were unable to think outside of their social norms. They were unable to think past their institutions. The result was what we have today.

If your goal is to have children without marriage or cohabitation, you don't want someone who is entirely dependent on you. That means that now women who make a lot of money, and are highly competent and responsible, are more desirable. You don't need to keep her dependent to ensure paternity; science has taken care of that.

CHAPTER 15:

The Culture War: Rape Culture or Theft Culture?

During the last few years, many have argued that "Rape Culture" exists. Rape culture involves normalizing and making excuses for sexual assault and rape. In general, I have quite a bit of sympathy for many of these ideas, although some people take it too far. It's hard to take comments like "All heterosexual sex is rape" very seriously. At the same time, the sheer volume of date rape, especially in colleges, shows there is something wrong with parts of American culture. Note that I am referring to situations in which a woman says "no" or says nothing at all, and is coerced.

The most brutal evidence of rape culture is among the police. There are, at the time of this writing, thousands of unprocessed rape kits sitting in police evidence lockers. According to NPR, in 2016 there were were tens of thousands of rape kits still left unprocessed. Texas alone had 20,000 untested rape kits.

When a woman is raped, she can go to a hospital to have evidence collected. This evidence should then be processed by the police. Going through this process is emotionally difficult, invasive, and uncomfortable. Few women work up the nerve to go through it. The fact that police don't even bother processing this evidence, while they have limitless money to go after non-crimes like drug use, has left many Americans furious.

This isn't the police saying, "Rape is okay." But it definitely is the police saying "Rape is less horrific than using drugs." If they have resources for the latter but not the former, there is no other way to look at it.

And yet, the vast majority of Americans do not think rape is okay. Most men and women consider rape to be a singularly abhorrent act. Among normal people, outside the police, rape approval is not a part of our culture.

Unfortunately, many who argue that rape culture exists have done so primarily by extending the definition of rape. For example, if a woman gives active consent while drunk, that is not, according to many university regulations, actual consent. Even if the woman initiates sex while drunk, even if she does so aggressively, that is still not considered consent.

Let me be clear. If a drunk woman aggressively initiates sex, the man tries to resist her, she is persistent, and he eventually caves, the man in that case is guilty of rape.

Thus, that sexual act, while it appears consensual by the dictionary definition of the word, is not consensual according to the regulatory definition. In an odd technical sense, many argue that it qualifies as rape.

Many people privately consider that preposterous, but rarely risk the social blowback of saying it aloud. But even if they don't say anything aloud, most people do not give that type of situation the same sympathy that they give regular rape involving no consent, drunken or otherwise.

Those who expect people to respond to that type of rape as angrily as they respond to stranger-in-an-alley rape do not have their expectations met. Their conclusion: people must think rape is okay.

The reality is that people consider stranger rape to be rape. They consider "I was drunk, so the consent I gave didn't count", or "the sex I aggressively initiated was actually rape" to be just a lack of responsibility.

When oil tanker captains are drunk and accidentally crash their ship, spilling thousands of gallons of oil and irrevocably destroying huge portions of ocean environments, we don't excuse that behavior. We don't say, "The crew should have noticed the captain was impaired and ignored his commands."

If a drunk pilot makes a mistake while flying a plane, we don't blame the flight crew for not taking control of the plane.

If a drunk surgeon makes a mistake, we don't blame the nurses.

If a drunk driver kills a kid, we don't excuse that behavior, saying it was not the driver's fault. If anything we are twice as unforgiving.

Rape hasn't been normalized. But most people are not willing to call irresponsible decisions made while intoxicated someone else's fault.

What About Blaming the Victim?

Many women argue that when women take brazen risks and then get raped, the woman often gets blamed for being irresponsible. Instead of getting sympathy, she gets scolded. Some women and their sycophants argue that this doesn't happen with any other crime. They argue men are not told to be careful to avoid crime, and blamed when they are victims of crime.

But the fact is that it actually does happen with many other crimes. Men are warned not to wear flashy watches or carry too much cash in particular areas. Those that do, and then get robbed, get zero sympathy from other men or women.

A man who gets pickpocketed is generally told to be more careful, and given suggestions on how to prevent future thefts. He is also generally berated for not doing those things in the first place.

A man who wears a flashy Rolex in a dangerous part of a city, and then gets robbed, is just chastised for being reckless.

Many years ago, two male friends and I went to Brazil. We were warned a couple of times not to wear any jewelry, and not to go on the beach at night. You know what we did?

We didn't wear any jewelry, and we didn't go on the beach at night. We were warned maybe one or two times. That's all it took. If we had gone to the beach at night, and been robbed, we would have gotten no sympathy at all. Our parents, our friends, our acquaintances would have asked, "Why did you go to the beach at night, when you were warned that it was dangerous?"

Compare that to the behavior of many women. They are reminded constantly to avoid situations that have a high risk of sexual assault. Those situations are laid out clearly, and there aren't that many of them. Most of them don't require major limitations on behavior. "Don't get drunk and pass out at a frat party," for example, isn't that restrictive.

These are not reminders given once or twice, but rather thousands of times. Women are given thousands of warning stories. They are told by their parents, grandparents, teachers, counselors, orientation leaders about what situations to avoid. And the vast, vast majority of women just listen. At a frat party, you don't see hundreds of women passed out from drinking a gallon of alcohol to get attention. You see maybe one. The other 99.9 percent of women take normal precautions that any sane person would.

When particular women get raped because they refuse to take the basic precautions that all men take with any property of any value, they invariably get some blame. It's not that people don't feel bad for them. It's that people cannot understand why anyone would put anything of value at such wanton risk.

A Better World

There are parts of the world in which wearing a Rolex is dangerous. Those are generally less good parts of the world. It is a major cultural achievement when you can wear an expensive watch and not worry about being robbed.

Would this be a better world if an unconscious man or woman had zero fear of being robbed or raped? Of course. Should we, as a culture, work toward that? Absolutely.

We would all prefer a world in which no person had to fear either robbery or assault. I reject the notion that rape culture exists, precisely because I do not think that most people consider rape acceptable.

Creating a world in which such fears do not exist is a worthy goal that we should culturally strive toward. The fact that we haven't achieved it yet doesn't mean that we live in a rape culture, any more than the fact that we haven't ended all carjacking means that we live in a carjacking culture.

CHAPTER 16:

How Theft Culture Defiles Us

The crucial thing about rape it that it's part assault, and it's part theft. It's not pure assault. The rapist gets something with a significant market value from the woman. He also assaults and violates her rights as a person, in a manner more intimate than property theft.

The theft aspect of rape will make it likely for the same reason that other types of theft are likely. Shoplifting, grand theft, burglary, and armed robbery aren't going anywhere anytime soon. When you have something of value, there is a chance someone will try to take it from you. Morally, they are wrong to even attempt to do so. Pragmatically, you should take steps to protect anything of value that you have.

Everyone knows that sex with women has a higher market value than sex with men. Women use this as a weapon, both personally and politically. They manipulate men in personal relationships, and they use male desire for sex to influence acceptable social behavior. On college campuses, some women use this to try to pressure men to support welfare statism. As mentioned earlier, it is not uncommon to see online dating profiles in which women aggressively indicate that they are interested in dating liberal progressives only.

That same value that allows that kind of manipulation also creates rape risk. This is no different from anything of value. If you have a full wallet, that both gives you power and puts you at risk.

The cultural expectation that people protect their valuables is not Rape Culture. It's not victim blaming. It's just common sense.

What would it actually look like if a particular crime were a part of culture? It would probably be so deeply ingrained in culture that no one would think twice about it. It would enjoy the kind of moral invisibility that comes from ubiquity.

If we really had a culture that normalized rape, rape would be a common means to an end. For example, you'd hear statements like, "I'm thinking about having kids, so I'll probably try to rape someone this weekend." Or, "I'm raping women to raise money for an important cause. Would you like to sponsor me?"

We don't see that, fortunately. But unfortunately we do see that with theft. People say, "I'm doing a scientific study, and I'm going to try to get government funding." That funding, of course, is money taken, through taxation, without consent of the taxee. That money is taken through theft. Theft is the first step of the scientific study, and it receives social approval.

We might see, "I'm working on a cool art installation, and I'm seeking a government grant." That grant is funded through coercive, non-consensual taxation. Again, the first step is taking money without consent, and doing so is socially approved.

If we had a real rape culture, there would be so much pervasive rape that people wouldn't even call it rape. I've never seen anything like that with rape. But we're all seeing that with theft.

Why do you, as an individual, pay taxes? Why do you pay sales taxes, income taxes, hidden taxes that drive up prices, property taxes (either directly or through higher rent)? For some readers, it's essentially a donation. Whether it was required or not, you would donate that amount of money to the government.

But the rest of us do so because we fear repercussions. We recognize that if we do not pay the taxes, men with guns will force us to. We don't have any choice. They don't wait for active consent. They don't wait for any consent at all. In fact, the taxes are taken over our direct opposition.

The word for having your money coercively taken over your direct objection is "theft." In our culture, theft has been normalized. It's not the kind of theft done by a man in a dark alley with a gun. It's the kind of theft that has become such a huge part of our culture that it is no longer seen as a necessary evil. It's seen as a good. In fact, today an associated act of theft actually culturally legitimizes an action.

For example, a person who starts a charitable organization gets some social approval. A person who starts a charitable organization with a taxation-funded government grant gets more social approval!

If that same person had robbed several middle class people to get the startup funding, he would probably get social disapproval. But theft through taxation gets social approval. Theft once removed gets more social approval than no theft at all.

That is unambiguously theft culture. Theft has been so normalized that it is seen as a positive, rather than a negative.

This is not limited to charitable organizations. A scientist who gets a taxation-funded grant to do research gets more social approval than one who does similar research without any associated taxation. The same is true of any other kind of research.

Art done with a taxation-funded grant gets more social approval than art done without it. In fact, almost any behavior done with a taxation funded grant currently gets more social approval than that same behavior without it. A thief who uses once-removed theft to fund his hobby is seen as superior to a non-thief who just pursues his hobby.

The existence of large scale taxation obviously erodes the comparative social power of men. As mentioned before, men cannot use the economic value they produce as leverage. They cannot choose to give or withhold the fruits of their labor in exchange for any particular behavior. This essentially limits male power in the same way that denying women the ability to give or withhold sex would limit female power.

The normalization of this type of widespread theft erodes this power even more. Men are no longer expected to view taxation-based funding as a necessary evil. We are expected to praise it as a social good. Theft culture, and its close relative grant culture, have become so dominant that they have not only normalized theft, but made it socially praiseworthy.

To fight that, we must first stop praising it. If someone you know gets a taxation-funded grant to research something, say, "I'm glad you're pursuing research in _____, but I'd be even prouder if you found a way to do it without taxation." Or, "The art you made is great; using taxation to support it is immoral. Have you considered Kickstarter or other voluntary programs?"

If that sounds harsh, take a look at what women had to do to gain value dominance. Post on Facebook something like, "Women should take basic precautions to avoid rape," and see what happens. Observe the immediate vitriol of the responses. See how aggressively people will respond. Then decide if the above responses are actually that harsh.

We need to de-normalize theft entirely. We can say, "Taxation is a necessary evil, to be used in only the most extreme circumstances." Or we can say, "Taxation is always wrong and never justified." Even the very simple, "Taxation is theft," gets the job done.

The political part of this, working against all forms of taxation funding of education, science, art, research, and hobbies is important. Vote only for candidates that will pledge to sponsor and fight for legislation to end all of that. We must work politically to end theft culture.

But we cannot just leave that in the political realm if we expect to win the personal war. This has to be something you fight personally. You can do it with grace, humor, cleverness, bluntness, understatement, overstatement, metonymy, alliteration, or anaphora. But, you cannot do it with silence.

Comparing Theft Culture and Rape Culture; The Sacredness of Work

When I have compared the mythical rape culture to the very real theft culture, the response is generally shrill rage. How dare anyone compare theft to rape? Rape is an invasion and violation of the inner, sacred part of someone. Theft is just money. It's not violating something inside you.

My question, then, is where exactly do you think work happens?

Economic work is not just force times distance, which is how work is defined in physics. Economic work is the culmination of your education, your passion, your effort, your concentration. Creativity, passion, excellence, and knowledge happen in the most sacred part of your body, in the most unique, personal, valuable part of your brain. That part of you is more sacred than any other part of you, including your genitals.

Work is sacred. It is divine. If you look at an iPad, it's just metal, glass, and plastic. But thanks to the innovation and labor poured into it, it has become a wonder just short of Aladdin's lamp. The divinity of labor transforms a hunk of wood into an ornate table. It transforms a person dying of cancer into a healthy person. It transforms an illiterate child into a critically reading adult, or a failing company into a successful one. The most sacred part of a person is their work. Whether that person is a teacher, sculptor, engineer, doctor, builder, architect - through work, they transform the world.

That divinity is something that should be respected and cherished. When we, as a culture, respect it, individuals learn to respect it. Young people understand that it is something to be respected and cherished.

The fruits of your labor are sacred. They are as sacred as your body, your thoughts, your sexuality. But today, they aren't treated sacredly. Today, the fruits of your labor are taken, through taxation, without a second thought, without an apology. It's never, "We know that you earned this with the most sacred part of yourself. We ask you to share some with us, for this vital project." It's not even, "We know that you earned this with the most sacred part of yourself. But this project is so vital, that we must take some of the fruits of your labor. We hope to never have to do this again, but this is a life or death emergency."

Nope. It's "Pay 'your' taxes. We'll spend it however we goddamn want." Today, the sacred fruits of the labors of men and productive women are stolen and given to women who can't even bother to treat their own sexuality and reproduction sacredly, or even concernedly. When you tell a young man it's normal and good that the fruits of his labor be stolen to pay for the needs of a slut with 9 kids from 9 different broke fathers, how can he possibly consider his labor sacred? If it's less sacred than that garbage, how is it sacred?

In that situation, it makes more sexual and reproductive sense to be one of the nine fathers than to be the sacred worker who is being robbed to pay for the nine kids.

Can you imagine sex being treated like that? If half of each woman's sexuality was assigned to whichever man "needed" it the most. Half the time she had sex, she would choose who to have sex with, and the other half of the time the government would choose. Or if the government did the same with procreation? How about if she could choose the father for half of her kids, and the government would choose for the other half?

First, it would be monstrous. And the way that work, which is just as sacred, is currently treated, is more monstrous. Work is more sacred than sex.

Work isn't just the application of mechanical force over a distance. It's the personal, intimate, creative process that makes that force meaningful. The person designing the next smartphone is not expending more external mechanical energy than an orangutan throwing a branch at a tree. It's what is inside him, what makes him unique and different from others, that makes his work more significant.

Our work, our thoughts, are far more individual than our genitals. There is some variety in genitals from person to person. There is a far greater variety in minds. Work is the fruit of the mind.

If women's sexuality were mistreated the way work is, if each woman were expected to have half of her sex with people assigned by the state, how would that transform women? Would they cherish their sexuality? Or would they learn to disrespect it, and find something else to value?

They would turn callous, unfeeling, and vicious. The fact that they were forced to have sex with those in need would not make them feel charitable. It would make them feel used and abused.

Today's disrespect of work is doing the same to men. They are turning callous, unfeeling, and vicious. Visit any Red Pill discussion board to see for yourself.

It doesn't have to be this way. We, as individuals, don't have to be this way.

The final step of the solution is obvious: end all involuntary taxation. If someone has a project that is worthy of funding, they can use

Kickstarter, Indiegogo, or another crowdfunding service. They can start a legitimate business that provides a vital service to people for a fee. If someone wants the fruits of your labor, they should ask. They should have to convince you, not force you. We don't tolerate people forcibly taking sex, and we shouldn't tolerate people forcibly taking the sacred fruits of our work.

But what is the first step? The first step is to understand that you are being violated. The sacred part of you, your work, is being taken without your consent. That's theft culture. Right now, you are probably rationalizing this by saying, "Well, my work isn't really sacred." Bullshit. Think of how hard you worked to develop the skill to do that work. Think of the thought and energy you put into that work. Your work is what makes you human far more than your sexuality does. Even a dog can have sex. The divinity, the sacredness in you is in your work, not your sexual desire.

If your work truly isn't sacred, start to find types of work that are. Find work that you value, that you are proud of. It will almost certainly require putting in effort. You may have to spend years learning, either through traditional or independent study. That's fine. That's how it's supposed to be.

When the fruits of your work are taken from you, understand that it is a deep and personal violation. It is not okay. It is not acceptable. You may need to tolerate it to survive, just as people in prisons tolerate rape to survive. That doesn't make it acceptable.

And then you must fight it. If you can use some non taxable form of income, like cash or cryptocurrency, do. If you cannot, then at least use your voice. Stop being polite to the people who are violating you, or supporting that violation, or benefiting from that violation. Every person using the welfare state, government grants, government contracts, even government schools is countenancing that violation. Every person taking a government salary is countenancing that violation. Every person using any optional government service is countenancing that violation.

That includes you. If you have a government job or use government schools, you are collaborating with the enemy. Start taking steps to stop. Connect with your local homeschool coop. Find a job that is not funded through stolen money.

And don't let people screw with you on "roads". Many pro-theft, pro-violation people will argue, "Well, you use roads, how is that any different?" First, it's different because of the percentages. Roads account for a tiny, tiny fraction of total spending. I agree that it is wrong to steal even a cent of the fruits of someone's labor. But it's more wrong to steal several thousand dollars.

Most importantly: you would be happy to pay for roads, through EZ pass or a similar service. You'd be happy to pay for them through Kickstarter, Indiegogo, or a similar service. But could the users or supporters of government schools or other types of welfare say the same? Sure, they are willing to rob and violate you to pay for it, but are they willing to just pay for it themselves?

That's the critical difference. Using something that you would be willing to pay for is vastly different from using something that you are only willing to steal for. If I had to pay for roads, I'd be happy to do so - as long as I could stop paying for welfare, government schools, medicaid, and the like. I'd be happy to pay directly for roads, as long as I could pay for only the kids I father, not the ones that I don't.

Work is sacred. Theft culture is morally abhorrent, politically and personally disempowering, and psychologically destructive. Those who forcibly take the fruits of your labor are violating you. Those who advocate for doing that are advocating to violate you. Let's work to stop that for good.

CHAPTER 17:

Example of Pulling Out: Art

Art and Watches

For centuries, art has been a central part of masculine culture. Like an architect creating a building, masculine artists created works of incredible skill and months of labor.

In general, the more skill and time a particular work of art took, the higher the price. This was true not only in realism and naturalism, but even in "modern art" movements like analytical cubism.

The great masters, from Da Vinci to Dali, poured both skill and effort into their masterpieces.

The price of art, like the price of all other products, reflected the skill and labor used to create them. Until it didn't.

In recent decades, the price of art has stopped reflecting the skill or labor put into it. Art that reflects neither skill nor effort is inexplicably astronomically priced; art that has both is often ignored.

Art, once such a central part of masculine culture, is finding less interest among men. Even the most obtuse among us can sometimes tell when people are obviously trying to manipulate us. As men lose interest in either buying or producing art according to the new rules, art has become increasingly politicized. Unskilled, zero-effort art that reflects the values of third-wave feminism, socialism, and social justice is supported and lionized. Art that rejects those values has no home.

It's gotten so absurd that normal people sometimes can't tell the difference between art and garbage. According to Gawker.com, in 2014 a cleaning woman at an Italian gallery accidentally threw out "art" by a New York artist. The art was designed to look like garbage. She figured it was.

Nor is this an isolated incident. The same thing happened in a British gallery in 2001 to an ashtray based art installation by Damien Hirst. And then again to another artist in 2015 in Italy.

The desire for art is still there. Men seek that connection with genius, brilliance, and excellence. But current, demasculinized art cannot fill that desire at all. Current art, like current marriage, demands that men treat material with obviously low economic value as if it were an economic prize. Men just aren't that interested in that. Marriage has, at least, social pressure helping it. Buying fine art doesn't have the same advantage. Many men look at today's art as ripoffs for fools.

But the desire for that close connection to genius, excellence, passion, and even meaningful symbolism hasn't disappeared. The changes in art left a void. But millions of men have found what they need in a completely surprising place: watches.

While the media has looked on in total bewilderment, millions of men have developed a fascination and even an obsession with wristwatches. Watches have taken the place of paintings and sculptures.

Unlike a $50,000 painting, which could be something that took less than 20 seconds to create, a $50,000 watch usually embodies $50,000 worth of labor and skill. More expensive watches generally take more time and more skill than less expensive ones. Sure, there is some branding that influences price, but the most expensive watches are generally the most complicated, take the most effort, and demand the most skill.

Watches, like any great art, built on elements of earlier great art, while bringing in more innovations. The visual elements in painting have been incorporated into the engraving, enamelling, and wood marquetry found on the dials of many great watches. Sculptural elements are, of course, a major part of any watch.

It's not just the aesthetic focus, the labor involved, or the intense effort allowing watches to take the place of other forms of fine art. Like other forms of fine art, watches are steeped in symbolism revealed through details and aesthetic decisions.

Take, for example, Audemars Piguet's Royal Oak watches. The decision to make them in steel, rather than gold, had obvious masculine symbolism. The later Royal Oak Offshore emphasized it's refusal to follow normal rules through its larger size, and its name. On the surface, "Offshore" indicates scuba diving. But, "offshore" is also the location of the bank where you hide your assets from ex wives and tax collectors.

Or consider Vacheron Constantin's watch "Philosophia". It has a 24 hour dial and no minute hand, but a chiming mechanism that allows the owner to determine the exact time on demand. It combines the masculine principle of timeless contemplation with the principle of exactness when needed.

Or consider the erotic watches made by Svend Andersen that hide brazen eroticism on the back of stately looking watches.

While painting and sculpture have been politically taken over by third wave feminism, "social justice", and socialism, watches symbolize masculinity and capitalism. Watches are often built using expensive materials, require incredible skill to create, and have prices that actually reflect the skill and time required to produce them.

The sheer amount of labor required to build a high end watch, in fact, serves much of the same purpose as the amount of labor required to build a church or cathedral. The huge amount of labor that went into building those religious buildings symbolized worship of the divine and dedication to the community. Watches, because they are worn by one person, inherently symbolize individualism and dedication to the self.

When art became increasingly useless, men (and plenty of women) at first argued against the the new art. Eventually, they got tired of arguing against pretentious, high-strung shriekers, and found a superior replacement. They told lazies and socialists that they could keep the old art forms, drag them through the dirt, and cover them with every kind of socialist propaganda. They simply moved on to a different art form, one insulated from that particular kind of idiocy.

Today, I see two methods of opposing garbage masquerading as art. Some people just stay direct and hostile: "A pile of garbage isn't art." But others are just sarcastic, dismissive, and condescending. People who have moved past painting and into watches say, "Hey, that's a really cool...um...sculpture?" or "That's a really nicely laid out pile of garbage, really reminds me of garbage." Then they turn their attention, money, and passion towards other art forms. Since garbage art is basically a tantrum against the hierarchies created by skill and effort, it only has meaning if the patriarchy opposes it. When the patriarchy stops really caring at all, the rebellion is meaningless.

Masculine culture has mockingly dismissed modern painting and sculpture. We smirk and say, "You guys can have painting and sculpture. Ruin it however you like, with our blessings. If you say that this particular pile of garbage represents the suffering caused by private property, and this other pile of garbage represents implicit white supremacy in the media, and this third pile of literal garbage tells us that women should have 3 years of paid maternity leave, we no longer care. If you guys are going to act like children having tantrums, we'll treat you accordingly. We won't fight or argue with you. We'll just mollify and ignore you."

When the proponents of garbage art showed their boldness by completely ruining painting and sculpture, men showed even greater boldness by moving on to another art form entirely. You can see this by comparing the relative popularity of art websites and watch websites. While watch websites have grown in popularity, art websites have become increasingly ignored. Watch sites enjoy higher rankings, more popularity, and more visitors.

To illustrate: artforum.com, the site of the most well-known art magazine in the country over the last several decades, is way down at the 28,000th most popular website in the U.S. On the other hand, Hodinkee.com, a blog about fine watches that is a few years old, started by amateurs who had an interest in watches, is much more popular, currently ranked as the 7,000th most popular website. It has many times more daily visitors, unique visitors, etc.

Today's watch aficionados didn't have to actively kill painting and sculpture to make it irrelevant. They just ignored it, and then took their passion, intelligence and money to an entirely different art form. Today, left in the hands of deadbeats, painting and sculpture have lost significance in male culture and the American culture of excellence. Few people can name a single living painter or sculptor, aside from personal friends. This is a radical departure from the past, when people like Dali, Michelangelo, Leonardo da Vinci, and even Picasso were legendary during their lifetimes.

Today's culture of horology is the worthy successor of the artistic culture led by those artistic giants. Watch culture has become one of the most important influences on the aesthetics and values of American and international culture.

The great civilizations of the future, when they look back at today's artistic achievements, will see capitalist watches, not social justice garbage, as the aesthetic and symbolic pinnacles of our era.

The Reverse Side: Dadaism and the New Communist Movement

Recently, I had the opportunity to discuss art with a leader in the anarcho communist movement. While capitalist groups have embraced the art form that requires a tremendous amount of skill and labor, communist groups have gone in the opposite direction!

In particular, Dadaist art has become popular. Dadaism has always been closely tied to the radical left, and embraces low skill randomness rather than high skill effort. It often focuses on randomly combining various objects, words, and images. It doesn't demand any particular level of skill or effort. That is the whole point. While only a very skilled few can make complex watches, anyone can do Dadaism. In the *Dada Manifesto*, Tristan Tzara explains how to make a Dadaist poem:

TO MAKE A DADAIST POEM

Take a newspaper.

Take some scissors.

Choose from this paper an article of the length you want to make your poem.

Cut out the article.

Next carefully cut out each of the words that makes up this article and put them all in a bag.

Shake gently.

Next take out each cutting one after the other.

Copy conscientiously in the order in which they left the bag.

The poem will resemble you.

And there you are – an infinitely original author of charming sensibility, even though unappreciated by the vulgar herd.

It's not an act of skill. It's an act of randomness.

Dadaism is completely egalitarian. It is a complete opposite to the elitism of watchmaking. While masculine capitalism has embraced an art form that demands high skill, reflecting our political and economic values, collectivism and anarcho-communism have embraced art that demands no skill or effort, reflecting their political values.

Backwards values defeat themselves. Welfarists, intent on stripping meaning from art, have left themselves in a world without the inspiration and meaning found only in true art. It was not enough to merely reject elitism and excellence; they have chosen to reject meaning itself. They have created a world bereft of inspiration, a world they assuredly deserve.

Obscenity Laws

Art operates differently from direct argument. Direct argument seeks to persuade you on what to think. Art seeks to expand your methods of thinking and feeling, showing you new ways to think.

Historically, many great types of art, including literature, music, comedy, painting and dance, have been persecuted by various cultures as obscene. They've been banned or blocked, their creators arrested. Those in power, whether part of the dominant political order or social order, understood intuitively that these new ideas posed a threat.

They were probably right about that. The art that historically has changed the way in which its audiences saw reality has affected the stranglehold on social and psychological reality that the dominant groups sought to hold secure.

Obscenity laws in America today primarily target pornography. For pornography to violate current obscenity laws, it must be patently offensive, violate community standards, and provide no political, artistic, or literary value.

I would argue that any form of art that violates community standards has artistic value. To you, specifically.

Today, many social justice feminist groups target pornography. They intuitively recognize that pornography is a direct threat to woman worship, which has been used to socially and culturally manipulate men into supporting policies that cannot possibly be in our self-interest. They argue that pornography alters the way men look at women. Obviously. That's the point of art: to change the way you look at things.

But it doesn't just alter the way you look at women. It alters the way you look at everything. Someone who watches porn regularly may be harder to politically trick than someone who does not. For example, a political distraction like "My opponent had a <gasp!> affair!!" may affect a porn aficionado less than someone else. When a porn watcher hears "My opponent has an illegitimate child!" he is more likely to ask the question that matters: "Can we change the laws so I don't have to pay for that child, or for any child, except for my own children?"

People argue that porn desensitizes people. True. In doing so, it makes them harder to politically manipulate through irrelevant distractions like extramarital affairs.

They say it makes people less willing to settle for "traditional" marriage. Sure. Although porn watchers who can read will discover that even marriage in the Bible was not always monogamous.

In the past, art that denigrated the Catholic church was persecuted and destroyed. It attacked the dominant religion of the time. Today, art that makes us question the dominant power is socially persecuted, and often legally prosecuted.

In doing so, the enemy has revealed its own weakness. Offensive pornography weakens its hold. The more patently offensive, community standard violating pornography we watch, the weaker its hold becomes.

I recommend considering all the types of pornography generally targeted as obscenity, and watching whatever you feel comfortable with.

Pornography helps you psychologically disengage from limiting social norms. It allows you to create your own individual standards, rather than being constricted by community standards. It removes the very restrictions used to keep you clinging to the institutions that are designed to disempower you.

The status quo fears that "obscene" art will permanently alter the way you think, making you impossible to predict or manage. Let's make their fears come true.

CHAPTER 18:

Capitalism is force

Proponents of welfarism and socialism often argue that capitalism is force. In a sense, they're right. The only purpose of money is to force others to do what you want them to.

Money allows you to compel a restaurant to give you a sandwich, an electronics store to give you a computer. Any time you spend money, you are forcing the recipient to do something for you. In fact, your action forces many other people to labor on your behalf. If you buy a computer, you are not just compelling the seller to give you a computer. You are forcing miners to mine metal, factory workers to assemble the parts, engineers to develop materials, stevedores to load ships with cargo, etc. Money is used to force people to labor. Without that monetary force, they probably wouldn't do that labor.

It happens to you too. One major reason you work, or build the skills for work, is that if you don't, you will not survive or thrive. We work, for the most part, because we have to.

And yet, capitalism is not force the way welfarism is. Capitalism doesn't involve taking anyone's money with a threat of violence, to spend it in ways he would not agree to. It doesn't involve the immorality of taking someone's money without consent.

Suppose you buy a TV. The only reason the store gives it to you is that you pay for it. The only reason the TV is built is that you and others are willing to pay to buy it. The only reason the TV factory pays its workers at all is that you might buy the TV they build. When you put it all together, the TV manufacturer and factory workers have two choices.

- Build you a TV.

- Starve to death.

Of course, they don't have to build you a TV. They can make you something else - a computer, a shoe, a pen, a yoga mat. But if they aren't useful to you, specifically, you aren't going to help them survive. If they aren't useful to anyone, then they probably won't survive.

The same rule applies to you. Either make yourself useful, or starve.

It's not a new idea. The Bible, in Thessalonians, says, "if any would not work, neither should he eat."

There are often things we'd rather be doing. Some of those might be fulfilling, in a personal sense. Perhaps you enjoy dancing. But unless you do it at a very high level, you probably won't expect people to pay you to do it.

In other words, you expect that if you are going to pay for something, it will benefit you. Even if you contribute to charity, you expect that to influence the world according to your preferences.

The important fact is that you pay for things that are useful to you. Not just useful to some person, but to you, specifically. It may benefit your neighbor to take a yoga class, but you probably won't pay for his yoga class unless you're getting something in exchange.

The same principle applies to children. If someone bears you a child, then it makes sense to pay to raise that child, and to provide for her, financially, emotionally, or in whatever mutually agreed upon way you like.

But if someone bears someone else a child, how does that benefit you? It's not that it's bad. If your neighbor takes a yoga class, that's probably good. But how is it your responsibility to pay for it?

Welfarists love to distort reality with arguments like, "we all benefit when kids are educated." That may be true in some really indirect way, but the benefits are not exactly equal. If you buy a Ferrari, I might benefit by maybe getting to see a cool car. But you benefit a lot more, as the owner.

Similarly, if your neighbor's kid is educated, that may benefit you in some small way. But it benefits him in a much larger way. He benefits in terms of social prestige, financial security, and his natural desire to have his personal child succeed.

If your neighbor took a yoga class. That might benefit you in some way. He may look more aesthetically pleasing, complain less, etc. However, it is ludicrous to expect you to pay for his yoga class. It would make sense for you to invest in a yoga class for yourself.

The other common argument: if you don't pay for other kids to go to school, then they might turn to crime. First, I doubt that. Most likely, their parents will pay for some kind of education for them, or homeschool them. But even if they do, how much crime? By attending government school, they are stealing over $100,000 per kid, via taxation. Is the minor increase in crime going to be greater than that enormous expense? I really doubt it.

In fact, my prediction is that crime will actually massively decrease if we end all welfare, especially educational welfare.

According to the book *Freakonomics*, one of the biggest reasons for reduction in crime over the last decades was legalization of abortion. Unwanted kids whose parents couldn't pay for them, or were generally unfit, were being aborted more often. Those kids were the ones most likely to turn to crime.

If we eliminate incentives for having kids that the parents cannot afford, it will encourage many people who can't afford kids without welfare to just not have kids. If having kids means paying for all of their needs, including education, those with no jobs and no spouses with jobs probably won't have kids.

Today, having kids means others pay for them. Sometimes, it even means that, as the mother, you get extra income from the government for yourself to live on. That creates an incentive for those who can't afford kids to produce them. But if having kids meant paying for them yourself, it would be a radically different situation.

Richer people would have more kids than poor people, which makes sense. The current situation, in which poor people have more kids, is completely illogical and backwards. Those who can't afford to pay for their own kids shouldn't have kids at all, but they certainly shouldn't be having more kids than those who can!

In the past, by the way, poor people had more kids than rich people. At that time, kids were a financial asset. They would work the land and look after you when you were old. Today, kids are a financial liability - one that the rest of us must pay for. While it may have made sense in the 1300s for poor people to have more kids than rich people, today it does not.

If we end all welfare, including government schools, we'll probably see a drop in crime similar to the one that came 18 years after the legalization of abortion, as jobless, spouseless parents just don't have as many kids, or any at all. The kids most likely to commit crimes just won't be born.

And if you're still really worried about your own safety, a $500 gun will probably do a lot more than spending hundreds of thousands of your tax dollars on other people's kids.

Unless someone is providing you, personally, with some benefit, it's preposterous to expect you to pay. A woman producing someone else's kid is not benefiting you. If anything, it is creating more competition for scarce resources for your genetic offspring. Why on earth should you pay a cent for it?

Do we expect Nike to subsidize the advertising of Reebok? Do we expect Intel to give money to AMD and get nothing in return? Why are you expected to literally pay for your genetic competition?

CHAPTER 19:

Financial Slut

One of your most important sexual rights is your right to say no. One of your most important financial rights is your right to say no.

You exercise that right all the time. A restaurant, store, charity, etc. has to convince you to give them money, usually in exchange for something you value. Apple, Netflix, or Toyota can't just take your money. They have to earn it. Your default answer is a "no". You don't give your money to most companies who ask for it. You don't buy everything you see offered for sale. You reject 99.9999 percent of the products you see.

As with sex, sometimes you withhold your finances for love. You might save sex for your spouse or spouses, or significant other(s). You want them to have something others don't. Similarly, you might dedicate your finances to your own kids. You want your kids to have things that others don't. Normal parental love means you want your kids to have advantages over others, to be ahead of others. That's not being selfish; that's being a parent.

No parent of a hard working athlete wants his or her child to come in "equal" place. Parents want their children to come in first place. That's why they try to give their kids what others do not have. That is a natural and fundamental parental right: the right to give to your kids and withhold from other kids.

Why else does paternity fraud matter? Why should a man be angry when he's tricked into raising someone else's genetic offspring? It is very simply wrong to force someone to act against their own natural interests, and trick them into pouring love, effort, and the fruits of his labor into someone he wouldn't want to.

And if it's wrong to do that by fraud, it is far worse to do it by force. To force parents to act against their fundamental nature and logical desires. To say to those working hard to help their kids get ahead, that they must now work hard to keep others at the same level.

You have the right to say no. Any access to your money, the fruits of your labor, requires active consent. Silence is not consent. "You don't want to pay, but you have to or you're going to prison" is definitely not consent. It is wrong to force you to share the most sacred part of yourself, against your will, against your interests, against your familial obligation, with the genetic offspring of your competitors.

What would you call a wife who has sex with the whole city? A slut? If it was required by law, it would be degrading to those who wanted to show love and respect through sexual fidelity. It would be turning honorable women, by force, into sluts.

So, what do you call a man who gives his financial resources to the whole city? Who doesn't try to give his own kids an advantage, doesn't reserve the sacred fruits of his labor for his own family, but rather gives it away to everyone? A financial slut? Today, that's required by law. It's turning honorable men, by force, into financial sluts. We're forced to give the most sacred parts of ourselves away. We are not allowed the natural and fundamental honor and integrity of reserving the best of ourselves for those we love. Instead, we're forced to pay for everyone, whether we love, like, hate, or are just indifferent to them.

Is it any surprise that so many men are turning into deadbeat dads? We're all forced to be deadbeat dads. We are prevented from working hard exclusively for those whom we love. Like a wife forced by the state to be a free prostitute, we are prevented from saving the best of ourselves for our families. Men who are repeatedly forced to act against their genetic instincts will eventually lose their genetic instincts.

We're robbed to pay for everyone else's kids, and then, having been so robbed, often end up turning, shamefully, to welfare ourselves. We've been so robbed that we cannot afford education, so we dump our kids, shamefully, into government schools. But even there, there is a light, as some of us wake up to the advantages of homeschool.

When we, so financially depleted, end up dumping our own kids into government welfare schools, we are already deadbeat dads. It's already happened. We've failed to provide for our kids. Anything we do after that just makes it slightly more official.

The idea of man as a powerful and exclusive provider no longer makes sense. That mighty fatherhood no longer has meaning. An actual good father, one who reserves his love and resources for his family, can no longer exist. So we pretend that a "good father" is one who plays catch with his kids.

A man who has a picture of his family at his desk, as a reminder of the people for whom he is working, is just lying to himself. He should have a picture of every entitled welfare queen on earth, fecklessly having kids, certain that his sacred work will be stolen and given to her. That man may want to provide for his family, to work hard for his family. But he's working hard for everyone else. For every ill-considered kid, for every nonsense government program, for every person and organization that has turned him into a financial slut.

He has been degraded. He can't reserve the best part of himself for those he loves. How can he love the best part of himself in such a circumstance? How can he respect that part of himself which has been so thoroughly disrespected?

The temptation for diversion and escapism becomes strong. We're tempted to spend free time drinking, playing video games, or watching TV. But that is the time you should spend sharpening your mind against your enemy. That is the time to be reading about ideas, learning about politics, figuring out how to dismantle those who have successfully degraded us.

If you like, put a picture of that enemy, or a symbol of it, at your workspace or at home. Get a picture of some smug, non-working, welfare queen with 9 kids that you're expected to support. Remind yourself that the other side, the degrading welfarist side, is working too. Remind yourself that they are not content with degrading the sacred parts of themselves; they want to degrade the sacred parts of you as well.

Speak to other men. Help awaken them. Organize. Fight.

Harriet Tubman once said, "I freed a thousand slaves. I would have freed a thousand more if only they knew they were slaves." While we can easily see, as outsiders, that they were enslaved, they could not.

Will history remember us as those who were degraded, then fought back and freed ourselves psychologically, spiritually, politically, financially? Or will we be just another indistinguishable phase of that degradation?

CHAPTER 20:

Financial Consent: His Money, His Choice

While third wave feminism's primary "contributions" have been to encourage promiscuity and welfarism, the movement has also brought forth an important concept: active consent. It has helped people understand that each sexual act requires active consent. Silence is not enough. No doesn't mean "yes". You must have actual, active consent for each act.

This has changed laws and reduced all kinds of abuse. As recently as 1980, marital rape, in which a husband forces his wife, was entirely legal. Today, that is no longer the case. A husband who forces his wife against her will is breaking the law and violating social norms.

Kissing is not consenting to sex. Marriage is not consenting to sex. Only consenting to sex is consenting to sex.

When it comes to abortion, third wave feminism has effectively emphasized the importance of self ownership. A woman owns her own body, and can do with it what she will. If she consents to having sex with a man, she is not also consenting to bring his child to term. She is free to take a morning after pill or have an abortion without the man's consent. She only agreed to sex, nothing more.

What about the man? His consent matters just as much as the woman's. If he consents to holding hands, he's not consenting to sex. If he consents to sex, he's not consenting to children, or child support. Just as a woman owns her own body and the fruits of her labor, the man owns his own body and the fruits of his own labor.

A man who signs a contract to support a child is in a different circumstance. He's signed a contract. The same holds with a verbal contract. He's consented to child support. He should follow through on that. Similarly, a woman who agreed to take a baby to term, either as a romantic partner or a paid surrogate should keep her word.

But consenting to sex is not consenting to children. Just as a woman can have a physical abortion, refusing to consent to the production of a child, a man has the natural right to a "financial abortion".

The obvious question here is why any man would want to do that. As men, don't we want to give our kids every advantage over other people's kids? Isn't the whole point to give our kids more, increasing their chance of succeeding over others?

From a masculine perspective, there's no earthly reason to want to deny your own kids advantages. Obviously, you would want to deny other people's kids advantages. You want your genetic offspring to be highly dominant over the genetic offspring of others. If we lived in a world based on principles of respect, consent, and fairness, there would never be a reason to not pay child support.

The problem today is that child support laws are being abused. Instead of men supporting their own genetic offspring, they are essentially subsidizing the lifestyles of women.

Current child support laws are based on percentages of the man's income. For example, 17 percent of a man's income may go to the first child, with the percentage increasing with more kids. In certain income ranges, that makes sense. In others, the man is paying much more than what is actually necessary for the needs or benefits of a child, and is being used to subsidize the lifestyle of the biological mother - and potentially her other offspring!

The actual financial needs of a child are relatively modest. Food, clothing, education, shelter, and books are the largest items on the list. Other expensive things, like video games, electronics, and fancy clothes are not generally to the advantage of the child. Spoiled, TV addicted children do not have an advantage over those whose primary source of entertainment is reading.

I won't deny that there are plenty of deadbeat dads out there, who don't want to pay for their own genetic offspring. Those men are unnatural, separated from their most fundamental genetic imperative, the imperative to give your offspring an advantage over others. Perhaps some of those men have been damaged by a culture that considers it a requirement to pay for the offspring of others. Perhaps those men have forgotten that paying for your own offspring to give them an advantage over others is a basic requirement of masculinity, and a genetic imperative in much of the animal kingdom. In a culture where we pretend it's normal to pay for the genetic offspring of others, perhaps we've too strongly deemphasized the moral importance and genetic self-interest of paying to support your own genetic offspring. Refusing to pay for some other person's offspring's education makes sense. But to refuse to pay for your own? That's as unnatural, as against genetic imperatives, as having sex with a first degree relative.

I have some pity for the men who have been so deformed that they have lost connection with their own genetic self interest. Those are men who will drag through life, obediently working to pay for the genetic offspring of others, while ignoring their own genetic offspring. What could be more broken and shameful? What could be more unmasculine?

Now imagine a cultural and legal change. Culturally, imagine if we embraced the idea that your job, as a parent, is to give your genetic offspring an advantage over others. Imagine if we let our culture be built on genetic truth and natural law.

We'd have far fewer deadbeat dads. We would remember that the goal is to provide for our genetic offspring, while refusing to provide for the genetic offspring of others. Men would proudly work to support their own biological offspring, and compete in the free market to help their own children have every possible advantage. Men would reconnect with the importance of children, recognizing, as all aristocratic and royal families in all of human history have realized, that children are essential to any meaningful legacy.

We need to connect with natural and scientific laws, and stop believing the lies of welfarism.

CHAPTER 21:

Silencing Opposition

When you have superior ideas, you welcome debate. After all, a calm, rational debate will help advance your ideas. For example, Galileo would have loved a calm, rational debate on the relative position of the earth and the sun. He knew he was right, and that in calm debate, the institutional beliefs would have been proven wrong.

However, when your ideas or goals are ludicrous, you don't want debate. You want to silence any opposition.

As feminist movements have pushed past the "achieve fairness phase" to the "more stuff for women, whether it's fair or not" phase, they are maintaining increasingly indefensible positions. For example, the argument that "All women should have the right to work," was pretty easily defensible. The argument that, "Companies should offer unpaid maternity leave to women", is also reasonably defensible. The argument that "Companies should be legally required to offer paid maternity leave to women, and also legally required to give women the same base salary and other benefits as men," is much harder to defend. The argument that, "Men should pay child support for the illegitimate byblows of cheating wives," is entirely indefensible.

The only way to defend an argument that insane is to silence the opposition. Feminist groups have resorted to two main techniques.

The first is one we are all familiar with: screaming, obscenities, hysterics, etc. in response to any deviation from absolute agreement with their viewpoints. Many get "triggered" in response to any disagreement, and devolve into tantrums and lunacy.

There's nothing complicated about that: if you raise the cost of disagreement high enough, people won't want to pay that price. If saying, "People should pay for their own birth control" is going to get 90 people shrieking at you for 3 weeks, you might choose to remain in fearful silence. If saying "All welfare, including government schools, is wrong" will lead to 3 months of that kind of shrieking, you might be tempted to keep your ideas to yourself. If pointing out that most people in prison are men will get you shrieked at, labeled a misogynist, and called a woman hater, you might decide not to speak up.

Further, if men know that disagreeing will decrease their likelihood of sexual success, then they will be even less likely to openly disagree.

Some women are more explicit. I've mentioned the online dating profiles that specifically say that they will not date anyone without the same political beliefs. These women openly have no qualms about using sexual leverage to enforce political obedience.

But one of the more interesting tools that women use is to say, "You cannot know what it's like to be a woman, so you are not entitled to have an opinion."

It's a clever silencing technique used by many groups who choose to push laws past the level of fairness or reasonability. Many minority groups use that type of argument right before they demand Affirmative Action, reparations, or other obviously unfair advantages. However, historically, black civil rights leaders didn't use that as a primary form of argument. They didn't need to, because their positions made absolute logical sense. Critical leaders of the women's movement also didn't need to use such arguments. They didn't say, "You can't understand what it means to be a woman, so you can't discuss voting rights for women." They didn't need to silence opposition, because their ideas would win in open debate.

The argument itself is preposterous. A man can't know what it's like to be a woman, but a woman can't know what it's like to be a man. A black person can't know what it's like to be Chinese. A 6'1" adult can't know what it's like to be 6'2", or even 5'8" as an adult. No one can know exactly what it's like to be anyone else.

That's what language is for. To explain experiences, discuss things, use logic, etc. That's why we have debate and discussion.

What should you do when people try to silence you? Should you slink away like a beaten dog? Should you respond with your own hysterics?

My recommendation: calmly, politely, firmly counter their arguments. Don't lose your cool, because that only means you lose the moral high ground. Don't act crazy, but don't back down.

If you're in public or on social media, this is especially important. Women may scream at you, call you all kinds of names, start spontaneously crying to try to shut you up. If that doesn't work, they will try the "you're not a woman, you don't know what it's like, so you don't get to speak," tactic.

Here are some things you can say if you are in public.

"No man can know what it's like to be a woman, just as no woman can know what it's like to be a man. However, that doesn't stop us from having a logical and calm discussion on the topic."

"I'm sorry that this topic is difficult for you to discuss. If you'd like to continue it later, I'm willing to."

If you want to be incendiary, you might try, "I don't know what it's like to be a German in the 1940s either, but I can still say that joining the Nazis is the wrong choice."

In public, most people will be silent, or will support the angry woman. Men, in particular, will support her. After all, she may provide them with sex, and you probably won't.

But after the fact, you'll probably get a few facebook friend requests, supporting emails, etc.

If all else fails, the woman will likely try to trick you into defending some lowlife. This common tactic is just designed to get you to take his side, so they can hammer you on those grounds. It looks like this:

Man: "Not paying for your birth control is not controlling your body. You're still allowed to buy birth control and have sex with whoever you want."

Woman: "Oh yeah? That's exactly the type of argument that supporters of <date rapist in the news> would say."

Stupid Man: "Well, marital rape isn't really rape." Or, "She shouldn't have been drunk if she didn't want to get raped." (At this point, the woman has tricked you into becoming a defender of rape, and will then hammer you on that point.)

Smart Man: "Rape is a tragic and despicable act. But, that's not really the issue at hand. Refusing to buy you something doesn't stop you from buying it yourself."

When women play the "male privilege" card, simply bring up the legal female privileges that happen at the expense of men. You can point out that men often have to pay child support for children that are the byblows of unfaithful wives. Bringing up issues like this is basically the same as the technique of tricking men into defending the current rapist in the news. You're tricking them into trying to defend an entirely indefensible position.

If you want, you can take it even farther. You can say, "As a woman, you cannot understand the concept of paternity uncertainty, the humiliation of being cuckolded, or the soul destroying nature of being forced by the state to pay for the resulting child."

But the most important thing: always, no matter what, stay calm. Don't say anything for which you might have to apologize later on.

The oldest debate trick on earth is to insult an unprepared debater in order to make him lose his cool and respond angrily, generally saying something stupid. Don't fall for that trick.

In relationships, women use basically one technique above all others. They get the man to say or do something stupid, make him feel guilty, and then punish him with his own guilt. In political discussions, they try to do the same. They will try to get you angry, and try to make you say something dumb. Don't fall for that.

Here is a list of common techniques women will use in political discussions to make you lose your cool.

1. Screaming, obscenities, tantrums, etc.
   The goal is to get you to yell back.

2. Suddenly refusing to continue the discussion.
   The goal is to get you to yell something like, "I'm not finished, you #@$%&."

3. If in a group, using multi-pronged emotional attacks. One person will yell, another will cry, another will stomp off, etc. Most men, who have never practiced any emotional control, get overwhelmed and say something that they later need to apologize for.
   The goal is to elicit that response and then use guilt against you.

4. If in a group, close themselves off to try to cause you social embarrassment.
   The goal is to get you to beg for approval.

If you have a lot of social confidence, you'll easily be able to handle the fourth situation by laughing it off and talking to others.

If not (and even if you do), a little preparation helps a lot. If you have one or two friends with you, that obviously erases the power of that kind of shunning. If not, make a few friends in a room before you get involved in anything. Demonstrate a high level of social dominance by meeting people, and most importantly, introducing people to other people. That can work even if it's people you just met. Make sure everyone knows that you can provide them with more social opportunities than any group of five or six women. It's not always that easy to do, so make sure you are able to laugh any situation off as a backup plan.

Bonus: A Common Advanced Technique, and How to Defeat It

Men often introduce a political policy with which they agree by associating it with a particular political figure. This is a bad idea, and leaves an easy opening for a well prepared woman.

For example, a man might say, "_____ is right: we need to abolish the NEA." At this point, the woman will derail the conversation by saying, "Oh yeah? You agree with someone who supports rape?"

A skilled man will bring the conversation back to the topic. An unskilled man will say, "_____ doesn't support rape, what are you talking about." And then the conversation becomes about whether or not _____ supports rape. Soon, this becomes a conversation about whether the unskilled man supports rape, and it goes downhill from there.

A general rule of thumb: present the idea or policy, but don't attach it to any specific person. Don't give the opposition the opportunity to rabbit trail the conversation into unrelated other attributes of that person.

Alternatively, you can say, "While I mostly disagree with _____, he is right about _____."

The same is true about countries. Instead of saying, "This works in Argentina", which will just allow the opposition to find some unrelated thing about Argentina. Instead, say, "I got to see how _____ worked in a recent trip to South America." If someone asks what country, you know they are planning an irrelevant attack, and can preemptively deflect an attempted shift to an irrelevant topic. You can say, "It even works in Argentina, which we all know has its share of problems."

CHAPTER 22:

Silencing Part 2: Marcusian Techniques of Intellectual Debate

Many young self-identified socialists and communists have recently extended the technique of silencing the opposition to areas in which civil intellectual discourse used to be the standard. At college lectures, they have focused on disrupting presentations by speakers that they consider "right wing." They have resorted to violence and arson in order to shut down events, loudly disrupt lecturers, etc. Some of the people that receive this treatment are highly provocative, deliberately offensive firebrands. But others are just calm intellectuals.

According to Jeffrey Tucker at the Foundation for Economic Education, this behavior is not just some kind of youthful lack of discipline. It's actually based on the views of early communist thinker Marcuse, who believed that all non-communist thought should be shut down. Among the rules he promoted can be found the following:

"They would include the withdrawal of toleration of speech and assembly from groups and movements which promote aggressive policies, armament, chauvinism, discrimination on the grounds of race and religion, or which oppose the extension of public services, social security, medical care, etc."[1]

In other words, if someone opposes welfarism, they should not be allowed to speak.

---

1) FEE: *Why Free Speech on Campus Is Under Attack: Blame Marcuse*

This system of forcibly shutting down opponents has influenced many self-identified socialist and communist activists, who use the tactic constantly.

They view opposing ideas as a direct threat, and with good reason. Those who hear the opposing ideas, who learn that they have the right to offer or withhold the fruits of their labor, who understand that theft culture is not okay, will often reject the culture that these socialists want to cram down everyone's throats. It's hard for such preposterous ideas to survive when people hear other ones.

It's not terribly different from the methods used in communist countries today, where all opposing ideas are silenced. After all, would North Koreans listen to Kim Jong Un's nonsense if they had access to any other ideas?

Today these techniques are particularly common at universities. In formal settings, we see guest speakers who don't follow the welfarist agenda shouted at, interrupted, etc. In informal settings, we see individuals who express views that go against welfarism and third wave feminism screamed at and shouted down. If you don't agree, they want you to shut the hell up.

To fight this, realize that you are not the only one they are silencing. Everyone who agrees with you is also being silenced. When you speak up loud enough for the silenced to hear you, you will be making allies.

Don't expect them to come to your rescue. If there is a room with 100 welfare warriors and 100 silenced individualists, and you say something against welfare, the 100 welfare warriors will scream at you. The 100 individualists will remain silent. Why? First, they don't know that there are 100 of you. They assume they are the only one, apart from you. They see you getting screamed at, and they don't want half of that directed at themselves.

But they will find you. People find me on facebook and twitter, speak to me after events, etc.

By the way, when you do this, keep calm. Don't lose your cool. You can speak with passion, fire, intensity, etc. But don't let people jerk you around by tricking you into losing your cool. Stay calm, respond to challenges and questions deliberately. That might mean deliberately provoking opponents, but it never means losing your cool.

If you use social media to speak on these issues, don't get thrown off by negative comments. Here's why: Facebook and twitter do not have "dislike" buttons. If someone agrees with you, they can click "like" or "love" or "retweet" or "favorite" or whatever. But if they disagree, they have to comment. That's the only way to express disagreement.

That means that on controversial issues, the comments will be mostly negative. Don't let that throw you. Instead, look at the number of likes, retweets, etc., and compare that to the number of unique negative commenters. Remember, you can like a post once, but comment 50 times.

Also pay attention to the new friend requests or followers you get from those controversial posts. As your communication improves, as you become less timid about telling the unadulterated truth, you will get more and more allies.

On my social media posts, I often get hundreds of negative comments. But a post that gets hundreds of negative comments usually has only a few negative commenters, each posting several negative comments. Also, I usually get as many new allies as negative comments, if not more.

Don't worry about the loud people. Find allies among the silenced. Make your voice loud enough for them to hear you.

THE POLITICAL IS PERSONAL

CHAPTER 23:

Studying Cultures; Building A Subculture

The common saying states, "If you're the smartest person in the room, you're in the wrong room." I personally believe that if you think you're the smartest person in the room - you've probably misread the room.

Unless you are the only person in the room, every single person in that room probably knows something you don't. Every single person has some area of expertise that you don't share.

What's true of humans is also true of cultures. Most cultures have flaws, but they also have good points. American culture is industrious and innovative; however, our food culture is a laughingstock, and obesity runs rampant. Ancient Greek culture brought individuals to their peaks; but they didn't have the organization or infrastructure for the kind of architectural greatness that the Romans had. The Romans were great at large scale projects; but that became their weakness when they overbuilt an empire, lost individual discipline, and alternated between hedonism and wasteful empire expansion.

At the moment, America is the largest economy on earth. Most other countries are economically far behind. And yet, there are still things we can learn from them. American arrogance can blind us to better ways of doing things.

Let's face it: third wave feminism, social justice warriors, and socialism masquerading as some kind of new free market capitalism are American problems. We can try to figure them out ourselves, but it may be wise to look at how other cultures handle this.

And what applies to our macro culture applies just as well to our micro culture. Family structures are different in every culture. Even when they share some surface similarities, they have vastly different behavioral roles and economic expectations. Cultures find different ways to make things worse, often with much less economic access than we have.

In some cultures, extended families and grandparents play a larger role. In other cultures, marriages are unspokenly expected to last just long enough to have kids, and a subsequent divorce is the norm.

There are many subcultures in America as well that we can learn from. Each culture that continues to exist over time has passed the Darwinian test of survival. In some way or another, that culture has worked. Some cultures are very matriarchal, where kids are raised by mothers and grandmothers, and the fathers are not a part of the household. In others, multiple generations live under the same roof.

Cultures change over time as well. American families in different decades and centuries have looked different. Some of those eras were more effective at raising offspring than others, but each of those eras has some valuable insights and lessons.

Learning about those cultures can prevent you from falling into the trap of thinking that what most people are doing right now in America is the only possible way. Realistically, what people are doing right now in America is about as bad as anything that has ever been done. Today men marry sexually used up women, raise about the dumbest kids in the history of the world, get divorced and robbed, and then sometimes repeat. If that's not rock bottom, I don't know what is.

There are almost 200 countries in the world, and thousands of cultures and subcultures today. If you include those of the past, the number is undoubtedly in the tens of thousands, or even millions. All of those things worked.

Today's American culture may not be the worst, but it's probably not the best, and it's certainly not perfect. Despite what welfarists and third wave feminists will have you believe, going along with this foolishness is not your only option.

As you study subcultures, you will start to build your own. After all, what is a family if not a subculture? Families have their own rules, norms, and styles of communication. Today, in America, we have monogamous families, polygamous families, and families in which parents live apart. Each family has its own subculture.

Learn from different subcultures as you create your own. Don't just blindly accept the rules some welfarist hands to you. Spend time figuring out your own rules. Try to understand the source of the rules in your culture and in others, how they were shaped, and what benefits they bring. After studying a rule's origin and benefits, you might decide to keep it, alter it, or throw it out. But it should be a conscious, intentional decision, not something you blindly accept.

Men, Morality, and Marriage

What is a moral marriage? Is it monogamous? Polygamous? Polyamorous? Open? Closed? Heterosexual? Homosexual? Traditional? Innovative? Religious? Secular?

To me, the question is better answered by asking, "What is an immoral marriage?" If we can avoid an immoral marriage, that's a great start.

A nonconsensual marriage is immoral. If a man or woman does not consent to a marriage, that marriage does not fall within the bounds of morality. For example, if you kidnap someone and force her to become your spouse, that is immoral.

A marriage that nonconsensually takes from others is also immoral. If your marriage requires that you steal to fund it, that is immoral. Whether that theft happens directly, through burglary, or indirectly, through taxation, is irrelevant. If your marriage requires taking money from others without their consent, your marriage is immoral.

This is especially true in the context of children. If your having children requires that you take from others without their consent, then your childrearing process and your marriage are immoral.

To me, political morality comes down to this: do whatever you want, as long as it harms no one else. If you are a man, and are married to five other men, that may be off-putting to some. But you aren't harming them. You aren't taking their money without their consent.

On the other hand, if you are married to one woman, and that means that you will have kids for whose schooling others will be forced to pay, you are harming others. You are taking their money without consent.

Don't rationalize it by saying, "It's my taxes paying for it." That's false. Your taxes pay for a fraction of the costs. The taxes of those who are not using government schools are paying for the rest. If your taxes were actually covering the full cost, then you would easily have the money for private school, rather than middle class welfare.

A welfare dependent marriage, such as a marriage that needs government schools, is not just unmasculine. It is immoral. It's violating the property rights of others, and normalizing a culture that will violate your property rights. When you use tax funded education, you cannot be surprised when someone else uses tax grants to fund their "art" or other hobbies. When you take money from others, through government, you cannot be surprised when others do the same to you.

Welfare dependency is immoral. Welfare marriages are wrong. They are both unmasculine and morally abhorrent.

But they are also avoidable. Just wait until you're ready.

Readiness might mean making enough money to buy education for your kids. Or it may simply mean learning enough about homeschooling to do it yourself. Even if you're very rich, you might follow Elon Musk's current example and use unschooling, a radical form of homeschooling.

Don't let lust or love make you irresponsible. The welfare queens so many of us look down on may have loved each of the 10 men with whom they had kids. But that doesn't make the welfare queens any less despicable. When you have 2 kids that are paid for through welfare, you are no different yourself.

If you're in your 20s, unless you are financially able to afford private schools or have done the research needed for homeschool, don't even consider marriage or kids. You'll just be supporting and encouraging the welfare state. You'll be setting a low standard of masculinity and morality for your kids, and for your culture.

The Morality of Monogamy, Polygamy, and Homosexuality

The most important moral rule for a marriage is do not create a theft-funded, welfare marriage. Do not have kids and make welfare plan A. And yes, government schools are absolutely welfare.

But what about the other questions? Sure, a theft and welfare fueled monogamous marriage is immoral. But does that make a polygamous, non-welfarist marriage moral?

Today, in many western countries, monogamy has become a deeply entrenched norm. Many people believe that one man and one woman are the only morally legitimate forms of marriage.

Those who have read the Bible know how strange this is. The old testament is full of polygamy. It even includes extensive advice on the correct and incorrect ways do do polygamy. Presumably, if polygamy was seen as always wrong, there wouldn't be that kind of advice. After all, Leviticus does not tell us the right and wrong ways to steal, or the right and wrong ways to bear false witness.

The New Testament is even more puzzling. The Gospels say little if anything on the issue. However Paul's after-the-fact writings fixate heavily on monogamy.

You may remember that Christianity spread aggressively only after the Roman emperor Constantine converted to Christianity. Here's what you might not know: Romans were intensely monogamous. It's hardly a surprise that when Rome and Christendom merged, monogamy became a major part of Roman Catholicism. It's the "Roman" part of Roman Catholicism, not the "Catholic" part, that gives us monogamy.

Obviously, Paul would see monogamy as the default. After all, he himself was a Roman soldier. It was a fundamental part of his culture.

Today, the tension between the polygamy of the Old Testament and the monogamy of Roman Culture continues. For example, the *Catechism of the Catholic Church* insists that "polygamy is contrary to conjugal love". But when discussing children, it specifically mentions two of the more famously polygamous marriages. When discussing an inability to have children, it says:

"Couples who discover that they are sterile suffer greatly. 'What will you give me,' asks Abraham of God, 'for I continue childless?' and Rachel cries to her husband Jacob, 'Give me children, or I shall die!'"

Jacob was famously married to Rachel and Leah. They weren't so much a "couple", as the above quote implies, as a "triad". Abraham's struggle shows just how much marriage was about succession, not sexual monogamy. His struggle about inviting another woman into his marriage bed is well known. However, the extent to which it had nothing to do with sexual monogamy or even resource fidelity is shown in the discussion of his estate:

"But unto the sons of the concubines, which Abraham had, Abraham gave gifts, and sent them away from Isaac his son, while he yet lived, eastward, unto the east country."

His famous moral struggle of whether to impregnate his wife's maid Hagar was not a question about producing biological offspring with other women. It was a question about who became his heir.

None of this is to say that monogamy is wrong or silly. It may be right for you. But you should be at least aware of where it came from, and what other historical, current, and potential alternatives there are.

Other religions consider things quite differently. Islam and Mormonism are most known for their open support of polygamy. Hinduism historically also supports it. I'm not just talking about the obviously polygamous sexuality portrayed in the Kama Sutra. Both the Mahabaratha and Ramayana are steeped in polygamous culture.

Monogamy may be very important to your family. But the fact is this: if you still need psychological approval from your parents, you are nowhere near ready for marriage. If you are still seeking their approval, chances are you are still seeking social approval in many other areas. You'll eventually fight your way past that character defect. But while you still have it, don't even consider marriage or kids.

What about homosexuality or bisexuality? Different cultures have had vastly different views. Among the Ancient Greeks, homosexuality was considered superior to heterosexuality. In *The Symposium*,

Plato argued that homosexuality was the highest form of love. Other cultures have clearly felt differently.

Many say that you should follow your instincts. I think that listening to your instincts is probably a wise step, but not a place to end. You must choose what kind of life you want. You might choose to follow your instincts fully, but make that a choice. Let your decisions define you.

Moral questions can be highly personal. They may be made in the context of your culture. However, they are often made against your cultural norms. Today, using government welfare schools is standard. Many of us are making a choice to not be part of that theft system. We are going against current norms in order to do the moral act, to act in ways we can be proud of, rather than ashamed of.

Religion and Marriage

For many people, morality comes from religion, rather than secular considerations. Most religions agree with the secular view that stealing is wrong, that a parent who depends on theft rather than work in order to provide has morally fallen short.

But many religions have additional requirements, ranging from monogamy to circumcision. For many, following those religious tenets is just as important as following secular moral codes.

The problem is that many of us receive our own religion second hand. Rather than reading the sacred texts for ourselves, we rely on summaries given by priests and grandparents. Often, those summaries end up as watered down justifications for the current status quo, rather than an honest representation of the religion.

Monogamy is often presented as a religious requirement, although it's supported by the religious texts of comparatively few religions. It's most directly supported in Christianity, although, as previously mentioned, that support comes more from Rome than from Bethlehem.

If you really like monogamy, or really like Rome, by all means, embrace monogamy. But if you are choosing monogamy because that's what you think your religion tells you is right, you owe it to yourself to explore your own religion. Read your own scriptures. Don't just rely on the summaries you get in "family friendly" sermons that primarily try to fit religion into the current social status quo.

If religion is important to you, see how marriage is described in your actual religion. Look at the respective roles expected from men and women in the actual texts of your own religion. See what it actually says.

Don't let others create some alternative version of your religion, where they keep the tiny parts they agree with, and reject the giant parts they don't like. If they, or you, want to reject religion entirely and live a secular life, by all means do. But don't let someone else's lies become your faith. Don't let someone replace your real religion with some self-serving counterfeit.

If your religion has texts (e.g. Bible, Quran, Mahabaratha, Tao Te Ching, Sutras, etc.) you owe it to yourself to read them directly, with your own personal eyes. Do not rely on bastardized summaries from those with agendas that run against your own interests.

When you do it, you may discover that your actual religion is quite different from what you've been told. If you try to embrace your actual religion, invariably people around you will try to argue that the parts that were left out no longer apply, but the parts they told you still apply. Perhaps they will argue that virginity requirements are no longer relevant today, but sexual monogamy is.

That's nonsense. Your religion is written down in your scripture. That's the real religion. That's why people wrote down scriptures in the first place; they knew that manipulators and liars would try to lie about it.

When you see your true religion, you may decide it doesn't work for you. You may decide it works even better for you. You'll be able to make an honest, authentic decision about whether to follow your actual, legitimate religion, not someone else's candy-coated fake.

Morality and Children

Getting married and having children, whether monogamously or polygamously, can be a sacred and powerful step to take in life. A real marriage, in which you provide for your children, demonstrates and builds responsibility, personal strength, and character. A real marriage also embraces the provider aspects of masculinity.

On the other hand, producing welfare babies does none of that. Welfare dependent marriages damage the self respect, integrity, character, and soul of the adults involved. They teach kids bad values by telling them that welfare is okay.

Welfare marriages normalize welfarism. Obviously, this damages male power, as it takes away the significance of economic power, and removes a man's economic right to say no.

As men, we don't want welfare families. We don't want to encourage welfarism, and we certainly don't want to be dependent on welfare. It's lowly and embarrassing. It's entirely unmasculine, and unworthy of respect.

The problem is that today, many of us are being tricked into welfare marriages. Many men are tricked into marriages that will, with 99.99999 percent certainty, lead to a welfare marriage, and welfarist methods of child rearing. The most anti-welfare young men are getting tricked into marriages heavily funded by welfare.

Today, over 90 percent of kids attend government schools. The fathers of those kids have accepted welfare-funded education. Sure, we tell ourselves that it's somehow different. We tell ourselves that since everyone uses government schools, it's not really welfare. We make mathematically bizarre claims, suggesting that the $2000 we're paying in property tax somehow funds the $10,000 per kid, per year government school costs. A father with 2 kids in government schools is essentially receiving a welfare check of $20,000 a year. If he's paying $2000 in property tax, and we assume that 100% goes to government schools, he's getting an $18,000 a year welfare check. He's educating his kids on welfare.

We all know it, so we go hugely out of our way to glorify public school teachers. We make outrageous claims, like government school teachers are "heroes", ignoring the obvious reality that they are just government workers who can't teach math very well. We fixate on a sentimental attachment with one or two (out of 40) of our own teachers that we had some bond with, and claim we want our kids to have that kind of experience. But the fact is this: we know we're lying to ourselves. We want to be great and powerful providers. We're ending up as welfare dependents.

How is this happening to us? A big part of it is coming from changing marital norms. These new marital norms have a staggeringly high probability of leading to welfare dependency.

In America, there are two pressures that are pushing us toward welfare. The first is not new. Americans believe in individualistic nuclear families, rather than extended families. It's not the norm for married couples to live with the parents of one of the people involved. We like to show our independence by living separately, having independent finances, etc. Obviously, a young couple that relies on their own small finances, often damaged by college debt, is not likely to have the money for private school.

The second pressure is new. It's the pressure to marry "age appropriately". The idea is that the man and woman should be around the same age.

This usually results in welfare dependency, most often dependency on educational welfare through government schools. Why? The simple fact is that most 25 year old men and women do not have the money for private schools. Sure, some do, like young internet millionaires. But the vast, vast majority do not.

At the same time, 45 year old women cannot bear children. By that age, many men and women are established enough to pay for private education. But it's not a realistic time for women to start having kids.

One solution that has worked for much of human history has been to have a significant age difference between the man and the woman (or women, for polygamous marriages). A 45 year old man may have the earning ability, and the 25 year old woman may have the reproductive ability. Interestingly, this is often a common form of a second marriage.

Another solution relies on extended families. Aristocracies often encouraged very young marriages, often for political reasons. However, that 13 year old prince was not expected to earn a living. He was part of the extended family. He had responsibilities to his clan, and his clan provided for him. Unlike the welfare dependent, he is part of a voluntary and reciprocal arrangement.

Today, we have a third solution, at least for education. Thanks to free online education, parents who take their responsibility seriously can homeschool their kids. Even without much money, they can still be legitimate providers. Unlike the permanently emasculated and embarrassed public school father, the homeschooling father can take pride in his work. Homeschooling fathers don't say things that only demonstrate shame and weakness, like "I get that your math teacher is bad, but just deal with it for this ENTIRE YEAR." Instead, they can say, "Yeah, this school is garbage, let's try something better."

The person who builds a house is just as much a provider as the person who buys a house. The person who homeschools is just as much a provider as the person who pays for private schools.

However, the person who lives in government project housing is not a provider; he's just a welfare recipient. The same is true of the government school parent.

Ending the Normalization of Welfarism

Having kids and sending them to welfare schools is publicly endorsing welfarism. It's normalizing the immoral system that disempowers men. Your actions are public propaganda for the welfare state.

Raising kids is hard, and takes a lot of maturity. If you haven't gotten to the maturity level at which you can either afford private school or do homeschooling, you probably aren't ready to raise kids. If you wait until you are financially and emotionally ready, you're doing the opposite. You are being the example of non-welfarist parenting that should be the norm.

Example of Pulling Out: Homeschool

Public schools are worse than useless; state-regulated private schools aren't much better. Their homework is basically busywork, their history books are mostly propaganda, and even their science books maintain political agendas. They teach math as idiotically as possible, currently through Common Core. Much of the homework, like writing "margin notes" all over each page just makes no sense at all. I got perfect GRE and GMAT scores, finishing both with about an hour and a half to spare. I developed a speed reading method for complex texts. I can tell you there is no bigger waste of time than scrawling gibberish in the margins of important literature.

To add insult to injury, schools blame their garbage results on parents. After accomplishing nothing at school all day, teachers then send kids home with about 15-20 hours of foolish homework per week. This gives schools the ability to blame parents for the school's own failures. They say, "The parents aren't doing their jobs." What they should be saying is, "The parents aren't doing our jobs."

Over the last decades, families started pulling out. They decided that if they were spending 15-20 hours of academic work at home anyway, if they were being blamed for the imbecilic decisions of teachers, they might as well just do the whole thing themselves. Instead of having their kids do nonsense busywork at home, they had their kids do academics that made sense: math that works, instead of foolish, inefficient programs like Common Core; unbiased history (I personally recommend the Cambridge history series); real writing, including fiction and useful nonfiction, instead of just useless literary analysis.

As with anyone who pulls out of the status quo, homeschooling families faced challenges. They had to figure out how to handle supervision, particularly of young kids. New communities created homeschooling groups in which parents rotated supervisory responsibilities.

They had to figure out how to provide education in various subject areas. Most parents aren't really able to teach all academic subjects. They formed homeschooling cooperatives to provide instruction. Some were free, some were paid. They learned about free online resources, like Khan Academy and MIT's OpenCourseWare.

They had to figure out how to handle socialization. Parent groups worked together to make sure kids interacted with others. In many areas, there are dances and athletic competitions, in addition to unstructured social interactions.

Have they overcome all challenges? Of course not. Just as your computer operating system updates all the time, homeschoolers constantly work to solve problems, improve their approaches, and innovate. Unlike the stagnant government schools that either cling to broken systems or lumber over to even stupider ones every few years, homeschooling families innovate continually.

Today, homeschoolers outperform those in public or state-regulated private schools. According to research conducted by Dr. Brian Ray, homeschoolers considerably outperformed the national average on the SAT in math and reading. At the same time, homeschoolers grow up in an environment that builds self reliance and self motivation, and build social skills on a foundation of self reliance, rather than on desperate approval seeking.

Homeschool parents can spend the same amount of time on in-home academics as they did before (about 15-20 hours of academics per week). Some spend even less, although others spend more. But now, instead of being blamed for someone else's incompetence, they are being rewarded for their own successes.

By leaving behind the security blanket of social approval, homeschooling families are learning more, controlling their destinies, and providing better education. Instead of worshipping the hand that smacks them, they have left to create something better.

CHAPTER 24:

Getting Started With Life

In discussions I've had around the country and on social media, I've heard many men discuss the difficulty of getting started with life. Specifically, they have discussed the difficulty of getting a solid enough financial footing to be able to provide for kids. Many have delayed having kids because of these reasons; others have decided not to have kids at all.

But why? It should be easier today than ever before to get started with life. Because of technological advances, each person produces more than people did in the past. It should be easier to get started than it was in the past.

What's changed? In today's world, you have to provide for everyone else's kids first. You have to pay for the welfare of poor kids, and the government schools of middle class kids. Through property taxes that drive up rent, through sales taxes, through income taxes, through so many hidden taxes, you're paying for everyone else.

At the same time, the prices of everything are also being inflated through taxation. You don't directly see the taxes businesses pay. You just see the price of goods. What should cost $2 costs $20.

So imagine this: your rent is much lower. Your taxes are much lower. The prices of everything are much lower. Your salary is the same, or higher, since your employer won't be paying as much in taxes. Would it really be that hard to get on strong enough financial footing then? If you were just providing for yourself and your own kids, instead of those of every irresponsible woman in the country, would it really be that hard? If, when you bought a steak, you were just paying for that steak, instead of that steak plus a ton of welfare and idiotic government projects, would it really be all that hard?

Many of us have taken the step towards using non-governmental, tax-avoiding cryptocurrencies like Bitcoin, Dash, Monero, and others. When you buy something in bitcoin, you are often avoiding some taxes. If you buy a computer, you just pay for the computer, not the computer plus some money for people who can't be bothered to pay for their own kids. You're defunding the welfare state a little bit. You're giving a tiny bit of power back to all of us.

Money is primarily important because it allows us to exchange one type of labor for another. An office worker uses money to buy a light bulb; the manufacturer uses that money to pay the worker in the light bulb factory. If we trade labor for other labor without having to also subsize welfare, we obviously get more for our labor.

Any action you can take to allow us to exchange labor without simultaneously funding the welfare state that specifically disempowers us is a good step. Learn to use cryptocurrencies, and keep searching for other methods to exchange labor without funding welfare. The end of the welfare state means a return of our full economic power, and of our sacred ability to choose to withhold the fruits of our labor from those who haven't earned access to them.

Example of Pulling Out: Cryptocurrency

The good thing about cash: government can't see cash transactions, and thus can't tax them to support welfare and idiocy.

The bad thing about cash: you can't transfer it digitally.

The other bad thing about cash: you can't stop its value from depreciating. The value of a dollar predictably goes down over time, since more are put into circulation by the Federal Reserve bank. A hundred years ago, $20 would get you a new suit. Today that same suit might cost $1000.

Thus, most digital businesses, remote businesses, shipping businesses, etc. have had to just accept that their money will be stolen for welfare. Most individual holders of cash have had to accept that the value of that cash will gradually decrease.

In the past, some monetary enthusiasts recommended that we start using gold or gold-backed currency. Historians quickly pointed out that in 1933, the government had seized all gold bullion, coins, and certificates in order to gain control of the money supply. They said: "In the past you could use gold or government money. Now you have to use government money." Holding gold bullion was illegal from 1933 to 1974, and by that time people were accustomed to government money.

Today, when people try to use gold or silver as currency, the government generally seizes the gold or silver, and fines or locks up the coin maker. You may have heard about the Ron Paul coins that were seized, and there have been other similar cases. They recognize that independent money is a major threat to their power.

Over the last years, various math nerds developed cryptocurrencies like bitcoin, litecoin, and ethereum. These can be used digitally, unlike cash. And, unlike dollars, these currencies are non-inflationary. That means that their value does not go down over time due to inflation (their value can rise or fall due to speculation, just as stock prices rise and fall). Over the last years, their value seems to have gone up, although it seems that some of the more extreme rises have come from speculation.

As more and more people test out cryptocurrencies, the government is panicking. The cryptocurrencies are designed to be anonymous. Innovators are working to make them even more anonymous and secure.

If the government declares an open war on cryptocurrency, they might lose, and encourage more people to self-identify as enemies of the state.

Thus far, they've found ways to allow people to pay taxes on cryptocurrencies, if they want. As it turns out, most people prefer tax evasion.

What if untaxable cryptocurrencies became the norm? That would mean that the only way a woman, child, or other man could get the fruits of your labor is if you chose to give it to them. Today, if a random woman has unprotected sex with a random man and has a kid, you, personally, have to pay for that kid's government school education, college aid, and possibly food stamps. That money is taken away from any kids you might have. Your kids may have fewer advantages because you have to pay for the bad decisions of someone you've never met.

But if our money was nontaxable, you would pay for what you wanted. You would provide more for your kids, and less for anyone else's, if you wanted. Or you could reverse that. The power would be yours.

Many point out that taxes are used for purposes other than redistribution. For example, just over 1 percent of taxes are used for road repair. However, the remaining almost 99% percent is wasted on welfarism, nonsensical military endeavors, pointless boondoggles, and the like. What would nontaxable currency do to that? If money couldn't be taken by force, what would happen?[1]

---

1) FRED Economic Data: *Total Construction Spending: Highway and Street* AND US Government Spending: *Current Government Spending in the US*

It would simply mean that you would only pay for what you wanted. Bitcoin isn't a license to steal. If you want something, you still have to pay for it with bitcoin. If you want to buy orange juice, an EZpass, or any other item, you have to pay for it with bitcoin. You just need to actually consent.

But if you don't want something, you can't be as easily robbed. If you don't want to pay for some random woman's (or man's) bad decisions at the expense of your own kids, then you don't have to. If you believe that a woman (or man) who wants your money has to provide something to you in return, ranging from legal help to housecleaning, then you can stick to that.

The pretend "right" to your money would be gone. You still would have to work to get cryptocurrency, and spend that currency to get products or services. But you wouldn't be laboring half the day to pay for someone else's kids, unless you really wanted to.

Today, cryptocurrency visionaries are working to rapidly advance this technology, to help make sure the government never catches up. There have been stumbling blocks and setbacks, and there will be more. But geniuses and innovators will continue to push past them, and work to give us back our natural right to determine what happens with the fruits of our labor.

We might be closer than we realize to a world in which active consent is required to take someone's money.

CHAPTER 25:

Pulling Out

Men cannot turn to the institutions of American culture for help. Those institutions have either abandoned us or actively turned against us. The medical institutions have abandoned our interests entirely, failing to bother to teach men the importance of paternity testing, and even putting lives at risk in order to prevent paternity knowledge. The legal institutions have abandoned us, treating men like tenth class citizens in family courts. The political institutions have demolished our ability to provide or withhold resources, and even to keep the fruits of our own labor.

As men, we can only rely on ourselves and our own ingenuity - and there's plenty of ingenuity to rely on. The ingenuity that drove the agricultural, industrial, scientific, and information revolutions is in our DNA. We must look at our situation objectively, not sentimentally. We must develop the perspicacity to find opportunities, and the courage to pursue them.

I'd like to begin with a well known example of "pulling out", and show how that mindset can apply to the personal sphere.

Historically, American manufacturing was the envy of the world. The assembly line, steam engine, ironclad boats, and countless other inventions were created here. The corresponding products were manufactured in America.

Americans were hard-working, skilled, and dedicated. Manufacturers could become rich by building factories in America, and there were plenty of manufacturing jobs.

Over time, things started changing. Labor unions started forming, and using their political power to change laws, drive up wages, etc. At first, these were probably reasonable. They negotiated safer conditions and reasonable wages.

But over time, they got more and more power. Their wages became inexplicably high for the skill level of the actual work. Prevailing attitudes and behaviors changed. Phrases like "lazy as a Teamster" became common (a Teamster is a member of the auto-workers union).

The earlier situation, with hard-working, skilled American factory workers was gone. Perhaps that original situation had over-favored the manufacturers. But this new situation was over-favoring workers. Specifically, it was favoring lazy workers, who were getting paid just as much as hard workers. Hard workers, the most likely to get pay raises and promotions, were actually being held down, given the same pay as lazy ones.

The problem was that the number of lazy, entitled workers was forming a larger and larger percentage of the workforce.

Manufacturers fought it. They lobbied for right-to-work laws, which allowed non-union workers to have factory jobs. Unionized labor fought that, insisting that union membership be a prerequisite for employment. Manufacturers fought the outlandish wage requests. But they lost one battle after another.

Eventually, they realized the solution was not to fight an unwinnable battle. It was to pull out.

They left. They built factories in other countries. The people there were only too happy to work hard, for a fraction of the inflated salaries American labor unions demanded. Even with the inconveniences caused by shipping and tariffs, it was easier for American companies to leave.

What manufacturers can do, individuals can do. Manufacturers built factories in America based on an assumption of the type of worker they would find. They expected to find hard-working, diligent employees, willing to start out low and work up to higher wages. While this was true, they kept factories in America.

When the type of worker changed, becoming lazy, slow, and entitled, the manufacturers reevaluated the situation, and left.

While women in America were chaste and helpful, it may have made sense to seek American women as spouses or life partners. When they became promiscuous, loud bullies, it made sense to seek companionship elsewhere.

I've met dozens of American millionaires with foreign wives. The same economic intelligence that made them millionaires drove them to find wives where better ones can be found.

But I've also met quite a few American men who pulled out entirely. They moved entirely to other countries in which their resources bought them power, not just status. Some weren't even that rich. Just like manufacturers, they took advantage of exchange rates. In a country in which a doctor makes the equivalent of $100 a month, a man who has a few thousand saved up, or just a job that allows him to work remotely, lives like an emperor.

Like the manufacturers who left, those men sacrificed some social approval. But the manufacturers who left weren't looking for social approval. They were looking for profit.

The men who left weren't really that interested in being given a pat on the head by a society they found irritating. They were looking for freedom, sex, and power. By pulling out, these relatively normal men get more of all of those than the average American celebrity.

Before major manufacturers relocated to other countries, they first did some site visits. Similarly, you don't have to start this by selling your house. Instead, take a look at some common expatriate destinations. South America and Southeast Asia are currently popular destinations for American expatriates. There are huge American communities with plenty of other Americans to hang out with. There are also many opportunities regarding women, whether you're looking to just have fun or to find something serious.

Money: Status or Power?

In America, money gets a man status. A high-earning man is seen as more accomplished and masculine. It also allows the man to provide some luxuries to a potential mate. For example, a man can take a woman to a nice restaurant. This makes the man more desirable.

In America, money can be used as an enticement or a show of masculinity. But in America, money does not mean power. Money is not legal freedom, the way it is in other countries. Even billionaires have to follow the law. It's not power over life and death; you're forced to pay for the needs and wants of every welfare baby producer in the country. We're living in a country where many people literally believe that internet and birth control pills are human rights - and that you have to pay for everyone to have them.

In many other countries, however, money can put you above the law. Affordable bribes mean you never get a speeding ticket, or go to jail for some victimless "crime." In America, even millionaires have to drive the speed limit, and can end up in jail for non-issues (drug "crimes", prostitution related "crimes", etc.)

Similarly, money in other countries can be the difference between life and death. Or between an unbearable life and a pleasant one. By unbearable, I don't mean that some people have unfulfilling jobs. I mean that people spend their days begging or prostituting themselves. If you have money, you can choose to radically change a person's life. That gives you more than just a fancy status. That gives you real power, real freedom.

Living abroad can also be more moral. Overseas, you may be rescuing people from lives of meaningless destitution. Your economic power will be more appreciated because it will do more good. Even if you run a business in America, you might, at most, give a few people slightly more interesting or rewarding jobs than they otherwise might have had. But overseas, every dollar you spend, every person you employ, every woman you invite into your harem, may be completely transforming a life for the better.

But ultimately, whether that's fair or unfair, good or bad, moral or immoral is not the central question. The questions you need to ask are: Does it benefit you? Can it be turned to your advantage?

Do you want to embrace the heroic life you were meant to live, or continue in the living death you experience here?

Will you play by some rules that the other side is refusing to follow? While leech women use every method of coercion against you, while they steal your money through taxation, while they force men to pay child support for children that are products of adultery, your playing "nice" is just playing the wrong game.

Spending time in countries in which money is actual power creates a whole different set of opportunities.

Stop wasting your money on status symbols that are supposed to indirectly attract women. First, they don't work. Second, if they work, they are attracting the wrong kind of women. But most importantly, you can just use that money to buy what you want directly. Whether you are buying wives, virginity, procreation, or just sex, there's no reason to be indirect about it. Take your money to where it matters; take your money to where you can buy those things directly; don't waste it on silly status symbols.

Make Dollars, Spend Pesos

There is a growing trend of people working to make dollars, and spend pesos. Basically, you try to get an American job that you can do remotely. Today, the number of jobs in that category is skyrocketing.

Then, instead of doing the job remotely in an American city, you do it from a city in a country with a weak currency. Even a moderate American income will allow you to live like a king in other countries. You will be rich enough that your money will give you power, not just status. In America, even Mark Zuckerberg is not that rich. He still needs to follow laws. In other countries, a $40K a year salary can make you rich enough to be above many laws.

So many Americans are already doing this that some major foreign cities temporarily maxed out their internet bandwidths! Fortunately, as bandwidth increases across the world, this will become less and less of an issue.

If you maintain your U.S. citizenship, you still have to pay your income taxes (if you report your income). But you don't have to pay U.S. sales taxes, property taxes, excise taxes, etc. You can also often avoid the value added taxes (sales taxes) in other countries if you are a U.S. citizen, especially if you pay in cash.

Your rent will be lower, food costs lower. You'll have money and freedom to do whatever you want.

Essentially, you'll be an Economic Conquistador. The original conquistadors used the superior technological knowledge of their home country to dominate the natives. Their steel armor, for example, was impervious to wooden arrows. Their firearms were far more deadly than the bows and arrows the natives had.

Similarly, you can use the superior economic power of your U.S. job to have power and freedom in an economically weaker area.

When you live in a country in which poverty presents a real survival threat, where welfare and social services are basically nonexistent, money means power. Money becomes the difference between life and death. Having money doesn't just make you a respectable husband or a cool boyfriend. It gives you the power to grant or withhold necessities. Winning your favor becomes a means of survival.

Even better: you're literally rescuing people from poverty and meaninglessness. You can provide more than food; you can provide access to information and ideas. You can open up a world that they could never have dreamed of experiencing.

Jealous American women will argue that doing so is taking advantage. If that's taking advantage, then the prince was taking advantage of Cinderella. Like the prince, why shouldn't you favor hard working, chaste, humble, decent young women, instead of selfish, loud, drunken, aggressive Americans who have taken their cues from Cinderella's step sisters?

You may have seen commercials that tell you that a few cents a day is enough to save a life in some country or other. Think about what that means. A few dollars gives you a massive amount of leverage. You don't need to live like the beaten down, henpecked American husband hiding in his man cave. The power will be so slanted in your favor that you can live like an emperor. And you can bestow kindness and favor on those who deserve it, rather than those who screech for it.

They say that the squeaky wheel gets the oil. But in an efficient enterprise, the squeaky wheel just gets replaced.

This situation is not some unfair twist of economics. It's how things are supposed to be. It's how life is if you are allowed to either give or withhold your resources, rather than having them forcibly taken from you. You've just gotten so used to complete disempowerment that having any actual power feels unfamiliar. Sometimes, unfamiliar is good.

If you want 9 girlfriends and 20 kids, you can do that. If you want a different girlfriend every day, or every month, you can do that too. If you want to find three or four special women, or only one, and give them a life they couldn't have dreamed of, that option is there too. Your financial power, if combined with psychological discipline, can give you what you cannot have in America.

The thing is, you have skills that are economically valuable. Most men around the world do not. At the very least, you know how to speak english and use a computer. You have work ethic and some ambition. You probably have some additional skills - or know how to build them. A quick trip around the world will show you how rare those qualities are.

One of my favorite speakers, Joel Osteen, often says, "Leave from where you're tolerated, and go to where you're celebrated." In America, you're treated like garbage. You've gotten used to it, but you shouldn't have to. There are many parts of the world in which you might be celebrated.

CHAPTER 26:

Changing World Politics

Let a Thousand Hong Kongs Bloom: End Foreign Aid

Imagine this: instead of around 200 countries on earth, there are 20,000 small countries. Each country would be competing for citizens, just as restaurants compete for customers. Some countries might run out of room or have waiting lists, just as restaurants sometimes run out of room and have waiting lists.

America might be 50 separate countries, as many have argued was the original intent of the founding fathers. Today, the word "state" has come to mean "province." But it's true definition is "country." America might be 5,000 countries for that matter, each competing for productive citizens.

What happens when countries have to compete? The same thing that happens when restaurants compete. First, you get efficiency. A restaurant that squanders its resources on nonsense goes out of business. Second, you get variety. If you already have 10 Italian restaurants on a block, a savvy entrepreneur might open a Chinese, Greek, American, Spanish, Ethiopian, Vegan, or other restaurant.

What would happen today if there were 20,000 countries, all competing? Either for reasons of efficiency or variety, we would get at least a few industrialized, modern countries that rejected welfarism entirely.

A rejection of welfarism means a recognition of the sacredness of your work, and an end to the general disempowering of men. You could provide for those you wanted to, and refuse to provide for others. Your progeny would have advantages from your work. Others would not.

Is such a thing politically possible? It's actually much more politically feasible than you might think.

In order to create a new country, you need sovereign land. Normally, when you buy land, you're buying land use rights, not sovereignty rights. You can't set taxes and laws on your property. Your land is not your own private country.

Historically, countries have sold sovereign rights to land, generally to other countries. The Louisiana Purchase, the Gadsden Purchase, and Seward's Folly (Alaska) are some you may remember from school. But today, countries tend to be pretty reticent to sell sovereign land.

Sovereign rights are incredibly valuable, but they also pose a financial risk to the country that sells them. For example, suppose a nation sold some sovereign land. The new owners of that sovereign land might just decide to set income taxes to zero, abolish all social welfare, etc. Immediately, the wealthy and productive citizens of the first country would want to move to that new area. It's culturally similar to the rest of the country, and you don't have to accept the theft of half of your yearly labor. Those who use welfare would immediately want to move to the original country, thus adding more drain. The original country would now have a greater financial burden, and a smaller group able to pay taxes. In order to compete, they would probably have to slash taxes and welfare too.

Thus, countries almost never sell sovereign land. In fact, other countries do whatever they can to prevent the sale of sovereign land too! Large welfarist countries don't want any country anywhere to sell sovereign land. They know that any non-welfare country can pose a potential threat to a welfarist country. As transportation becomes easier, as internet becomes ubiquitous, a non-welfarist country does not need to be adjacent to a welfarist country to pose a threat. A country halfway around the world, that can maintain basic infrastructure and rejects all welfare, poses a threat to welfarism everywhere.

Countries generally sell sovereign territory when they desperately need money. In other words, if we make countries desperate enough, they will sell sovereign land, creating the possibilities of many new countries.

Making mismanaged countries run out of money isn't complex. They usually do it all by themselves. If it wasn't for outside intervention, many countries would already be selling sovereign territory. The problem is that through foreign aid, the World Bank, and the International Monetary Fund, countries like America keep those countries afloat, preventing the need to sell sovereign land.

If we shut those programs down, countries will sell sovereign land. Sovereign land is incredibly expensive, and an ideal way for a country to fill a budget shortfall. It generally takes groups of investors to even be able to conceive of affording a small amount of sovereign land.

The good news is that foreign aid is pretty much the least politically popular program that exists. If people understood that without foreign aid we would have many new countries competing to offer less welfarism and better lives, I imagine foreign aid would become even less popular.

The even better news is that new countries are often quite successful, often disproportionately more so than the parent country. Hong Kong, in the short time it has been free from the communism and foolishness of China, has become a financial and cultural powerhouse, with a much higher average standard of living than its abusive parent nation. Imagine if each current giant nation had a thousand

Hong Kongs surrounding it, some of which would inevitably reject welfarism entirely.

This is a politically winnable fight, and one whose consequences could be incredibly beneficial and empowering. Through new, competing startup countries, we could force even old countries to abandon welfarism, and to once again start treating work as sacred.

Pulling Out Example: Brexit

A recent example of pulling out shows exactly what happens when countries separate and compete. In 2016, Britons had had enough of EU regulation and taxation. They were tired of having to pay for the degenerate financial irresponsibility of nations like Greece. So, they voted to leave the EU.

As of this writing, Britain is struggling between two versions of itself. One possibility is that Britain remains a welfarist European nation, with high taxes and heavy socialism. The other possibility is that it becomes a low tax mecca, attracting businesses and productive people from everywhere.

It's made some minor hints towards reducing taxes to become more competitive, although whether it will make any serious strides towards less welfare is still in doubt.

In response, their former teammate and new competitor France has already slashed some of its own socialist regulations, including some of those that make it insanely difficult to fire unproductive workers.

When cartels and monopolies are broken apart, they compete by lowering costs, improving quality, and caring about customer service. When big countries or cartels of countries like the EU break apart, the result is similar. They compete for useful citizens by lowering taxes and nuisance regulations, while generally slashing various forms of welfare. Preventing businesses from firing useless workers is one example of such welfare.

Imagine if provinces seceded from countries, and cities seceded from provinces. Imagine if economic competition between these thousands of competing nations forced them all to abandon all welfare in all its forms. You would see a complete return of economic power. The destruction of economic power, the only type of power men have, would be reversed.

Any secession, any separation of nations, anything that increases competition between countries is good for men (and productive women). We should do everything we can to encourage all secession and separatism, while advocating to end all foreign aid.

Example of Pulling Out: The American Revolution

The most historically famous example of pulling out is the American Revolution. A few independent, motivated colonists left the mightiest empire of the time. They set up their own rules, their own culture, and their own economy. They left behind the hidebound and lazy culture of the British monarchy, and created a meritocracy that became the most powerful economy in the world. America isn't perfect, and it's lately been hijacked by welfarists, but it's a pretty impressive achievement.

Today, Americans work with Britain from a position of obvious dominance. Americans today are harder working and more innovative, just as the early colonists were. It has made our country more powerful, at least for now.

That process wasn't easy. America had to fight an empire, then fight the same empire again in 1812, and then face itself in a Civil War. The process involved mistakes, trial and error, internal struggle. But the results speak for themselves.

At the time, leaving Britain was seen as lunacy. Leaving a dominant culture always is.

But Americans realized that they had more than what Britain could offer. They saw their own value, and realized what their value could become. They refused to settle and be the second rate dogs of a stagnant aristocracy.

They had the option of obedience or mutiny, safety or greatness, the familiar or the excellent. We're all lucky that they chose wisely. Even today, we look up to them as examples of courage and wisdom.

Can we do the same? Can we set an example that our descendants will be proud of?

Trade Protectionism

U.S. based companies often try to keep out goods produced by foreign competitors - especially when the foreign competitors are better. They lobby to increase tariffs, create import quotas, etc.

The effective and competent American companies don't need to resort to that. But the most incompetent, bloated, trashy companies often do.

In the marketplace for women, a similar pattern can be found. American women often lag behind their foreign competitors in critical and high demand areas. Most American women these days are not virgins at the altar. Those who seek virgin wives often look to other countries. The same is true for those who seek women unaffected by America's obesity epidemic, or who want wives who provide emotional support rather than an emotional drain. The socio-political insanity so popular among many groups of women today (third wave feminism, social "justice", etc.), also encourage many men to look elsewhere for more calm, sane wives. Men who want women who are refined, demure, and classically feminine have started to look outside of America to find them.

While those seeking fat, sexually used-up, loudmouthed, socialist drunks probably consider America a paradise, many American men are looking elsewhere. And as so many incompetent, worthless companies have done in America, American women have sought trade protectionism. Third wave feminist groups have lobbied hard to create laws trying to stop men from marrying foreign women. After all, a man who can marry a foreign woman will almost certainly not be interested in marrying a third wave feminist/socialist. Unfortunately, at least one of these, the International Marriage Broker Regulation Act, has passed.

The passage of this law, and attempts to pass others, lets us know one thing: third wave feminists believe that they cannot survive against foreign competition. In this case, they know best.

It also lets us know how large the international marriage industry has become. After all, why bother to lobby against something insignificant? As the industry continues to grow, it will either put pressure on American women to improve, or simply place them out of the market entirely.

Personally, I don't recommend marriage to anyone. But if you must marry, don't marry American. Women from other countries demand less and offer more.

CHAPTER 27:

What We Can Learn From the Gay Rights Movement

For centuries, gay men were treated like tenth rate garbage. Alan Turing, the hero who helped crack the Nazi code, the man who did more to help the Allies beat Hitler than anyone else, was persecuted by the country he helped save for being gay. He died young, probably from the stress of persecution, social abuse, and imprisonment.

America, just a few decades ago, was still treating gay men like trash. Over time, however, gay men learned how to fight back, take their rights, and achieve value dominance in critical areas.

As a simple illustration, one of the major discussion points during the gay marriage debate was the rights of gay people to visit their partners in the hospital. Normally, pretty much anyone can visit someone in a hospital; however, at some key times, only close family and spouses are allowed.

The gay movement fought relentlessly for gay spouses to have the same visitation rights. It became a central talking point in the news, on social media, and in private discussions. Those who opposed gay marriage became monsters who didn't want people to see those whom they loved at a critical time.

Eventually, this and other points were hammered home hard enough to change social perception, and then to change laws. The gay movement won the day. Having learned that socio-cultural warfare works, they continue to fight on other issues.

But realistically, what's more significant: the ability to visit someone for a couple hours right after a medical procedure, or the ability to not be forced to pay for someone else's kid for 18 years?

Today's culture is saying that it's barbaric to make a gay man wait for an extra couple of hours to visit a partner in a hospital, but it's totally fine to make a straight man suffer 18 years of being forced to pay hundreds of dollars a month for the products of paternity fraud against him.

I'm not saying that gay people shouldn't be able to visit spouses in the hospital. I believe that they absolutely have that natural right. But that right is frankly smaller than the right to not be forced to pay for the products of paternity fraud for years.

For much of the history of the gay rights movement, gay men didn't really publicly fight back. The public told them they were tenth rate degenerates. They made them feel lowly and ashamed. At first, they hid, denied who they were, and stayed in the closet. Eventually, they learned to take pride in who they were, to stand up publicly for their natural rights, to stop hiding who they were for fear of the social backlash.

With straight men, the silencing technique is different. We're told that we're always the oppressors. No matter how much evidence we can see to the contrary - fewer men than women going to college, men being silenced in colleges, men being forced to pay for products of paternity fraud, large scale genetic sequencing being blocked to prevent people from finding out about paternity fraud, being disempowered by losing our economic right to say no - we're told that we're the oppressors. We're told that any incursion on our rights is irrelevant, since we have privilege, and use that privilege primarily for oppressing people.

This leaves many of us afraid to say anything, or ashamed to say anything. We're like gay men from decades ago. We say, "We should be happy that society tolerates us at all. We shouldn't push for more." That was a losing strategy for gay men, and it's a losing strategy for straight men.

If we're being disempowered, if our natural rights are being trampled, it's up to us to fight for them. Gay men waited for someone to defend them; that someone never came. They had to do it themselves. They had to stand up, be proud of who they were, admit that they deserved their natural rights, and then fight for them. Straight men need to do the same.

It is not, in any way, okay for us to be robbed to pay for kids we didn't produce. It's wrong for us to be forced to pay for others without our active consent. It is wrong for us to lose our economic right to say "no".

No one is going to fight for that for us. We need to do it ourselves.

I've often said that men are being silenced by society, culture, feminists, social justice warriors, etc. But the truth is, we're silencing ourselves. We aren't being physically gagged; our vocal cords have not been removed. No one has cut off our hands to prevent us from writing.

What silencing do we face? People shrieking at us for voicing opinions they don't like? So what? Do our lungs not work? Do our vocal cords not make noise? If someone yells at us to shut up, can't we just yell back louder? Do third wave feminists have some unique ability to shout that men don't have? Do they have some special access to social media that we don't? If they write a political post on social media, can't we write ten? What are we afraid of? That some shrieky used up woman won't have sex with us? So what?

Don't fall for the lies people tell you about masculinity. The biggest lie is describing a man as the "strong, silent type", and suggesting that such behavior is masculine. "The strong, silent type" is not a description of a powerful man. That is the description of a well trained donkey.

The great men of history were not silent. They were orators, like Cicero and Demosthenes. They were political writers, like Douglass, Mill, and Locke. They didn't just shut up and carry stuff. They used words to change reality.

Most of us were taught how to do everything but that. In school, instead of being taught to write political persuasion, we were taught to waste time on literary analysis. Instead of learning debate, we wasted time on Powerpoint presentations and oral reports. Even those of us who joined debate teams just learned to talk fast, because of the insane scoring system used in competitive debate.

Those of us who spoke out were either punished or drugged down with Adderall. We learned the value of shutting up and not making waves.

In college discussions, we learned how to accept the current cultural premise, to seek approval of the group, and only debate within paradigms. Instead of learning how to shatter deeply held assumptions, we learned to parrot back professors' ideas on papers and in discussions.

But there is nothing stopping you from learning now how to fight back, how to speak out. Practice writing on social media, websites, or through letters to the editor. Watch famous speakers on youtube, and practice whenever you can. Watch politicians doing town halls, speeches, and question and answer sessions, and learn what you can.

Most importantly: don't be afraid to fail. The first 100 times you speak out, you'll probably just be shrieked at. But no one can shriek you into silence. Only you can silence yourself. Keep practicing, keep improving. Soon, instead of shrieking at you, people will be telling you how what you said made them cry. That's getting closer.

Keep going. People will try to use every kind of social and sexual pressure against you. So what? Sex with non-virgins can be had cheaply in most countries; sex with virgins is more costly, but less costly than your soul. Just being American can be a huge attractant in many countries. And if you put your effort into exercising and developing social dominance rather than into seeking approval from your cultural enemies, you'll have even more options. Don't give up who you are in order to get access to the used-up genitals of an angry nag.

No one but you can silence yourself. No one but you can speak for you.

Gay men stopped responding to social pressure, found their voices, and created one of the most powerful socio-political movements of the last century. Let's learn from them.

CHAPTER 28:

The Personal is the Political

The behaviors of individual consumers and businesses shape the economy. Micro behavior shapes macro behavior.

The same is true in political reality. Personal reality shapes political reality. The dynamics of our personal relationships alter the dynamics of our political relationships. The social reality created in our private interactions shapes our political interactions.

Today, American political debates discuss inexplicable tax funded benefits for women, while ignoring violations of the natural rights of men. Today, for example, many women's groups argue that birth control pills should be tax funded. Many others believe that recreational sex should not be funded through theft. Either way, it's hard to legitimately argue that not having your recreational sex subsidized is a violation of your natural rights.

At the same time, currently the gross violations of male natural rights are essentially ignored by political debates. Consider how often you've seen loud debates demanding taxation funded birth control. Now consider how often you've seen discussions about allowing men to not pay for other people's kids? Or even allowing victims of paternity fraud to not have to pay for the products of that fraud?

The micro level mimics the macro. Inside of relationships, it's men who are routinely "in the doghouse" for various transgressions. While research suggests that women do, on the surface apologize more frequently, the apologies tend to be routine and minor, not about anything that delves into the realm of values.[1]

Within relationships, when it comes to value warfare, women often have the upper hand. Men with dissenting political, personal, or sexual views usually face heavy emotional artillery from significant others. Silenced by shrieks and tears, men lose one value battle after another.

You may have felt that way - constantly apologizing, just not bothering to broach any topics in which your values disagree. You end up feeling like you're constantly in the wrong. You may face a bizarre mix of modern and traditional views. You're supposed to follow "traditional" rules about monogamy, but her elaborate sexual past is totally fine, because that is supposed to be judged by modern, permissive standards. She's not going to apologize for that, of course. That was just "serial monogamy", which, while obviously a type of polygamy, should not be judged as such.

Why are men losing these personal and political value battles? Why are men losing at the macro level and the micro level? Why are we being silenced at home and in the public sphere?

Those two spheres are fundamentally connected. Losing value battles at home, and losing value battles in politics are not mere coincidences. We are losing the public battles because we are losing the private battles. We are having our reality deformed in our private lives, and operating within that deformed reality in the political sphere. If we are going to regain our natural political rights, our fair economic power, our financial ability to say "no", we need to learn how to fight those personal battles more effectively.

For generations, women have learned to operate cleverly and subtly. They had no choice; they had no political or economic power.

---

[1] The Week: *Why women apologize more than men*

Cleverness was their only option. They learned to be the "neck that turns the head". They developed effective personal and social strategies. Those principles remain part of their culture.

But those strategies never became part of male culture. Men didn't need them; after all, they were given every possible advantage. Affirmative Action makes people weak, and no one in history has gotten more Affirmative Action than men did. For centuries, all political and economic power was reserved for men. Men didn't need to develop clever strategies. While challenges were making women more clever, advantages were just making men weaker.

Today, the tables have turned. We have been dispossessed of our basic political and economic rights. But we have not yet learned cleverness, or even reasonable personal strategies. The result is that more and more of our rights are trampled. Men are forced to pay for the biological offspring of their unfaithful wives' lovers. We are forced to pay for the offspring of women we've never even seen. And while we struggle haplessly, women charge ahead with increasingly unjustifiable demands. Today, for example, women are demanding a combination of paid maternity leave and laws that demand that men and women have the same nominal salary. In other words, men and women get the same salary, but women get an many extra vacation days.

Can you imagine men demanding something as ludicrous today? Can you imagine men demanding the same nominal salary, but five times as many vacation days? Maternity leave might be six weeks or more. Are we supposed to pretend that six weeks of paid leave is an insignificant benefit? With most jobs giving two weeks of leave a year, paid maternity leave would be a huge financial benefit.

We're learning to be politically silent because we've learned to be personally silent. We don't stand up for ourselves in our private lives, and have learned not to stand up for ourselves in our public lives. We're letting others shape our private reality, and letting that deformed private reality shape our politics.

If we're ever going to have laws that respect our rights, we have to learn how personal reality is shaped, how we can reshape it, and how to prevent our reality from being deformed.

Whether you plan to only have casual relationships, marry one woman, engage in polygamy, or follow some other path, you will gain from understanding how personal and political realities are shaped. Whether you choose to live a middle class life in America, or live like a king in some country with a weaker currency, the same principles will apply.

1984

Near the end of Orwell's 1984, the main character Winston has been captured by the government. He is about to be tortured by a member of the ruling party. The man says:

'Do you remember...writing in your diary, "Freedom is the freedom to say that two plus two make four"?'

He then holds up four fingers, but demands that Winston see five. He keeps torturing Winston.

Winston tries to lie, and say he sees five, but the torturer knows that Winston is just lying. He continues the electric shock torture.

Winston finally cries out that he wants to see five, but he cannot. The torturer asks:

"Which do you wish: to persuade me that you see five, or really to see them?"

Winston replies, "Really to see them."

The torture continues in intensity. Eventually Winston says, about the number of fingers, "I don't know. I don't know. You will kill me if you do that again. Four, five, six--in all honesty I don't know."

At that moment the torturer rewards Winston with a pleasure inducing drug.

The most fundamental freedom is the freedom to perceive and speak the truth. As Winston puts it, it's the freedom to say 2+2 = 4. If you can control a person at that level, if you can change his fundamental perception of reality, then you can control him completely.

Many men can identify with the above process. Challenge a perception of reality, torture the person until he either agrees with a different reality, or admits he has no idea what reality is anymore, and then reward him with pleasure.

Imagine this: a man and a woman are dating. He expresses some political or personal opinion that she doesn't share. It could be significant and political. It could be minor and personal.

The woman attacks, verbally and psychologically. She uses everything in her arsenal. Yelling, stomping off and making the man chase her, crying to make him feel guilty, dark cloud silent treatment, etc. Every kind of emotional artillery is unleashed. At first, the man fights back. But eventually, he gives in to the onslaught. Maybe he says, "No, I didn't mean that."

She says, "You're just saying what you think I want to hear. You don't believe it." She's right. The onslaught continues. Hours, days, whatever it takes. Eventually, beleaguered and exhausted, he says, "I don't know. Maybe I didn't mean that. Maybe I did. I have no idea any more."

And then she rewards him with physical pleasure, makeup sex, or just psychological pleasantness.

Consider your dating history right now. Consider all the times you've had makeup sex. Now ask yourself this: did that happen after you convinced her, or after she convinced you? Were you rewarded for being right or for being intellectually obedient? Were you being respected for having the right view and convincing her, or were you just rewarded like an animal for doing what your trainer wanted?

The actual issue you give in on may not even be that important. After all, it doesn't really matter how many fingers a person is holding up. But reality matters. Control of reality perception definitely matters.

Just like an animal tamer getting a tiger to jump through a small hoop, the woman may choose a very minor issue on which to have the initial battle. The subject will be insignificant; the response will be disproportionately massive. The goal is to get the man accustomed to adjusting his reality to suit her. The first hoops are minor. They grow and grow, until eventually the man is agreeing to all kinds of dysreality.

When you concede on a minor issue, it seems like you've lost nothing of consequence, but you've actually lost the most important thing. Like Winston, you've lost the freedom to say 2+2 = 4. Just a little bit. But enough. And the process continues. If you step out of line from her version of reality by an inch, she will respond with everything she has.

For many men, the process continues until they wander through each day like zombies, beaten and depressed, and not even really understanding why. They become psychologically dependent on their new arbiters of reality.

Some men fight back, but almost 100% of men make the same mistake. They lose control over their emotions, say something idiotic and cruel, and then feel guilty. Once the man feels guilty, the woman pushes hard on that guilt, making him feel even more guilty, while continuing the reality assault. Weakened by guilt, unable to handle the onslaught, the man who tried to fight back eventually gives in. Like the judo expert, the woman uses the man's guilt force against him.

The result: men spend so much time pretending, they end up living in a fantasy world. They end up believing things that are either false or impossible. Once you've lost your authentic perception of reality, you've lost yourself.

Fortunately, this can be prevented or reversed. Even if you've fallen into this trap, even if your reality is so distorted that you have lost yourself, you can save yourself. Even if you're banished to a "man cave" in a house you're paying for, even if you're adopting political views you don't really believe in order to appease others, even if your personal or sexual reality is being denied and silenced, it's not too late.

I'll first discuss prevention, and then use that discussion as a basis for the discussion of a cure.

CHAPTER 29:

The Basics of Social Reality

Man is a pack animal. We survive in groups and tribes; alone, we struggle. Even the most introverted and independent among us cannot thrive in total isolation.

In prison, solitary confinement is one of the worst punishments. Separated from human contact, we psychologically wither.

Some part of us seeks to be included in tribes and groups. Most groups are at least partially defined by their social reality - their value systems, political reality, and social culture. We often adopt these elements of social reality in order to avoid being rejected from that tribe.

There is often a sexual element to that, but that element can be overstated. It's true that we may be tempted to adopt particular value systems, group markers, etc. for sexual advantages. But this usually goes deeper than sex. Our brains, designed during a time when acceptance by a tribe was necessary for survival, seek that tribal acceptance even more than we seek sex.

When warning teenagers, we use the oxymoronic phrase, "peer pressure". But that phrase itself makes no sense. Peers are, by definition, equals. How could an equal possibly exert any major social pressure on an equal?

What teenagers experience is just the same desire for tribal acceptance that all people feel. If the tribe of teenagers around them hold drinking alcohol as a core value, they will be inclined to adopt that value in order to gain that tribal acceptance.

Individuals adopt the values of nearby tribes in order to gain tribal acceptance. Even entire subcultures will often accept the values of the dominant culture in order to gain cultural acceptance from the dominant culture.

I saw this during my time as Vice Chair of the Libertarian Party. The Libertarian party rejects government taxes and regulation. At a philosophical level, any Libertarian should reject the existence of government schools (public schools). And yet, rejecting that core value of the dominant culture was usually too much for members of that subculture. Even though Libertarian ideology and philosophy unambiguously lead to opposing the existence of government schools, expressing that view would lead to rejection by the dominant culture, in which worship of government schools has become a required value. One sitting Libertarian state legislator, who identified as an anarcho capitalist (a person who rejects the existence of any government), even stated that openly opposing public schools would be social suicide. In other words, refusing to accept a core value of the dominant culture would lead to rejection by that culture.

As we begin to understand this impulse, we can begin to free ourselves from it. It's a vestigial instinct. We don't need it. In today's capitalist economy, we don't need tribal acceptance to survive. We just need a product or service that others are willing to pay for.

But it will feel like you need that tribal acceptance. Large scale industrial capitalism has existed for maybe 100 years. Our brains evolved tens of thousands of years ago. Our brains still believe that we need tribal acceptance to survive.

But, there's good news: that part of your brain is quite easy to manage. Normally, other people manipulate that part of you. In college, you may have pretended to believe in third wave feminism and social "justice", because that part of you had been manipulated. That part of you responded to your social surroundings, and adopted the

It's a pretty effective technique. But the good news is that for many women, it is literally their only technique. If you can defeat it, you can defeat her. She has no other weapons. She's never needed any others.

Some women combine this technique with the aforementioned technique of emotional over-response. Big deal. So they have two techniques instead of one. Neither is that hard to block.

The even better news is that the same basic technique defeats both the emotional over-response technique and the guilt judo technique.

I call that technique masculine politeness. Despite being male (if you are), and despite being told your whole life to be polite, you've probably learned very little about masculine politeness.

As a kid, you probably were told that being polite is about being nice. We're told to be polite in order to avoid hurting people's feelings.

Later, you may have learned a "customer is always right" type of politeness. That's the kind of politeness that is automatically submissive to the opinions of anyone else. It's just agreeing to get something out of someone. In retail, it's just agreeing to get money. In personal relationships, people do the same to get sex. The difference is that retail transactions take a few minutes, while relationships can drag on for months, while your reality is beaten down into nothingness.

But you might never have learned about masculine politeness. Masculine politeness is not about sparing people's feelings, or being obsequious long enough to get something out of them. Masculine politeness has one purpose: defeating the emotions of others.

Emotions are weapons. If you've ever felt the misery of dark cloud silent treatment, of being cried at, of being guilt tripped, you've felt the sting of those weapons. They are far more devastating than fists. If

the mountain, having others adopt your reality, or beaten down in a man cave, having adopted someone else's reality. Or you might build a shared reality. As a tip: if the other person has not adopted a single part of your reality, it's not actually a shared reality. It's just a reality you've been psychologically beaten into that has then been incorrectly labeled as a shared reality.

We've discussed one technique already: a disproportionate emotional response to get you to bend some important part of your reality, followed by a sexual reward. It's a common technique, but not half as common as using your own guilt against you.

Here's how that works:

- The woman provokes the man into saying or doing something cruel. In this phase, she will use insults, emotional explosions, leaving in the middle of a sentence, physical violence, etc. The goal is to needle the other person to provoke an attack.
- The man foolishly falls for the trap, and says or does something cruel.
- The man feels guilty once he's calmed down.
- The woman beats the man into submission using his own guilt.

Like a judo expert, she uses the man's own force against him. In that feeling of guilt, the man is willing to give up any part of his reality to show his apology. He feels so bad about himself that he doesn't even think he deserves to fight for his reality, or even to have one. If his reality lets him be a cruel monster, then how much value could it have?

This process is repeated a few times, until the man is obediently buried in his man cave, broken and pathetic.

eral countries with polygamy and no income tax right now. It's not impossible. It's just different from what you grew up with.

The dominant reality you grew up in conditioned you from an early age. It was the reality that shaped your understanding. Your brain grew up in that reality. It's almost impossible for it to imagine anything else.

How do we begin to see differently? Books can help. For me, *The Fountainhead* and *Zen and the Art of Motorcycle Maintenance* were particularly eye opening. But in a broader sense, the ability to change reality comes from understanding that every single part of reality, with the exception of the laws of physics, can be changed. And the jury is still out on the laws of physics.

Once, women who had kids out of wedlock were sent to homes for unfortunate girls. Today, that's just a part of the generational welfare lifestyle. Reality changed. Once, virginity was an expected part of marriage. Now it's not. Reality changed. Once, there was no income tax. Today, there is one. Reality changed. Every single part of today's reality that is different from that of the past has changed. That means that each of those parts of reality is, obviously, changeable.

In recognizing that something has been changed, we must, at least, accept that it can be changed. It can be reversed, moved in a different direction entirely, or maintained. It is not a permanent fixture. It is malleable.

Reality changes are most noticeable at the macro level: passing the income tax; normalizing marriage to women who have already had sex; the relative position of heterosexuality and homosexuality; the comparative position of religiousness and atheism. But most reality battles happen at the micro level.

Some of your biggest reality battles will happen in the context of romantic relationships. You will either find yourself on the top of

CHAPTER 31:

The Fluidity of Reality

The idea of social reality may be new to you. You may be thinking, "Isn't reality just reality? How can there me more than one reality?"

Here's a simple example. In parts of Ancient Greece, homosexuality was not only normal, it was preferred. Plato wrote about how superior it was compared to other types of love. In the late 20th century in America, it was seen as evil and degenerate.

That's a huge, major part of social reality. The question, "What is better, heterosexuality or homosexuality?" has had two completely different answers in two major cultural powers. Ancient Greece and modern America are two major centers of culture, thought, and ideas. They exerted influence on many other cultures. And yet, on something so big and fundamental, they had different answers.

Whenever a particular reality achieves dominance, it acts as if that is the only way that the world could possibly be. Monogamous marriages and income taxes are seen as permanent. But many ancient and modern cultures had polygamous marriages, and the U.S. only adopted income taxes in the early 1900s. For most of American history, there was no income tax.

That's what reality dominance looks like and feels like. A dominant social reality feels like an unchangeable fact of life. It makes sure that we can't even imagine an alternative. If I ask you to imagine a world with polygamy and no income tax, you might say, "Sounds great, and also impossible." But the simple fact is that there are sev-

large ones are secret, but you probably have a friend that can add you. You can also just search "dark humor."

Dark humor expands your mind past the constraints put on it by the social politeness that welfarism depends on. If you can learn to laugh at the sacred cows of welfarist ideologies, those ideologies can't hold you down. If you can broaden your humor past the cages of social restrictions, then you won't need to spend your life in someone else's constructed reality. More importantly, you're making important steps towards destroying that fake social reality.

Harvard and other welfarist institutions cannot control laughter. It's a threat to the shield of fearful politeness they have built around their welfarist ideologies.

And that applies not just to the central institutions of welfarism, but to all parts of welfarist culture. We can fearfully stay silent, and pretend that people who have nine kids and no job just can't help it. But we can't help laughing when great comedians mock that view. For example, it's hard not to laugh when Chris Rock declares, "A black woman that got 2 kids, going to work everyday busting her ass hates bitches with 9 kids on welfare. Bitch! Stop fucking, put the dick down. Get a job holding dick. Whatever you do, get paid to do it."

Dark humor, politically incorrect humor, any humor that doesn't fear the shields of social politeness around welfarism, social justice, and other nonsense is a powerful tool. It opens your thinking.

If you don't like dark humor yet, don't worry about it. It's an acquired taste, but one worth acquiring. I'm reminded of this quote from Bruce Lee:

"Some martial arts are very popular, real crowd pleasers, because they look good, have smooth techniques. But beware. They are like a wine that has been watered. A diluted wine is not a real wine, not a good wine, hardly the genuine article. Some martial arts don't look so good, but you know that they have a kick, a tang, a genuine taste. They are like olives. The taste may be strong and bitter-sweet. The flavor lasts. You cultivate a taste for them. No one ever developed a taste for diluted wine."

To get started, you might consider playing a game like Cards Against Humanity. Or you could just search for funny examples of Cards Against Humanity on Google images. There are plenty of dark humor groups on facebook. If you want something somewhat political, join a few "anti-SJW" groups. If you want dark humor for its own sake, see if you can join one of the "Pimps of the Hood" groups. The

nonprofits get together and play Cards Against Humanity, everyone on earth watches porn that would have been illegal a few decades ago, and dark humor has become the norm among politically influential groups like the alt-right. Considering all this, kicking kids out for memes seems like a major overreaction.

That tells us that Harvard, and other social justice and welfarist institutions, recognize that dark humor is a threat.

On an absolute level, light humor can be funnier than dark humor, just as candy can taste better than high cuisine. But dark humor forces us to think and laugh outside of normal social rules. And when we are free to think outside of those social assumptions, we can better question them.

Why would Harvard fear thought outside of social assumptions? Perhaps there's a social assumption they don't want gone. Perhaps it is, "College is necessary for success."

When you think inside social politeness, you think things like, "Soldiers are heroes", "Public School Teachers are heroes", "Affirmative Action isn't racist", and "College is necessary for success". When you think outside of social politeness, you can see the unfiltered truth.

Harvard can control many parts of social reality through social pressure. They can create a culture in which everyone is just too scared to say anything against welfarism, "social justice", and third wave feminism. Silence is voluntary. You can choose to be silent if you don't want to deal with the repercussions of speaking out.

But laughter is involuntary. You can't not laugh at something sufficiently funny anymore than you can convincingly laugh at something unfunny. Laughter connects you to reality, no matter how many layers of nonsense are in the way. That's what makes it so powerful.

Harvard doesn't bother with this since drunkenness doesn't really threaten them. If anything, it probably helps. Just as most people need to be drunk to tolerate the tedium of most sporting events, drunkenness encourages people to tolerate the mind-numbing idiocy found at "elite" colleges. Alcohol isn't a threat to Ivy League dogma, so they leave it alone.

In fact, Ivy League colleges actively embrace alcohol culture. Even the most arguably uptight of the Ivy League colleges, Princeton University, had the second largest single alcohol purchase in all of 2011, according the PrincetonScoop.com. That massive purchase of alcohol was used for its reunion, which lionizes alcoholism, unsubtly reminding all of Princeton University students that heavy drinking is the Princeton Way. The only event that entire year that had a larger purchase of alcohol was the Indy 500.

Alcoholism doesn't threaten Ivy League culture. It does contribute to date rape, alcohol poisoning hospitalizations, and other problems, but it doesn't threaten the social justice and welfarist value systems. They don't bother actually trying to challenge the culture of alcohol.

What does threaten the social justice culture that dominates the Ivy League? As they recently revealed, it's politically incorrect dark humor. In the spring of 2017, Harvard rescinded the admission offers given to ten students. Their crime: posting dark humor memes in a private facebook group.

For context, this group was an invite only, secret group. To get into the group, you had to first be in another group, and get invited from that group into the secret group.

That secrecy didn't stop Harvard from finding out, and then rescinding the admissions of those kids.

I've seen and laughed at those memes. In modern context, they aren't particularly noteworthy. Today people who work at charitable

It's no surprise that social "justice" warriors and third wave feminists have so aggressively gone after humor, suggesting that some humor is right, and some humor is wrong. But with humor, there is a scientific way to measure it. If it makes you laugh, it's funny. If it's supposed to make you laugh but doesn't, it's not funny. If it's not supposed to make you laugh, but it does, then it's funny.

Powerful humor can undo years of careful indoctrination in a few seconds. People who understand that both respect and fear the power of humor.

The Roman Senator and historian Tacitus said, ""If you would know who controls you see who you may not criticise." I say, if you want to know how to destroy a power, see what it overreacts to.

Harvard and other Ivy League colleges have plenty of problems. Alcoholism, drugs, date rape, etc. Many of these are pretty easy to solve, but Harvard and other Ivy League colleges don't even begin to make serious attempts to solve them. Sure, they make some pretend attempts to discourage alcoholism and drug use during freshman orientation, but that's about it. At the same time, many colleges actively encourage drinking among 22 year old seniors (e.g. through Bar Crawls and similar events designed to encourage people to leave with positive memories.) They even more strongly encourage drinking among alumni when seeking donations to fund their safe space culture and "research" on social justice and related nonsense.

Realistically, it would be easy to essentially eliminate drugs and alcohol from a college campus, if you were so inclined. For example, you could monitor social media, since people post pictures of themselves drinking pretty regularly. You could set in a system of progressive fines. For example, if a student gets caught drinking, you could fine them $5000 for a first offense, $10,000 for a second offense, $20,000 for a third offense, etc. You could tie financial aid to a complete sobriety requirement. The list is endless.

CHAPTER 30:

Humor

Laughter is involuntary. If something is truly funny, it's impossible not to laugh. If it's not funny, it's impossible to genuinely laugh.

Humor connects us to our true reality. It goes deeper than the part of us that seeks tribal approval. It doesn't adopt the values of whatever tribe happens to be nearby. Humor is real, honest, and personal. If something makes you laugh when you are alone, then it is a connection to your actual psychological reality.

Logic, on the other hand, is pretty flexible. Martin Luther said, "Reason is a whore," because logic can be used to justify anything. You can, in response to personal desire or social pressure, rationalize all kinds of things.

Maybe, when left alone, you're stalwart in defending men's rights to keep any money they earn, and give that money only to those they want to. But what happens if you're talking to the most attractive woman you've ever seen? You know her beliefs are different. Maybe her views aren't that bad after all? Maybe there is some merit to the idea that we all have shared responsibilities. And why should men have any economic power? Isn't it wrong to coerce others, using money?

See how easy it is? Reason is a whore. When your hormones are interfering with your values, you can rationalize anything.

But humor is a lot less whorish. If something is funny, you can't help but laugh. If it's not funny, you can't laugh. Sure, you can force a chuckle, or force a cackle at something the group you're trying to be a part of is supposed to find funny. But you don't really laugh.

make that desire manageable. When I'm speaking, I don't need to try to get acceptance from the people in the room. Instead, I can basically view them as people from some foreign culture that I don't care about. I can speak as brazenly as an American capitalist might when speaking to a group of Russian communists visiting America. By recognizing the people in the audience as not my tribe, and remembering that I do have a tribe, I can manage and redirect my desire for tribal acceptance. I can remind myself that what I say in that room matters to my real tribe, and that I need to speak in a way that they would accept, not in a way that this irrelevant group of a few welfarists might accept.

That's not to say that the desire for tribal acceptance gets erased. It's just managed enough. I can navigate DC, the welfarism capital of the country, without giving in to its value system in part because the acceptance seeking part of my brain is neutralized. But it's not easy. Nothing worthwhile ever is.

Note that this should not be confused with surrounding yourself with yes men. That is never a good idea. You should talk to people who challenge your beliefs. You should not close yourself off from the logic or evidence of other arguments. That's just deliberate ignorance.

But you should try to neutralize that vestigial part of your brain that will lie to you in order to gain tribal acceptance. That part isn't responding to logic or evidence. It's responding to fear. That part of your brain is not an ally. It's just a liability. Keep it under your control, so someone else doesn't keep it under theirs. Use social media to saturate that part of your brain with a tribal culture that shares your current values. If your values change, they should change because of logic and reason, not because of a fearful desire for tribal acceptance.

surrounding values so that you would be accepted by the tribe. Today, you may be doing the same. You may be going along with welfarist values, pretending that public school teachers are somehow "heroes", not just embodiments of welfarism and incompetence, because that's what is needed to be accepted by the dominant culture around you. Your brain is adopting the values needed to get that tribal acceptance.

But you don't need that tribal acceptance. In the modern era, it's totally useless. Instead of letting others manipulate it, just manage it yourself!

Thanks to social media, you can quickly connect to thousands of people who share pretty much any view. By intentionally spending a small amount of time each day with people who share your reality, you can control the part of your brain that seeks tribal acceptance.

For example, every day I spend a few minutes on my favorite facebook page, Anarchyball. In the culture of the Anarchyball tribe, it's normal, and even required, to reject all forms of government welfare. The part of my brain that seeks tribal acceptance sees the more than 100,000 people on there, and decides it's okay for me to keep believing that government welfare, including government schools is wrong, and that such beliefs don't pose a threat to my survival.

Throughout the day, I'm going to interact with at most fifty people, most of whom think government schools are a necessary part of reality. But those fifty people cannot affect my brain as easily once my brain knows that there are 100,000 people who agree that government schools are welfarism that just destroys male power.

On some days, I might have a speech or presentation. There may be 500 or 1000 people in the room, most of whom believe in welfarism. The desire for tribal acceptance in such situations can be incredibly high. But using social media to remind that part of my brain that there are many thousands of people who reject welfarism can

you've had your own emotions turned as a weapon against you, you've seen how much damage a skilled warrior can do with emotions.

Masculine politeness gives us a powerful shield against these weapons. It flows from a simple principle: never, ever do or say anything you might need to apologize for later on. Don't yell. Don't say anything obscene. Don't use physical violence. Don't say anything vicious that you don't really mean. Don't say anything vicious at all.

It's easy to see why masculine politeness is often so hidden from us. On the surface, it looks a lot like the "be nice to everyone" kind of politeness. The actions are nearly identical. The motivations and intentions, however, are quite different.

Masculine politeness is a tool of social and interpersonal warfare. It's a way to keep the upper hand.

You've seen it at work in political debates. If someone loses his cool and says something in anger during a debate, we recognize that he lost the debate. Skilled debaters might intentionally try to provoke an emotional response from their opponents, in order to make them look weak.

We see it in film and literature. *House of Cards'* Frank Underwood is never more powerful than when he's in control of his emotions - and never less powerful than when he gives into them and says something intemperate.

The comedian Michael Richards destroyed his career when he angrily started using racial epithets against some hecklers. He didn't follow the core rule of masculine politeness: never say anything you might need to apologize for later.

In your personal life, where major parts of your personal and political realities will be shaped or deformed, this principle is even more important.

The fact is, no one actually has the power to conquer, or even slightly alter, your personal reality. In order to do that, they need your help. If you refuse to give that help, you're impervious to their ideologies.

The only help they need is for you to lose your cool. Once you do that, they will use your guilt to hammer your reality. By themselves, they don't have the power to do anything to your reality. With your guilt as a weapon, they absolutely do.

Imagine this: suppose your goal was to provoke someone into saying or doing something stupid. What might you do? Perhaps you would find ways to emotionally exhaust them, and then attack, knowing that in their worn out state, they will slip up and say something inappropriate. Perhaps you would rudely leave while the other person was speaking, knowing that they will say something stupid like "Get the #@$% back here." You might even physically hit them, provoking some kind of physical or verbal response.

If you're really smart, you'll wait for them to get drunk, or even encourage it. When drunk, they are more likely to do something stupid, and less likely to remember what really happened.

Once they feel guilty, you might then threaten to leave unless they change. Desperate and guilty, of course they're willing to change. They're willing to compromise their principles, change their political views, move their stuff into a man cave, etc.

Now consider, strategically, what the response would be. What should the other person do to avoid being provoked?

First, he needs to realize that resisting provocation is an active and ongoing process. Any idiot can give in to anger; most idiots do. It takes discipline to respond to rudeness with politeness. But a person who can respond to rudeness with politeness has discipline and power. He is as easy to negotiate with as a steel wall.

You must practice and master the art of resisting provocation. You must be able to patient, stand your ground, and keep your cool when someone else stomps off mid sentence. You must be able to calmly stand your ground while you are being insulted, yelled at, given the silent treatment, made to feel sexually jealous, etc.

Usually, when you don't respond to normal levels of provocation, people will just increase the level of provocation. When you still don't respond, people become extremely respectful and compliant. The display of calm discipline and politeness in the face of provocation and rudeness commands respect.

This is not just about how women perceive men. It's also about how men perceive other men. We expect our leaders to be unflappable. If someone tries to provoke a political leader, and he gets provoked, we see him as weak. If someone loses his cool in business or politics, we see him as weak.

The same principle applies in your personal life. Using politeness to defeat provocation shows power, discipline, and strength.

Mastery of that kind of masculine politeness is an active, ongoing, lifelong process. It takes as much practice as any other difficult skill. There will be setbacks of many kinds, and new techniques you will learn. Here are some to get you started.

1. Practice resisting verbal provocation and Ad Hominem Attacks

The simplest way to anger someone enough to do something stupid is to insult them. The better you know someone, the easier it is to find and use their emotional triggers. You know exactly what to say to set them off.

This will often happen during arguments about political or social reality, and usually take the form of an ad hominem attack. In debate, an ad hominem attack is attacking the other person, instead of debating the point. For example:

A: "Taxation is immoral because it is nonconsensual."

B: "You just think that because you're a misogynistic asshole who can't even get a promotion at work."

Note how person B's reaction has nothing to do with person A's statement. It's only designed to provoke person A into some foolish over-response. If person A does the over-response, he will then later end up apologizing, getting hammered with his own guilt, and probably conceding the issue. It will look like this:

"I'm so sorry for how I acted. I don't know what got into me. I know that taxation isn't really nonconsensual and immoral, I just got carried away."

As part of the apology, person A ends up conceding some of his reality, in order to make up for his idiotic behavior.

Instead, he should have stayed calm. He should have said, "I appreciate that this upsets you, and it is an emotional topic. Let's discuss this later, when our nerves are less frayed." He should have refused to get provoked, and used masculine politeness as a shield against the verbal attacks.

Obviously, not all verbal attacks are part of political discussions. They can happen at any time for any reason. Their only purpose is to get you to say something stupid, so you can then be hammered with your own guilt, and concede some part of your reality during the apology.

If you refuse to get provoked, you constantly maintain the upper hand. A man who won't defeat himself in a disagreement cannot be defeated. If you simply refuse to hand the other person the weapon that is your guilt, they cannot affect your reality.

2. Stay prepared

For this, preparation is just as important as practice. If you're tired, hungry, or drunk, you will more easily get provoked. Having a ready supply of food and sleep is essential. If nothing else, get some energy bars to keep with you at all times. People often lash out and say insane things when they are hungry (or "hangry", to use the popular neologism). The same is true when they are tired.

If you aren't getting enough sleep, work or play less. Make time for sleep.

A common technique among cults is sleep deprivation. According to cult counselor Steve Hassan, cults will have introductory sessions that last 16 hours a day, and then add homework assignments. They will keep their members always slightly sleep deprived, never able to fully recuperate and consider their situation. Sleep is absolutely essential.

Solitude is also important. You need some kind of fortress of solitude, other than the bathroom, where you can be alone. If you have a house, take the absolute best room in the house, and make it your library/office. It should not be a man cave full of video games. It should be an office with a desk, a place to think, and books. An adult man should have a library, not a man cave. If you prefer an e-reader, as I do, then have that instead of a bookshelf.

Sobriety is another way to prepare yourself for battle. Most people don't step into a boxing ring or political debate while drunk. Why would you step into a reality battle without your full wits?

That's not to say you should never drink. Just don't drink in a way that predictably leaves you vulnerable to doing something stupid, apologizing, and then conceding your reality. If you want to get drunk, do it with your male friends, in a different city, with your cell phone locked away. Make sure you cannot physically contact anyone you're dating while drunk. When you're drunk, you are the most likely to do or say something stupid, end up feeling guilty, apologizing and conceding your reality.

The same is true of drugs, obviously. If you want to get high on bath salts and meth, cool. Just make sure you cannot reach your phone, or interact with anyone you are dating at all.

Getting drunk or high around someone you're dating is essentially a guaranteed way to end up getting hammered with your own guilt, apologizing, and conceding your reality.

3. Practice resisting the pull away.

One easy way to provoke someone is to walk away while they are speaking. Just wait for them to be about to make a point, and then walk away. Or just say something provocative, and leave before they can reply. This will make most people furious.

It takes very little skill to do this; people of any level of intelligence can do it. Given its ease and effectiveness, it's something you should learn to defend against.

When someone storms off, do not yell, try to restrain her physically, or chase after her. Let her leave, maintain calm politeness, and then wait. In a few days, or a few minutes, once she knows that technique won't work, she will be open to rational discussion.

Be ready at all times to handle this technique. Practice with a friend, or visualize these scenarios. Your personal and political realities are at stake.

4. Recognize and ignore false urgency.

One of the easiest ways to cause someone to make bad decisions is to create a false sense of urgency. Con artists and advertisers use this technique all the time ("This is your last chance ever to get such an amazing deal which is about to be gone!")

In order to provoke idiotic responses, people will often try to create dramatic urgency. It may involve creating an immediate fear of loss: "If you don't do _____ right now, I'm leaving forever." It may involve manipulating sexual jealousy, "If you don't do _____ right this second, I'm going to go have sex with _____."

False urgency can easily be resisted once you realize it's false. Any disagreement today can be handled tomorrow, or next week. You don't have to do anything under the kind of falsified pressure designed to provoke you into doing something stupid, and then apologizing and conceding some part of your reality.

In a Vice Presidential debate in 2004, Dick Cheney indicated that he needed more than two minutes to address a topic. The moderator said he only had two minutes. Cheney simply refused to discuss the topic with that time constraint. Like Cheney, you can simply refuse to act within constraints that simply don't work. Rushed and panicked decisionmaking is rarely necessary. Unless something is actually physically on fire, don't make rushed decisions. Take your time, discuss the issue calmly, and take as many days as you need.

One particularly misunderstood bit of advice I've heard spread around: don't go to bed angry. On a very literal level, it's good advice. There's rarely a need to get angry at all. Stay calm and try to solve the problem.

The way this advice is misinterpreted, however, is that people believe they need to solve the issue before they go to bed. That's insane. Some issues can be solved in a few hours. Some take a few months. Attempting to solve a 6 month problem in 3 hours will almost certainly get you the wrong answer.

Go to bed when it's time to go to bed. You don't have to solve the world's problems, or even all of your own problems first. Don't let someone trick you into sleep deprivation, or rush you into a bad decision.

Do not act under someone else's fake time constraints. Don't let their artificial desperation provoke you into saying something stupid.

These are starting points for a lifelong practice of self improvement and increased personal power. The ability to be unfazed by the emotions and provocations of others gives you a huge advantage in fighting for your reality. It's also obviously a vital skill in business and politics. As you develop this skill, you might find other parts of your life improving. Masculine politeness gives you an advantage in your personal and professional life, and is the most important tool for shaping social reality.

It's Easier Than You Think to Resist Emotional Provocation

Have you ever seen a very small child in a checkout line with candy in it? They often reach for every single bit of candy in the aisle. Often, grocery stores advertise that a particular aisle has no candy, so that parents don't have to deal with that.

It's no surprise that little kids reach for the candy. Some of the best minds in the world design the packaging of candies specifically so that little kids will desire them!

Now consider yourself going through that same aisle now. That packaging is designed to appeal to you. Some part of you wants the candy. But you're not really affected by that part of you. It's not like every time you walk past a candy aisle, you buy 50 pounds of candy.

Some of the finest, most manipulative, most ruthless minds in the world work in advertising. Their job is to try to get you to buy things.

And what percentage of ads do you actually respond to? Like one in every 10,000? Fewer?

You realize that an advertisement can't make you buy something. It can invite you to buy something. It can entice you buy something. But an advertisement, created by a team of experts, psychologists, designers, copywriters, sociopaths, and manipulators can't make you buy anything. It can only invite you to buy.

The same is true of emotional provocation. No one can make you angry. No one can make you jealous. No one can make you happy either.

Someone can invite you to be angry. You can accept that invitation, or turn it down.

You've learned to do this with candy, consumer products, cars. You constantly turn down provocations to act with barely a thought. Just as you learned to do this with products, you can develop the ability to turn down emotional invitations as well.

And you can do that with your values and understanding of reality too. No one can actually browbeat you out of your reality. They can invite you to give it up. But the actual decision is yours.

CHAPTER 32:
Creator Rights and Preemptive Action

In one season of *The Sopranos*, mafia boss Tony Soprano is splitting up with his wife. Normally, in such circumstances, the man is expected, and often legally required, to leave the primary house. But as a powerful mafia boss, Tony doesn't feel like he needs to follow the rules. The police won't enforce any such rules; he operates above the law.

So he stays. It's his house. He paid for it. He has no fear of the police. Why should he leave?

The situation becomes more and more tense and uncomfortable. Eventually, he moves into the pool house. Even that is too close. Soon, he leaves his property entirely.

He wasn't forced out by the state. There was something deeper at work here.

The house he lived in was paid for by him. But it wasn't created by him. He didn't pick out the decorations or the linens. He didn't choose the furniture or the kitchen equipment. He didn't pick the color of the paint, or the style of the wallpaper. His wife did that. Sure, he paid for it. But she created it.

We remember that Leonardo Da Vinci painted the Mona Lisa. Do we remember, or care, who paid for the commission? We know that Michelangelo painted the Sistine Chapel ceiling. But most of us don't remember who specifically paid for it. Creator rights are far more fundamentally powerful than owner rights. The artist who creates a work is far more deeply connected to and associated with the work than the person who commissions it.

A house is a work of creativity. The person who creates the home has a far more primal claim than the person who pays for the house.

We all instinctively know this. Even if a woman moves into a man's house, she intuitively starts changing and decorating it, making it her own, laying a primal claim to the space. If a couple moves into a new home together, the same thing happens even faster. Within a few days, the woman has made enough decorating decisions to have a creator claim to the house. It doesn't matter who pays for it. It's her house. If they split, he will leave.

Let's revisit the Tony Soprano situation again. What if every inch of the house reflected his decisions and his personality. Imagine he had creator rights. He designed every detail, he picked every decoration, on his own. It would have been his house. It would have been absurd for him to leave. It would have been truly his house. What claim could she have had?

If you want that primal claim to your own house, you must fight for creator rights. And be ready for a battle. Women know how important creator rights are. They won't give them up easily.

In fact, women often win the creator rights battle so far in advance that men don't even know what's going on. Suppose a couple is getting married. The bride registers somewhere, and picks out the gifts. Those are linens, equipment, decoration. They are gifts for her, chosen by her. They are cutlery and plates and sheets and appliances. They are decorations and styles.

The couple might not even be living together yet. But she's already won the battle over creator rights. It's her home now.

Men often make fun of women for planning weddings decades before they meet the groom. They may pick out everything from the color theme to the types of napkins. They'll pick out the location, the type of music, the wedding favors, everything. And they haven't even met the groom yet!

Men laugh at this, considering it silly. Then, when their lack of preparation meets the woman's preparation, they wonder why they lose the war. The years of planning the wedding, planning the registry, and planning the house decorations, pay off. With blitzkrieg-like speed, the woman fully creates the home, gaining complete creator rights, while the man dumbfoundedly wonders what happened.

This battle is hard to win. But you can turn it into a tie. You just need to fight tooth and nail for every single part of everything.

Men who don't understand the importance of creator rights generally don't have opinions. They say, "Sure, pick whatever color you like, whatever silverware you like, I don't care." Those men should expect to be dispossessed of their houses during the divorce - or relegated to a man cave if the divorce never comes.

But men who do understand the importance of creator rights have nothing but opinions. They have as many opinions about paint color as Leonardo or Michelangelo did. They care more about patterns than Faberge did. It's not because they are effeminate, but because they are establishing a creator claim over every inch of the house.

You should fight to change literally every single thing. Every silverware pattern, the color of the walls. Hire your own interior decorator if you can; consult with your friends if you cannot. If you move into a new place, your friends should be there every day, helping you make decisions. You should take control like a combination of a foreman and an artist.

If you plan to get traditionally married, either insist on having primary say over the registry, or refuse the registry altogether. When it comes to planning the wedding, take the lead role, or have your friends or hired help do it. Do not let anyone else pick the color of a single drop of paint without fighting for it first.

Within the house, pick your library/office. Hint: it should be the absolute best part of the house or apartment.

This isn't about divorce proceedings. Creator rights don't really figure into that in any significant way that I know of. This is about shaping reality. If you've shaped the surroundings, it will be your stronghold, allowing you to increase value dominance. If someone else has shaped the surroundings, you're just a guest. You will lose value dominance.

If you are colorblind, or just aesthetically challenged, get an advisor. And then fight as hard as you possibly can. Shaping your world begins with shaping your home. Your home should be your castle, not someone else's artwork.

Preemptive Battles

Preemptive battles and creator rights are not limited to paint color. If you plan to have kids with one or more people, you should have open, clear discussions about any issue you can imagine.

Understand that many people will use indirect approaches when it comes to childrearing discussions. For example, instead of saying, "If my three year old son decides he's a girl, I will raise him as a girl," they may say, "I believe gender is fluid, and not limited by biology." You, not realizing that the conversation has any possible relevance to your future, may respond with some noncommittal, "Sure, makes sense."

A few years pass. You've forgotten that conversation. You have kids. One day, your two year old son puts on his mom's shoes. Instead of saying, "Haha, fun joke," she gleefully declares that her son is trans, prepares to relish the social attention, and gets ready to psychologically confuse and/or chemically castrate your son. Note that the disease Munchausen's by Proxy, in which someone seeks attention by making a child ill, affects primarily women.

Maybe on a first date someone tells you about a friend who is a free spirit and artist, wandering the earth. To be agreeable, you say, "Yeah, sounds cool." That date goes well, you end up having kids. Twenty years later, you have a weed addict rotting away in your basement. You told her that being a lazy, "free spirit" was okay. She took you at your word.

When it comes to discussions with a significant other, there are no theoretical conversations. Absolutely anything can be applied to specifically you and your offspring. You must discuss everything you can think of beforehand. Even then, I promise some things will slip through the cracks.

If you expect academic excellence, make it clear. Make it clear that you expect your kids to practice multiplication tables at home. If you expect your male children to be raised as boys, make that clear. Discuss every situation you can imagine.

This doesn't have to be playing defense the whole time. You can instigate the discussion.

For example, let's say that you believe that ADHD drugs are the wrong solution to an inability to focus. Bring it up. You can bring it up politely, as in, "What do you think about ADHD drugs?" Or you can be more blunt: "I'd rather shoot my kid than stunt his brain with ADHD drugs."

Or try the middle ground: "Attention is a skill that is built through reading, yoga, and exercise. It is eroded through video games and TV. I would use every non-drug method, including homeschool, getting rid of TV, switching to a low glycemic, high vitamin diet, moving to a different part of the country, and moving to a different country entirely, before considering ADHD drugs. Too often, parents are unwilling to make those kinds of decisions, since they cannot tolerate any disruption to their status quo. I am not such a person."

If you don't want to pay the rent of your alcoholic sister in law, make it clear that you believe every adult is responsible for providing for themselves, and that alcoholism is not some uncontrollable disease.

If you don't want to have your in-laws stay at your house for 6 months, make sure you make it clear that you do not want that, and instead you believe that people who visit friends or family should stay in an hotel.

Obviously, you have to follow your own rules. You can't say that bit about alcoholism and responsibility, and be a lazy, jobless, drunk yourself. You have to live up to your own standards.

Reality wars are won on the details, and won long before the questions are applicable. Make your opinions known early. Do so gracefully with some reasonable amount of social intelligence. But it's better to do it gracelessly than to not do it at all.

EPPs; Lessons from Military Culture

For certain types of scenarios, most men know they need to be prepared. Consider the last time you were with a date at a restaurant. What would you have done if there was a sudden fire at your table?

The second I asked that, you started thinking of ideas. Maybe you'd fold the tablecloth over to cover the flames, starving them of oxygen. Maybe you'd pour your cup of water on the flame, or cover it with your jacket.

If it was a large fire, maybe you would work to get your date and yourself out of the restaurant. Maybe you'd have some plan to get older or injured people out.

Mentally, you're prepared with some pretty good ideas on how to deal with the fire.

Now imagine yourself at the same date, and your date starts crying. Maybe you said something offensive. Maybe she just wants to embarrass you. Maybe she's upset by something that has nothing at all to do with you.

What do you do?

The most common answers I get are: "Ummmm...hold on, let me think about this one", and "Shit, absolutely anything to get her to stop".

Most men are psychologically prepared for highly unlikely physical threats, and not at all prepared for highly likely emotional situations.

In any situation, most men are psychologically ready for fires, snipers, shooters, and nuclear war. But they are not at all prepared for the emotional situations that they actually face.

Most men haven't been in a restaurant fire, or even met anyone who has. But quite a few have been in a situation in which a date or significant other starts crying and they didn't know what to do.

What about if it happens again? Most men still don't know what to do. They know it's a possible concern. They had it happen before. And they still don't have any kind of action plan!

Can you imagine a man who'd been in a restaurant fire, who didn't come up with some action plan just in case it happened again?

In fact, most men have no action plan for handling hysterics at all. When faced with an emotionally upset woman, they generally either get angry, making the problem exponentially worse, or immediately cave and sacrifice some part of their reality.

The result is that all a woman has to do to force those men into another reality is cry. This doesn't show female weakness. It shows male weakness. If someone just needs to cry to get you to abandon your basic sense of reality, then you aren't very firmly rooted in your reality.

You know why so many men get caught cheating? Because women expect it. They know that a pretty high percentage of men cheat, so they are always on the lookout. As soon as they see something, they investigate.

This is not because women are paranoid. It's because men actually cheat a lot. In fact, for most of human history, it was expected and tacitly approved of. Today, it's still expected, just not accepted.

Similarly, understand that roughly 100% of women will try to browbeat you into changing your perception of reality, and then reward you when you give in. Even the ones who aren't as smart as you. Often, people figure out how to do it through instinct and observation of parents and friends, rather than through metaphysical contemplation.

You must expect it. You have to know it's coming. You have to be psychologically prepared and tactically prepared. You need a specific action plan. If you are in a relationship or marriage, this will definitely happen at some point.

Many problems are highly predictable. I call them Easily Predictable Problems, or EPPs. For any problem that can reasonably be predicted, you should already have a solution, or be actively working on a solution.

In Hollywood movie shoots, there is always backup equipment for everything. That's not because equipment is supposed to fail, but rather because it sometimes does. It might fail, so there are backups. Equipment failures are EPPs, so production companies have planned solutions.

Chances are, one day you might forget an anniversary, birthday, etc. It's an EPP with an easy solution. Just always have a couple backup gifts ready, if it's part of your relationship culture to give gifts on those days.

I was once at a get together at a large family's house. Midway through the evening, they realized that it was one of the sibling's birthdays...and they had forgotten. But this was a family that knew how to handle EPPs. Within seconds they had out a birthday plate, candles, and a slice of cake. They knew that there was a chance of forgetting someone's birthday, and they had backup plans.

If you're an engineer, or have any job of any kind, you probably already do this at work. You have plans to handle EPPs. You have specific protocols on how to handle faulty machinery, upset customers, power outages, etc. You have backups to your backups. But many men don't bother to do that in their personal lives...and they pay the price for it.

Bars and Restaurants know that people are most likely to get problematically drunk on Fridays and Saturdays, so they are ready for it. Do you know what days relationship fights are most likely? I do. Thursdays. That's the day that the strain of the week has built up the most, but it doesn't have the psychological release associated with Fridays.

Many men's Thursday plan is to get blindsided by an emotional attack, say something insane, get hammered with their own guilt, and then concede part of their reality. But now that you know it's coming, what can you do instead? How about creating a positive, calm, enjoyable evening for next Thursday...and then working on how to advance your own reality?

Don't forget that reality battles go both ways. Your reality can be advanced too, you just have to stay calm, use masculine politeness as a shield, calmly present your understanding of the world, and change it only for logical reasons, not because of emotional pressure.

As an example of the level of constant preparedness you should have, consider military culture. Military recruits are often given zero warning for parades, formal dinners, etc. The only way they can possibly be ready in time is if they are always ready. They must always have their uniforms ready, shoes polished, etc. This extends to a general principle of constant readiness for any situation.

This is one of the most fundamental and long standing principles in military culture. The American minutemen were soldiers who could be ready in a minute to fight the British.

I'll be the first to admit that today's U.S. military is mostly involved with unstrategic nonsense. The last thing you should do is enlist to be part of it's idiotic and pointless non-strategies. But we can all learn from the principle of constant preparedness.

If you are prepared, you're less likely to be blindsided and end up doing or saying something stupid. You are aso in a position to advance your own personal and political reality.

CHAPTER 33:

Engineering vs. Behavioral Solutions

When two people meet, there will be reality conflicts. For each area of conflict, either one or the other person's reality becomes dominant, or they simply agree to disagree.

Now imagine each of these two situations, and predict whether the man's reality is likely to be advanced.

Situation 1: The man is disorganized, emotionally undisciplined, unprepared, and lives in a giant mess. He spends his time playing video games, and rarely reads or exposes himself to new ideas.

Situation 2: The man is organized, ready for any situation, and knows how to get things done. He's prepared for both emotional and practical situations, with clear protocols on how to handle most.

The man in situation 1 is a hapless child. The man in situation two is obviously more powerful.

The second man also has real maturity. Real maturity essentially means ability. If you have more real maturity, you have more power and freedom, as well as the ability to advance your reality. If you have more real maturity, you make more of the rules and determine more of the norms. If you have less real maturity, you follow someone else's rules and norms.

This is strikingly different from what many others will have you believe maturity is. Their fake "maturity" basically involves accepting the status quo, and ceasing to fight it or go against the grain.

Their version of "maturity" is just obeying authority and settling for a pointless and tedious existence.

That's not maturity. That's resignation. That's failure.

Real maturity is competence, ability, freedom, and power. Fake "maturity" is obedience, resignation, and living by someone else's rules.

Many of us have been lied to about our options. We've been told that we have a choice between a perpetual adolescence of video games and alcoholism, or resigned obedience to the status quo. That's picking between powerlessness type 1 and powerlessness type 2.

Do not pick between two types of powerlessness. Instead, choose competence and power. Be better at life than other people. Be more organized, more disciplined, and more effective. Have your life running more effectively than other people's. Given that most Americans are lost, confused, and in debt, this is not as hard to achieve as you might think.

One principle that can be helpful is to realize that most problems are engineering problems - including the ones that initially seem like emotional or interpersonal problems. To use a simple example: I always forget to put the toilet seat down in my house. This would often lead to problems. In my early 20s, I'd debate about the logic, indicating that what reduced the total number of lid movements was just people moving the lid themselves. I ended up in all kinds of arguments about respect, roles, etc.

Then, one day, I decided to look at it differently. The goal people had was that the toilet seat be down. They didn't care if I personally engaged in the unpleasant task. So I looked at it from an engineering perspective. Several trials later, I had found something that worked: an electric toilet seat, that put itself down.

Instead of wasting time discussing respect, rights, kindness, roles, love, like, and all that, I should have looked at it from the start as an engineering problem.

Today, I do my best to look for an engineering solution, rather than getting emotionally worked up. Sometimes, there isn't one. The other 99% of the time, there is. I've put in alternate toilet paper dispensers so no one runs out, found ways to increase white noise for when people go to bed at different times, put in an automatic door closer to eliminate disagreements about a closet door, etc. Rather than letting things turn into emotionally symbolic things, I try to solve as many things with pragmatic solutions as I can.

Successful businesses do the same. Amusement parks, for example, figure out how far people will walk to throw something in the trash; they make sure that there are enough trash cans nearby so people don't lazily throw things on the floor. Rather than having littering police and environmental lectures, they seek engineering solutions. According to "Disney Myths: What's True and What's Correct" by Nicholas Karafilis, Disney World keeps trash cans no more that 27 feet apart. In addition, they don't sell gum at any of the shops, to prevent it from being stuck to the sidewalk, people's shoes, the undersides of chairs, etc.

Most people intuitively turn to engineering solutions when dealing with infants. Instead of explaining to infants the principles of electricity and why we shouldn't stick our fingers in the electric socket, we just block the electric sockets. Most people of average intelligence can make a house safe for infants - as long as they have an engineering mindset.

Each engineering puzzle you solve will make you a better problem solver. You'll learn how to ignore emotional baiting, and go directly to a solution.

Sometimes the solutions may require you to learn new skills. One of the most important skills I've learned is how to write with interruptions. I've learned to be able to stop writing when I need to address something, and then pick back up from where I left off.

Other times, the solutions just require installing something simple, or even just rearranging what you have in the room. This usually involves simple changes involving Command Strips, not complex things like rewiring your house.

An effective approach will always require keeping a neat, clean, and organized space. This is often well achieved by getting rid of anything you don't absolutely need. You'll be surprised how much calmness of mind you can get from getting rid of the nonsense you have cluttering up your space.

Competence helps achieve value dominance and reality dominance. Seek to improve yourself and your surroundings.

Family Management and Star Trek

Many challenges are engineering problems. But some do require behavioral solutions.

Many entrepreneurs who become successful enough to hire employees realize that management is its own challenging skill. Great managers work on improving interpersonal interactions and creating positive and effective environments.

In business, many men strive for competence in this area. We read books, take classes, even pursue degrees to enhance our skills.

Competent management isn't just part of our real goals; it's also reflected in our fictional culture. Great leaders, even in entirely fantastical environments, demonstrate great management skills. They listen, stay calm, and find better solutions.

In fact, one of the best examples of calm, competent management comes from Captain Picard in Star Trek! If you're a fan, you've probably noticed that Captain Picard is always ready to give his undivided attention to any of his officers or crew. Anyone who asks to see him privately gets a private meeting. He takes seriously what every person on his team says.

You won't see his crew yelling at or nagging him. They don't need to, because he listens and tries to actually address the problems. If his first officer alerts him to a problem, he takes it seriously and takes actual steps to actually address it. If a low ranking crewman alerts him to a problem, he takes it seriously and takes actual steps to actually address it. In fact, the only time he gets nagged is if he is avoiding a medical checkup! The second he stops taking problems seriously and addressing them, he starts getting nagged.

Now imagine what Picard's life would be like if he ignored his officers when they brought something up. They'd learn to repeat and nag. Even before he got the chance to ignore them, his officers would henpeck at him, repeating things, harrying him. By ignoring his team, he wouldn't just be encouraging nagging; he'd essentially be requiring it.

Quite a few men make exactly that mistake. They ignore information, requests, and issues presented by their significant other(s), essentially forcing them to repeat themselves, nag, and henpeck.

The ideas of responsive, effective leadership are already a part of male culture. And yet, we often forget to bring them into our own homes, where they matter the most.

Consider this: what if you treated the people close to you the same way Captain Picard treats his crew? What if you gave people your undivided attention when they asked for it, listened to problems, and addressed them? Would anyone even need to nag you? Of course not. There would be no point in it.

That doesn't mean it's your role to play therapist, or always have time to listen to prattle devoid of content. This isn't about being nice. It's about being competent. When a problem is brought to your attention, listen, and then do something. Not all problems are going to be fixed immediately. But something as simple as "That's an important issue, and I think we can get to it by next month" is far better than boredly ignoring the problem in a way that is guaranteed to encourage nagging.

It's not an easy ideal to achieve, but it's easy to make the conscious choice to pursue it. It's not easy to be a great leader, but it's easy to make that a real goal. You can become a better, calmer, more competent leader day by day, year by year. As your competence increases, your options, freedom, and power will increase too.

That's not to say that Picard does everything people tell him to. Sometimes, his answer is no. But it's a considered no, a no that includes some clear explanation. He weighs the pros and cons seriously, and makes a calm, rational, decision. Often, his officers disagree. That's okay. He doesn't need to please everyone. He just needs to listen to the information they provide.

Instead of seeing interpersonal conflicts and challenges as a nuisance, see them as a way to make yourself a more powerful and effective leader. Each interpersonal challenge you face will make you better at this.

Whether you do monogamy, polygamy, or something else, competent leadership is essential. Your private life is just as important as your business life, and demands just as strong a dedication to skill and excellence.

A great place to get started is by studying Marshall Rosenberg's theories on Nonviolent Communication. Most men have read at least one guide on dating or seduction. This is more important. Whether you do monogamy or polygamy, it's more important to be good at building and leading a family (either on equal terms with your partner(s) or as the unofficial leader) than it is to be good at picking up women.

Example: Division vs. Redundancy of Labor

In the 1950s, division of labor gave married men advantages over single men. Married men gave 100% of their efforts to the business world, and women focused on the household.

Married men were well fed, psychologically supported, and ready to take on the business world. Single men, on the other hand, were borderline starving, subsisting on saltines, ketchup, and whatever else they could put together.

At the time, men and women existed in different worlds and cultures. During the workday, men and women were physically separated. The rest of the time, they were still psychologically separated. They had different educations, friends, and interests. This allowed psychological space and tranquility.

Today, men and women inhabit the same cultural space, for the most part. They also have the same skills. Today's young women are no better at cooking than today's young men. Today's young men are no more college educated than today's young women. In fact, women today attend and graduate from college at a slightly higher rate than men do.

That means the division of labor and specialization of expertise, which in the past gave married people such a huge advantage over single ones, is gone. Instead of division of labor, we now have duplication of labor.

How is it different? In *The Wealth of Nations*, Adam Smith explains that division of labor, in which each person focuses on a specific part of the overall process, allows for much higher total productivity. Two people doing division of labor would produce much more than twice as much as a person doing all parts by himself.

But if two people just do the same things, they wouldn't have that advantage. Two people would produce just twice as much as one person. Assuming their consumption rates were the same, the net percentage benefit would be zero.

With division of labor turning into duplication of labor, those advantages of marriage are gone. What about the psychological ones?

Today, married men are often psychologically beaten down, relegated to man caves, and sexually imprisoned. Married men in the past came home to soothing words and a hot meal. Married men today are expected to provide the soothing words and hot meal to permanently unhappy, incessantly nagging harpies.

In the past, single men came home to an empty house. Today, single men still come home to an empty house. But today, an empty house offers much more happiness and comfort than a house with an angry nag dissatisfied with her workday.

That empty house can be filled with friends, women, or whatever else you want. When they become tiresome, you can kick them out.

Single men now have the psychological advantage. They are well rested, psychologically undrained, and spiritually free.

That is, as long as they are self sufficient. As long as they don't need someone else to make them food and do their laundry.

So, in this particular area, I agree with the angriest feminists. Men should learn to cook, clean, and do laundry (or hire someone to do it). Not because it's nice. Not because of equality. But because it makes you free of nagging chains.

CHAPTER 34:

The Unspoken Demons: Depression and Anxiety among Men

A 2016 study in the Journal of Counseling Psychology that was popularized in the Washington Post indicated that men with "sexist" values have more depression than those with "progressive" values. The interpretation that researchers and journalists are trying to force down our throats is that normal male culture is both wrong and also a precursor to mental illness.

But the more likely and obvious explanation is much simpler. When you're values are in conflict with the dominant values, it puts a major amount of mental strain on you. Obviously life is easier if you agree with the current ideology in power. If you believe in welfarism, life is simpler for you than if you don't. If you believe that you shouldn't have to pay for someone else's kid, obviously your life is going to be harder. It's psychologically easier to go along with whatever ideology is in power. How is that news?

The researchers, of course, have suggested that those men with normal values just give up, embrace welfare worship, and find "happiness". But I don't think that giving up your reality is really going to make you much happier.

Emotional fluctuations happen in response to many social and political changes. As Vox reported in early 2017, liberal users of Match.com had a significant drop in activity. Apparently, when they were no longer at the top of the political hierarchy, it affected their emotions. What a surprise!

Many researchers, most of whom spend their lives seeking welfarist government grants, say we should change our "toxic" masculinity (the kind of masculinity that opposes welfarism). But do they apply the same logic to their welfarist allies? Do they tell welfare-state supporting liberals to just change their political views in order to improve their libidos? Not so much.

But, the study did point out something important: men with male values were less likely to seek help.

Instinctively, many of us avoid those in the mental health field, since we can easily see that many of its members don't have our interests at heart. They seem entirely unconcerned with helping us achieve our authentic goals. Instead they seem dead set on trying to make us comply with society's latest norms and idiocies.

Many of us, as kids, intuitively recognized that government schools are more about teaching us to be obedient, not powerful. Many of us didn't take very kindly to that. That same male culture that drove the founding fathers to rebellion, that drove Socrates to philosophical greatness, that has driven countless artists, thinkers, writers, and inventors to think beyond the rules, burns in all of us. We're not interested in being broken down and made docile. We know that isn't real education. We know education is supposed to make you more powerful. It's not supposed to turn a wolf into a dog; it's supposed to turn a wolf into a scarier wolf.

In response to our early refusal to obediently go along with that kind of intentional disempowerment, the mental health field has been weaponized against boys. According to "The Drugging of the American Boy", which appeared in Esquire in March of 2014, about 20 percent of boys are diagnosed with ADHD, and 2/3rds of those are drugged down with Adderall or a similar drug. Boys are 3 to 7 times as likely as girls to get the diagnosis.

And yet, that doesn't mean that mental health is not important. It is vital to us, and vital to our movement. If we're depressed and beaten down, if we can't get out of bed or control our anger, how are we going to change anything?

We have a mental health crisis in the men's movement, both among those who consider themselves part of it, and those who simply agree with the ideas of ending the welfare state and rejecting "traditional" norms that were made up a few years ago. Rage, anxiety, and depression have become overwhelmingly common, and they are blocking our greatness. Refusing to address these issues at all is like refusing to address a broken bone.

Yes, a societal compliance mechanism masquerading as a mental health field is an enemy. But that doesn't mean mental health doesn't matter. It means that we should avoid one particular set of approaches to it, specifically those that are putting current and foolish social norms above our authentic reality.

At the root, this is an issue of collectivism versus individualism. The parts of the mental health field that we intuitively avoid are just putting the collective goals above our goals. In school, they want boys to comply so they can easily continue their charade of obedience training masquerading as education. With adults, they want men to comply with welfarism and third wave feminism, so those immoral and insane ideologies can continue unchecked. The collectivist impulse to devalue individual needs is nearly identical to the collectivist impulse to devalue individual rights and autonomy. The collectivism that gave us the welfare state, a government that not only fails to protect our property rights but also actively violates them, has also given us a useless mental health industry that not only fails to help us achieve our authentic desires but also actively suppresses them.

Just as we can seek alternatives to government nonsense, through bitcoin, homeschooling, alternatives to subsidized colleges, etc., we can seek alternatives to this kind of anti-individual, collectivist approach to mental health.

"Men's" Therapists; The Seduction of Acceptance

It is an undeniable fact that early 20th century masculinity was not successful. In open competition, it lost. It was defeated by every kind of welfarism, and a denial of male reality.

When any people are conquered, they have a choice. One is to learn to live with that condition, to "maturely" accept it. The other is to refuse to. The first allows a kind of calm. The second does not.

When women were culturally enslaved, the "balanced" and "mature" women accepted their fate, resigned themselves to it, and found happiness within it. They learned how to navigate their enslaved condition with charm and grace.

The "unbalanced" and "immature" women, however, refused to. They fought what was unfair, unjust, and immoral. The accepters of the status quo, as they always do, probably called that courage immature, dangerous, and deranged, as a way to make themselves feel better about their own cowardly failings.

Today, within the men's movement, there is a growing number of therapists who focus on helping men navigate and come to terms with their current condition. They aren't trying to help men achieve their real goals; they are trying to help men come to terms with the current state. A few hundred years ago, they would probably have been helping slaves achieve emotional balance while remaining slaves.

What makes these therapists dangerous is what makes cults like Scientology dangerous. New initiates into Scientology go through a process of facing childhood repressed traumas. It's a mostly effective process, used by many different forms of therapy. The effectiveness of this simple method allows Scientology to gain the victim's trust.

With that trust, they have the victim believe every kind of idiocy imaginable.

Their initial, technical advice is good. Their philosophical advice and their perception of reality, is not.

Most popular men's therapists are similar. A lot of their tactical advice is good. Their tips on how to listen in relationships, to understand the psychic wounds of your inner child, to avoid letting childhood parental patterns create emotional triggers in adult relationships - are all usually great advice.

But their philosophical perspective is not.

The famous serenity prayer says, "Grant me the serenity to accept the things I cannot change, the courage to change the things I can, and the wisdom to know the difference." The men's therapists will have us accepting the things we can change, that we don't need to accept.

Their default assumptions -- that stifling marriages are the only mature path for heterosexuals, that any possible arrangement is mature for homosexuals, that erasing every aspect of heroic or effective masculinity is the path to emotional wisdom -- are the problem.

I encourage you to remember this: the communication skills these therapists recommend can be applied to situations of your own choosing, including ones that go against social norms. The skill of giving a wife your undivided attention can also be applied to a mistress, concubine, or harem. The skill of saying, "This is not okay" to a parent can also be applied to resisting the welfare state. Language skills, charm, and charisma are just tools. They can be used to accept your current state, or to make a different method work better.

You can use effective skills and uninterrupted attention to adapt to someone else's reality. Or you can use it to create your own.

Instead of doing what those popular therapists say, just do what they do. They use language skills to change social reality. They might be using those skills to attack the reality you actually believe. But they are changing reality. They aren't accepting it. They aren't saying, "Oh, I guess men still think harlotry is disgusting, and don't want to pay for kids they didn't father, I'll accept that men think like that." Instead, they use careful persuasion to try to change that.

You can start doing the same. Don't say, "I guess people think it's okay to economically violate me, I guess I'll accept that they think that way." Instead, be like those therapists. Try to help people see that what they are doing is stealing and violating. Help them see that the reality they are unquestioningly accepting is wrong.

Normalization

Among women, miscarriages are extremely common. According to an October, 2013 article in the *Huffington Post*, about 20 percent of pregnancies end in miscarriage. If you have 4 pregnancies, you have about a 59% of at least one miscarriage.

However, since people are terrified of talking about miscarriages, when women have miscarriages, they think they are the first person in history to be so terribly cursed. Thus, they don't talk about it, and the cycle continues. What should be seen as normal and not a big deal instead turns into a huge drama of shame, tragedy, and humiliation.

Today, men are doing the same thing with mental health issues. We're supposed to be tough, so when we face anxiety or depression, we obviously hide it. Thus, men view depression and anxiety the way women view miscarriages: we think we're the first man in history to face these issues.

In reality, anxiety and/or depression affect roughly 100% of men at some point or another. It's just usually not reported (obviously). We need to realize that facing anxiety or depression doesn't make you weak, any more than getting the flu makes you weak. However, refusing to address a problem does make you an idiot.

As kids, we're essentially taught to force down all emotion. In some settings, this is good. In business and politics, you don't want to show emotion, unless you're doing so very deliberately. But the result of this training is that many of us are essentially taught to be afraid of our own emotions. We brutally suppress them when we feel them, and often just wait for them to explode as rage, smolder as anxiety, or use up all of our energy as depression. We ignore the information and guidance that those emotions contain, and thus end up going along with idiocy we know, deep down, is wrong.

Earlier in this book, I pointed out that work is sacred, because it is produced by the most sacred part of you: your mind. Work isn't just mechanical force times distance. A violation of your mind, through stealing the fruits of your work, is just as much a violation as a violation of your body.

For the same reason, a mental injury is more significant than a physical one. Your brain matters more than your body. If you broke a bone, or even sprained your pinky, you'd do something about it. You wouldn't just rely on inaction. You wouldn't say, "I sprained my wrist, it is proof that I am weak, let me get drunk and wallow."

Men address problems. We don't ignore them. As far as I know, it's not part of male culture to drive around with flat tires, to not bother to set broken bones, to leave burned out lightbulbs unreplaced.

Of course there are many different ways to approach each challenge. Some focus on the act of attaining calm, through yoga or meditation. Others rely on experts - life coaches, therapists that focus on individual goals not just social obedience, etc. Others rely on reading books on how to handle these issues. But they all have one thing in common: they are active attempts to try to address a problem.

Not every attempt will succeed. If you are an engineer, programmer, or entrepreneur, you know that the first try, second try, or even tenth try rarely works. But with persistence, we find ways that work.

One useful principle is that emotions are information. They are a way for your body to communicate information to you. Sometimes that information is distorted and useless. Sometimes it is accurate and insightful. Learning to listen to those emotions, to understand them, will help you become more yourself. If you like, go ahead and listen to them right now. Close your eyes, feel the emotions in your body, and feel what they are trying to tell you.

It can be, at times, easier in the short term to repress them, because it is usually easier to go along with the dominant value system. But living that kind of inauthentic life is a guaranteed recipe for a gradual emotional implosion.

Many men work out to improve their bodies. We learn things to improve our intellect. Let's work on emotional excellence with the same diligence, and make ourselves strong enough to live authentically and fight the battles we can win.

A common saying is that just because you don't take an interest in politics, that doesn't mean politics won't take an interest in you. Many people who avoid any political activity realize that they still get robbed and violated through taxation.

Similarly, just because you aren't interested in your emotions, doesn't mean they aren't interested in you. If you don't seek awareness of them, someone else probably will, and use them to manipulate you. It could be an advertiser selling you garbage, a politician selling you welfarism, or another person directly manipulating you. Even if no one else manipulates them, your emotions will affect you. Ignore them at your peril.

MEN AND MASCULINITY

CHAPTER 35:

Rites of Passage

Those in the transgender movement often say, "my genitals don't define my gender." They're right. There is much, much more to being a man than having a penis.

Male culture is one of the oldest cultures on earth. It is also one of the most diverse, with many different traditions that vary over time and region.

And yet, there are certain significant commonalities, certain universal lessons that we can benefit from considering. These are not rules to lock ourselves into, but ideas to consider as you define what your masculinity means to you.

I want to begin with one of the most common male traditions, how it has been hijacked, and how you can make it authentic to you. That tradition is the right of passage.

In rites of passage, a boy becomes a man, usually by some test of will, daring, strength, etc. You'll find these rites of passage in history, fiction, and in the modern era.

The nature of your right of passage will define your perception of what it means to be a man. If your right of passage involves courage, then you'll see a man as more courageous than a boy. If it involves ingenuity, you'll see a man as more clever than a boy. If it involves physical feats, you'll see a man as stronger than a boy.

Today, college and the military have replaced true rites of passage. The resulting perception is that once you go through college or the military, you will be transformed from a boy into a man.

College is often referred to as a modern rite of passage, especially when it involves living on campus. Colleges even tap into the ritualistic side of rites of passage by having people wear literal *robes* when they graduate, as if they were druids or religious initiates. While taken at face value that attire appears outlandish and insane, when we consider that robes were historically often parts of religious rites, it makes more sense.

The military was once seen as a major male right of passage, and continues to pretend to be. In one of its commercials designed to trick dupes into joining its idiocy, the military shows a male model fighting a dragon. The voiceover says, "It is more than just a trial by fire. It is a rite of passage." By the end of the commercial, the male model is transformed into a male model wearing a marine uniform. Even though the commercial is preposterous, it's still emotionally effective. The psychological manipulation works by tapping into that nearly universal principle of a rite of passage from boyhood to manhood.

Both college and the military are rites of passage based on obedience to the establishment and status quo. They are not about individual self-definition, independence, power, or freedom. They are about becoming either sycophants or servants to the collective. In this process, they trick us into believing that establishment worship is somehow part of masculinity. They want us to believe that a man is more subservient to the status quo than a boy.

This myth has become dangerously widespread. According to the myth, boys rebel against authority, men bow to authority. This couldn't be more false. Men should have more independence of spirit, more ability to write their own rules, and less subservience to the status quo than boys. Men should be more powerful than boys, not more docile.

This myth also flies in the face of what we see in the animal kingdom. In the animal kingdom, young males challenge (and often kill) the established males for dominance. Human masculinity is built out of independence, dominance, and freedom, not obedience, servitude, and collectivism. Masculinity is about independence, and sometimes overthrow. It is never about serving the establishment.

The good news is that there are many, many other rites of passage that men can use.

In business, making your "first dollar" is a rite of passage. Small, medium, and large businesses often frame and display their first dollar. In my family, the first dollar is generally given to the oldest living member of the family, emphasizing both clan loyalty and the importance of entrepreneurial determination.

Writing a first book, making your first art piece, selling your first art piece, etc., are also common rites of passage. I remember the sheer disbelief I had when someone actually bought my first book, and how freeing it felt to be able to achieve that without being commanded or forced.

Note that these all have something in common: they don't involve obedience. Instead, they involve initiative. No one commands you to write a book or start a business. That's the point. By commanding yourself, by acting without being ordered, you go through a rite of passage of true, self-driven, independent masculinity, not obedience masquerading as masculinity.

I've spoken to many who have been employed by the military, and asked them why they took that job. In public, most people talk about defending the constitution, fighting for freedom, etc. But in private, the answers are usually different. A big one: they thought it was the best opportunity available. Some thought it was the *only* real opportunity available. They saw a choice between joining the military and working in a fast food restaurant forever, and they chose the military.

Many were also tricked by the "We'll teach you valuable skills" argument the military loves. Those who leave the military often find that there are not that many tank repair jobs in the private sector. Some of the skills do transfer over to fixing cars, but not half as well as, for example, spending four years working as a private sector car mechanic. Some of the very specialized skills used in the military do not transfer at all.

Today, post 9/11 veterans face higher unemployment than the national average. This is a striking change from the past, when veterans were more employed than others. As people increasingly consider military actions to be counterproductive, as more in the military get PTSD instead of the promised right of passage into manhood, employment and employability drop. This comes after the huge preference given to veterans who are applying for government jobs.[1]

Those on a college path look at that decision-making mockingly. Of course tank repair skills are useless. What kind of an idiot would sacrifice years to learn a skill with no real financial value at all? If you get really good at tank repair, the only thing you can possibly do is maybe teach tank repair.

So what exactly can you do with most college majors? Is there some major demand for anthropologists and amateur philosophers? Even the "practical" majors like biology and economics mostly confine you to research and teaching. Some people use them as stepping stones for medicine or an MBA (the single most pointless degree in existence), but the actual skills you actually learn in actual undergrad are actually commercially useless.

---

1) Military Times: *Despite decreasing veteran unemployment rate, underemployment remains a problem*

The few applicable skills that are mentioned are so heavily filtered through the lens of "social justice" as to provide no personal advantage at all. And those skills you could learn independently in a tenth of the time for no cost.

Many poor families see the military as the only option. Many rich families see college as the only option. I don't know which group is more wrong.

Reject both. You don't need to be a government worshipper and you don't need to be an academia worshipper. You don't need to serve the State or the Academic establishment. You don't need to learn skills that can only apply to academia or military obedience.

Screw that. Serve yourself. Learn skills that benefit you. Get the advantages that benefit you.

Learn what you need to learn. Learn it quickly. Start your own business, and then start a few more. Most businesses fail. So start at least a few. Life is far more a test of perseverance than of ability.

Learn as you go. That means read. Read hard stuff, even when no one is ordering you to. Read *The Wealth of Nations* and *The Fountainhead*. If you have time to read this ridiculous book, you should have time to at least read the beginnings of those. Read books on business, ideas, inspiring fiction, philosophy - and do it without anyone telling you to.

Launch ideas on Kickstarter. Work on creative pursuits. Develop the ability to pursue excellence without being told. Free yourself of their grasp.

Their most powerful hold on you is not taxation or laws. It's the psychological hold. It's inside your head. Breaking free of that is the real mutiny. The doors of that prison are unlocked. Just walk out.

If you want to prove your academic ability, verify it with professional level exams. These are discussed in the next chapter.

Make your right of passage worthy of the type of man you want to be. Even if you've already gone through a military or academic facsimile, it's never too late for the real thing.

A real rite of passage should be self-motivated, self-created, and self-beneficial. It should be an expression of your independence and initiative, not weak obedience. You should become more yourself, not less. It should be you deciding your own values, not following someone else's.

As they say, you were born an original. Don't die a copy.

CHAPTER 36:

Examples of Pulling Out: Non College, Non Military Options

Colleges have become centers of welfarist indoctrination. According to the Washington Times, liberal professors outnumber conservative professors 12:1. Libertarian and anarcho-capitalist professors, presumably, didn't even statistically register.[1]

A few of those professors are dedicated to open exchanges of ideas. The rest - not so much. On their papers, a welfarist perspective is often the only one allowed. In their discussions, you're only allowed to support the status quo.

The thing about colleges: they are really good at psychological manipulation. You might have seen how effectively they indoctrinate other people. But you may have missed how effectively they have indoctrinated you.

In particular, colleges have convinced most of America that a college degree is both necessary and sufficient for success.

But the fact is, it is neither. There are plenty of non-degree ways to prove your ability, and many jobs now require additional training beyond, or instead of, the standard four year degree.

Most of the non-degree methods of proving ability require work and initiative. So does all of life. If you are "unable to self-motivate",

---

[1] The Washington Times: *Liberal Professors Outnumber Conservatives Nearly 12 to 1, Study Finds*

then you need to fix that far more than you need to learn about theoretical physics or gender studies.

One option: an academic education that is outside of a college. To prove to future employers you've learned the material, you can take challenging exams on those topics.

If you want to prove your math ability, consider the legendarily difficult first actuarial exam. If you can pass that, you've proven your math skills. To prove your abilities in the humanities, you can take the Foreign Service Officer's Test, which the State Department uses in order to gauge the knowledge of potential diplomats. It's hard as hell, but passing it proves your ability. Pretty much anyone can get a degree. Very few people can pass the FSOT.

The GRE, GMAT, and LSAT are other exams you can study independently for. There are also financial sector exams, environmental engineering exams, IT exams, computer programming exams, and many others that you can use to prove your ability.

But you don't need to be limited by an academic education. Consider entrepreneurship. If you have a big project in mind, consider the Thiel Scholarship. Peter Thiel, founder of Paypal, felt that he was successful despite his Stanford education, not because of it. So, he created a scholarship to help people see how much they could accomplish without college. The scholarship is $50,000 a year...to not go to college for 2 years. Thiel wants you to see how much you can accomplish without college. As a tech entrepreneur, he's seen many successful tech entrepreneurs without degrees. Mark Zuckerberg, Steve Jobs, and Bill Gates are the most famous ones, but there are many, many more.

Want to try entrepreneurship that is more freelance oriented than large project oriented? Check out freelancer.com, or 99designs.com, or fiverr.com. Learn business responsibility, reliability, and other relevant skills that matter.

Want to be involved in the intense discussion of ideas? Consider politics. The world of politics is huge, full of ideas and debate, and always looking for talented, creative, and charismatic people. You'll learn more about ideas by being involved in politics than you will almost anywhere else. I've certainly learned more about ideas through politics than I did at an Ivy League college.

Let other people waste 200k on colleges that teach them to conform, become drug addicts, and shut the hell up when they have a thought that opposes the welfarist status quo. You don't need to support that world at all.

The fact is, you don't need college to be financially successful. You definitely don't need it if you want to openly discuss ideas. Today, colleges are the last place to openly discuss ideas, as any non-welfarist perspectives are either ignored or shouted down.

If you are going to college to make more money, first see how much money you can make without college. If you are going to explore ideas, explore them without someone screeching at you to shut you up.

Right now, colleges depend on undergraduate tuition to pay for graduate students and "research". You don't need to be someone else's cash cow. You don't need to pay exorbitant prices so grad students can get paid to study social justice. Use that money to develop skills, start a business, and actually explore ideas. Not only do you, individually, get ahead, you also help defund the primary bastions of welfarist propaganda.

Parallel Example of Pulling Out: Military

College is, today, what military service was in the past; it's the thing you do when you turn 18. Having a military record was almost essential for political involvement or social respect.

But, that is no longer the case. Today, military service is no longer necessary for social respect or politics. Our last several presidents had no military record of significance, and our last two presidents as of this writing (Trump and Obama), had no military record at all.

In fact, many political analysts, including me, believe that a military record is actually a drawback when running for president. Currently, military service is seen as a mark of lower socioeconomic class. Those who currently join the military are seen as either too poor or too stupid to go to college. Sure, airlines still give military personnel early boarding and call them heroes, but they do the same with people in wheelchairs. Some people still say "Thank you for your service," sincerely. But the rest are saying it with exactly as much actual emotion as "I'm sorry for your loss" when speaking to a stranger about their grandparent's death.

Among wealthy classes, roughly zero percent of kids plan to join the military. In my education business which heavily caters to the socioeconomic elite, we have roughly 100 kids who want to go to an elite college for every one kid who wants to go to a military officer's academy. Non-legacy military is even rarer: those who want to go to military academies generally have parents who are military officers themselves.

Some of this disdain for soldiers is driven by increasing disdain for what the military actually does. They are no longer fighting the British Redcoats for American sovereignty and freedom. Instead, they are bombing hospitals and creating enemies. Some are building schools in recently bombed areas, presumably as useless as government run schools in America already are.

Much of it comes from the intuitive importance of self interest. Why would someone risk his life on an idiotic mission?

The result has been that, as of this writing, military recruitment is well below the military's targets - even though the military is open to both men and women now. According to Richard Sisk's April 2018 article in Military.com, the Army was forced to lower the year's recruiting target from 80,000 to 76,500. In order to reach the standard they had set...they first had to lower it.

More and more young men are realizing that a rite of passage should be meaningful, not foolish. It should involve proving independence, not subservience. Just as men are pulling out of college to seek something that benefits them, men are pulling out of the military to seek something that benefits them.

A true right of passage should be a right of self determination, intelligence, and independence of thought. It should reflect true masculinity, not some lie that pretends that masculinity is just a brand of subservience. As men, we must learn to shape our destiny, not follow someone else's wants. We must learn to shape ourselves, not be beaten into someone else's mold.

Our true rite of passage, our true fundamental challenge, is to break those molds, to ignore those expectations. The men we need today are those that shape culture, not serve it, that dismantle institutions, not support them. Our rite of passage into true masculine independence is no longer a symbolic test; it is the true trial to become who we are meant to be.

CHAPTER 37:

Chivalry and Warrior Culture

The discussion of men opening doors for women has become surprisingly large. What was once seen as an insignificant courtesy has become a focal point of debates about gender roles.

I often hear third wave feminists arguing that women are physically strong enough to open doors, and don't need to rely on men. I hear men arguing that because men are stronger, they have the duty to open doors. In the context of male culture, both groups are totally wrong.

You can't separate male culture from warrior culture and military culture. Even today's U.S. military, which squanders resources on worthless and endless activities, still maintains the core ideas of male culture and military culture.

In military culture, who opens a door? The strongest person? The mightiest person? The highest ranking person?

Obviously not. It's whoever matters the least. Privates open doors for Generals. Generals open doors for Commanders in Chief.

A lower ranking person goes in first, to make sure it's safe for a higher ranking person.

In any warrior society, women are more valuable than men. They can produce new members of the tribe. One man and a thousand women can repopulate. A thousand men and one woman cannot. Men open doors for women because, in a warrior culture sense, women matter more.

To look at a parallel, in warrior cultures, chivalric cultures, and aristocratic culture, it is often common for men to stand when a woman walks into the room, just as generals stand when a president walks into the room, or enlisted men stand when an admiral walks into the room. That's not because men think women are weak, and standing somehow addresses that. It's showing respect for the most critical part of warrior culture.

If you want to see how closely chivalry, politeness, and military culture are intertwined, you might enjoy watching *Downton Abbey*. You'll see how constant readiness and absolute hierarchies are the common basis of both military culture and aristocratic chivalry.

If the goal was bullying, men wouldn't open doors for women. They would threaten harm unless the women opened doors for them. A bully doesn't say, "Let me get the door for you." He says, "Open the door for me, or I'll hurt you."

How That Relationship has Changed

Today, when many men think of women, they don't consider them the sacred core of a society, those with the vital ability to create life. Instead, there is a hue of hostility.

But why? Biology hasn't changed. Don't women still have the sacred ability to create life?

In a sense, they do. But today, when women create life, they are often not really creating something beneficial. Instead, many are now producing mountains of human garbage, dependent on one kind of welfare or another. The children are now an excuse to rob you, not the people who will one day fight alongside you. Poor women produce children that suck up food stamps (paid for by you), middle class women produce children whose schooling you must pay for.

U.S. military members take an oath to protect the constitution from enemies both foreign and domestic. I can't tell you how many soldiers have told me that they feel that the real enemies of our freedom are in our own government, not in some other country. The enemies at home restrict our freedom and steal the fruits of our labor.

And in today's welfare state, women are producing children dependent on it. We don't feel the same deep respect we once did, because they are not doing something respectable. They are not producing kids that they or the child's father will take full financial responsibility for. Instead, they are just producing burdens.

To use a parallel, imagine a world in which police officers were helpful and useful. For example, Imagine if they prevented theft, or quickly found stolen property. In that case, most people would respect them highly. On the other hand, if they focused primarily on annoying and robbing us with speeding tickets, or pursuing non-crimes like drugs and prostitution, we'd consider them a nuisance. Today, many people find police an irritating burden, not valuable members of society. The same has happened with women. We don't respect them as wives and mothers because they are not respectable as wives and mothers.

Our instinct to not respect them isn't new. In past eras where chivalrous behavior was the norm, people did not give any respect at all to women who produced children that were burdens. Women who bore children without husbands were treated like garbage, since they presumably were creating burdens and future criminals. A woman who kept on breeding unwanted burdens would have been unthinkable, not worthy of respect.

Today's behavior of producing children that everyone else has to pay for is not worthy or respectable behavior. It's just being a leech, a burden, and a drain on others.

The non-chivalrous instinct, interestingly, is spreading to entirely unexpected areas. According to a May, 2016 poll at YouGov.com, 61 percent of men believe that women should be required to register for the draft, with 27 percent opposing. Women feel quite differently. Only 40 percent of women believe that women should be required to register for the draft, with 43 percent opposing. The male instinct to protect women has been replaced with the desire to use them as more cannon fodder.

The point of all this, by the way, is not to discourage chivalrous behavior. It's not worth fighting a battle over door opening. It doesn't matter that much. Open doors for women when they seem okay with it, and don't when they do not. Grace and calm are usually the best way to go.

But seek to understand why men today do not feel toward women the way men of the past did. Don't cling to outdated perspectives on modern women. See what's actually in front of you, and then determine what amount of respect you consider right.

CHAPTER 38:

Classical Warrior Culture as an Alternative to Middle Class Culture

We've talked about rejecting the dominant middle class culture, and indicated that there are many possible alternatives. In this section, we'll explore one possible alternative. It's not the only one, or the best one; just a different one. I call it warrior culture, or warrior-king culture, since it derives from the warrior societies of the distant past.

American culture is predominantly a middle class, consumerist culture. The unstated goals are to gain individual status and to get things.

Generally, we tend to apply these principles to our personal lives, and to our romantic and sexual lives. Those that follow the middle class status principle try to seek the types of marriage that society approves of. Those that seek the middle class acquisitiveness principle seek as much sex from as many different women as possible.

While superficially different, these are both middle class, consumerist drives. The middle class consumer isn't buying a new pair of sunglasses for some purpose relating to advancing his family, tribe, or culture. He's buying them to have them. Much of middle class spending is for status. Some amount is for convenience. Only a tiny amount is for advancement.

Even education is affected by this consumerist mindset. Families don't spend money to educate their kids to take over the family business, or to start a business. They spend money for higher status

- a higher SAT score, a chance to get into a more prestigious college, etc. Often, there is no particular educational goal attached to that college. It's not, "I want to get into this elite college so I can gain knowledge to advance this agriculture, semiconductor, or service business." It's, "I want to get into this college to get a degree from this college."

In other words, we don't seek education to advance a pre-existing task or goal of our own family or tribe. Instead, we prepare ourselves to be part of some external thing.

Middle class values, in fact, actually create a stigma against education that advances a family enterprise. A young man who seeks education to advance his family's business is seen as inferior to one who seeks education just for general advancement. A young man who contributes to and advances his family business is often seen as, bizarrely enough, less masculine than one who takes a job somewhere else.

The second man, after all, is getting third party approval. Someone outside his family enterprise is willing to hire him. And what do middle class values elevate more than approval? Those in the middle class seek approval, validation, status.

Implicit in this is a trust of the values and opinions of the general society. We put society's opinion above our own. It is, "Go prove that you can survive in their society." It is not, "Let us expand our values and power over a greater portion of this earth." We are taught to seek approval from outsiders, rather than advancing our actual tribe.

Even among the ultra-wealthy, middle class definitions of masculinity still stand. The ultra wealthy don't view their family as a tribe or small kingdom. They don't see their kids as heirs that will expand the power of the family or tribe. Their kids, at best, will start from zero and prove themselves just as their parents did. The wealthy man says, "I proved myself to society and earned social respect. Now you should prove yourself similarly." The child doesn't start from where the parent left off, and increase the level. He starts from zero and catches back up.

Obviously, this keeps family power weak and limited. If you need to start at the beginning every time, you can only go so far.

The state loves this. What could be a bigger threat to the state than families that rivaled the power of the state? Britain's great houses could force the king to sign the Magna Carta precisely because they had power rivalling his. Had they been as weak as the wealthiest families today, they wouldn't have been able to. The weaker the families, the stronger the state.

Society loves that too. When a family's values oppose those of a society, and the family has the power to maintain those opposing values, society really hates that. When individual families and tribes are too weak to maintain any real value opposition, society loves that.

Today, middle class values even dominate "royalty." The "royalty" of England are now just famous people. They don't attempt to increase political, economic, or cultural power, reach, or influence at all. They are just people who do their best to live up to social expectations. They have moved entirely from the mindset of warrior-kings to the mindset of the middle class. And this is not unique to Britain. The kings of many middle eastern countries, including the UAE, Jordan, and others do their best to show how modern and progressive they are, how well they can cater to our middle class values. The world's literal royalty has become thoroughly middle class.

Consider how vastly different middle class approaches to masculinity are from the definitions that came from the warrior-king cultures of the past. King Philip of Macedonia didn't want Alexander to prove that he could live independently, without family support. We don't call him Alexander The Great because he managed to live independently, but because he so massively expanded his family's power and holdings.

Today, we're tricked into jumping through societal hoops, rather than spending that energy advancing our tribe, our family. We squander our wealth and energy on middle class approval seeking, rather than on advancement of our tribe.

Consider, for example, how we look at education. We don't say, "Let's look at the tasks we're doing, and see what type of knowledge might help advance those tasks." We don't say, "Our family enterprises could use some expertise in DNA manipulations, some of us should study genetics." We don't say, "There are opportunities in _____, let's invest in knowledge in those areas."

Because we aren't seeking knowledge for a particular purpose, we rarely even look at a variety of ways to get that knowledge. In today's information rich age, there is rarely any reason to look past the internet for knowledge. Most knowledge can be had for free or cheap, and we all already take advantage of it. As soon as we need help in a particular task we're working on, we turn to free or cheap stores of knowledge online.

Thus, when we worship Academia, we beggar ourselves on approval-seeking masquerading as education. We go into debt to get college degrees of dubious relevance. Supposedly, we're seeking the knowledge to help with our tasks, but for many of us we haven't even decided what the tasks are before we start college! And while humans can be silly sometimes, it is inconceivable that most of us are that willing to put the cart before the horse, to pick some random selection of the infinitude of human knowledge to study without deciding on what task that knowledge will be used for. If the goal was seeking knowledge for a task, I can't imagine that we'd go into debt to study the knowledge before deciding the task.

Colleges have become aware of the fact that we are realizing just how silly that is. They have now started emphasizing that they teach critical thinking, giving students the ability to question deeply held assumptions. They argue that they're teaching us critical thinking skills that can be applied to any of the situations we might encounter.

Two issues. First, they are not. Socialist indoctrination in an alcohol-fueled culture is not teaching critical thinking. Being shrieked into silence every time you disagree with third wave feminism is not learning to think for yourself.

Second, that skill can be found literally anywhere. It is a normal part of the human experience. Reading books, getting involved in politics, entrepreneurship, watching documentaries, and having conversations actually develop critical thought.

And we all know this. We know that college training won't help us with any task in a way that looking up what you need on the internet can't. Those who are going into law or medicine need to get undergraduate degrees, but that's correctly seen as a foolish requirement, not a legitimate educational need. The actual learning happens during medical residency and in law school, not while getting an undergraduate degree in social justice.

We know that you can learn to think critically anywhere. Our college obsession is just middle class approval seeking. We seek knowledge not for power, not for the enhancement of any particular enterprise, but for a degree that confers some social approval.

And this doesn't start in college. Much of the education we receive at the secondary level is intentionally gutted to make it both tedious and commercially useless. As a simple example, the types of writing that are most commercially and culturally significant are fiction and nonfiction. The least commercially and culturally influential type of writing is literary analysis. Most schools fixate on literary analysis, and teach neither fiction nor nonfiction writing. They make sure to take up all the energy that young people could put towards any actual enterprise, and squander it on total foolishness.

In other words, rather than seeking education that helps with any current, or even conceivable, task, we go for education that grants a degree or other form of social approval. We seek not economic power, but social status. We seek education from a middle class value perspective, and we get that kind of education. We don't adopt the warrior mindset, so no one bothers to offer us warrior education.

Even those that successfully take on major enterprises then slip right back into the middle class mindset, the mindset in which we view ourselves as subservient to society rather than independent of it, seeking its approval rather than granting it (or withholding) our approval. Consider the common phenomenon of men making huge amounts of money, and then basically giving the vast majority away to a charitable endeavor. Such an action perfectly embodies the middle class masculinity. The person has made plenty of money, which he sees as something that gives him social status, personal freedom, and access to things and experiences. He gives it away to have more fame and social respect. His name becomes part of history.

But his family doesn't continue to rise in power by any stretch of the imagination. The mindset isn't to first buy a house, then a town, then a state, then a country. His family doesn't become economic conquerors, continuing to expand. Depending on his parenting style, his kids generally become worthless hedonists, or basically start from scratch. Many wealthy parents want their kids to independently prove themselves (seek social validation). This parenting style is clearly better than the "Here's some cash, go become a spoiled drunk" style. But, it is still radically different from the warrior-king parenting style, where the kids understand that their goal is to increase the family power and legacy. Their upbringing is imbued with a sense of purpose; it is not directionless. Children recognize themselves as having both access to the family's power, and a duty to expand it. They seek education not as a grudging social necessity, but as a way to advance their tribe over other tribes.

This is not to say that warrior-king cultures lacked any aspect of proving yourself. Even among warrior-king cultures, there were still symbolic rites of manhood. Tests of courage, independence, strength, etc. The difference is that these tests usually lasted a day or two, not an entire lifetime. You proved your manhood, and then set out to advance your family, your tribe, etc. Yes, you sought approval and validation, but you didn't waste an entire lifetime seeking those things. It wasn't, "Make enough money to be respected, and then give it away to be more respected." It was, "Prove you can function as a man, and then let's go conquer."

In the modern era, the idea of a warrior-king family seems a bit weird. It would be challenging, to say the least, to conquer new territory by force.

But the ideology doesn't really change; only the weapons do. In the past, people used bronze weapons. Then they used steel weapons. Then they used firearms. Today, we use economic weapons.

What would a warrior-king ideology look like today (assuming you don't live in a violent part of the world, in which case it would just look like it always has)? Let's start with education. It wouldn't be about seeking a degree. It would be about learning the skills to increase your family's holdings. Those skills might be learned on the job, through formal education, independently, through apprenticeships, through online earning, or even through scientific research. You wouldn't be pursuing a degree. You wouldn't be stuck in some foolish and outdated system. You'd be pursuing actual knowledge. The symbolic value of the degree would not matter; the actual value of the knowledge would.

How about sexual, marital, and romantic relationships? In the middle class value system, these are largely for social approval or acquisition. Middle class culture tells us we need a certain type of wife, or some number of sexual conquests. We follow those imperatives as assiduously as we seek college degrees. The symbolic value often massively outweighs the actual value.

In the warrior-king mindset, women exist for a purpose, generally the increase and strengthening of the family or tribe. They are wives, mothers, innovators, strategists, business advisors, engineers. They are part of your team, helping to advance your tribe.

Some manipulators, aware of the power of warrior-king and tribal culture, are attempting to convince young men that their tribe is their entire race, generally the white "race", which actually incorporates many different subraces, religions, ancestral languages, etc. That is completely absurd. Your tribe is not every person on earth with the same skin color as you. That's just bizarre. It's your close genetic relatives and their spouses.

Don't let those collectivists replace one kind of welfarism for another. A woman of the same race as you, who has kids with someone other than you, deserves zero dollars from you. Women who procreate with you, or otherwise directly benefit you, should be rewarded by you, no matter what their race is. Women who do not, should not. We don't expect Nike to pay the employees of Reebok just because they are both shoe companies. Reward those who benefit you, only.

Single race welfarism is just as bad as multicultural welfarism. No one has any right to the fruits of your labor unless you voluntarily give or exchange them. It doesn't matter what skin color a person has; someone who is not serving or benefiting you specifically, is not plausible someone you should feel financially responsible for.

Male power has been diminished because we're forced to give the fruits of our labor to women who have not benefited us at all. Being forced to give the fruits of your labor to women with the same skin color will have the exact same effect. If we want to gain the natural power that comes from economic usefulness, don't give a cent to any woman who hasn't earned it from you, specifically.

Many of the women shrieking men into silence on college campuses are the same race as the men at whom they are shrieking. This has nothing to do with race, and everything to do with individual power. This is fundamentally a battle of the individual or family versus the large, faceless collective. Racial tribalism is not warrior culture; it's just collectivist welfarism, and will erode male power just as much as collectivist welfarism always does.

Open Borders; No Welfare

Racial Tribalists and White Nationalists have become increasingly opposed to immigration. Depending on how you look at it, immigration can either be hugely helpful or hugely disadvantageous to our access to our natural rights.

In the context of a welfare state, obviously open borders would be problematic. Instead of paying for the kids of every feckless American woman that you didn't procreate with, you'd be paying for the kids of every woman on earth that you didn't procreate with. People would flood in seeking welfare funded by your work - government schools, medicaid, food stamps, etc. You'd end up working endlessly to pay for kids that weren't yours. You'd be increasingly forced to operate against your natural genetic interest and common sense.

Today, as American welfarism becomes world famous, immigration, particularly illegal immigration, has changed to reflect this. According to a May, 2018 article in the National Review, "For the longest time, illegal immigration was driven by single males from Mexico. Over the last decade, the flow has shifted to women, children, and family units from Central America." Single men know there is little reason to sneak into a bastion of welfare. I've personally spoken to a few single men who left America for Mexico, so they could pay lower welfare taxes![1]

---

1) National Review: *The Truth About Separating Kids*

As America became more the land of welfare than the land of opportunity, this change happened. If we change it again, people will instead be sneaking in to work for you, serve you, buy from you, benefit you. Imagine if the women who were sneaking into America didn't already have kids that they expected you to pay for? Imagine if they were coming to America to, for example, bear kids for you? In that world, why not open the borders, and turn that trickle into a flood?

Some argue that open borders, even in the absence of welfare, mean that we will face economic competition. For example, if you are a software developer, you would face competition from foreigners. But realistically, you're already facing that competition. If you are a computer programmer, you're already facing competition from computer programmers in other countries. The same is true if you are an engineer or involved with any kind of manufacturing. At the moment, however, those competitors are not buying much from inside of America. A programmer stuck in Pakistan isn't going to buy much from American grocery stores, restaurants, clothing stores, etc. Right now, people in other countries are competitors, but they aren't spending their money here.

When it comes to many jobs, you'll have a huge advantage over foreign competitors if you speak fluent English and understand American culture. It will be an advantage in most parts of the service sector, many parts of management, etc.

If you're an entrepreneur, you'll have more potential customers. If those Asian computer programmers are now living in America and spending in America, they might spend some of their money at your business. If you have a job, they might spend money on the products or services your company produces, helping it grow and creating more opportunities for you.

Now consider what it means for sexual competition for women. Today, many American women have made themselves about as unpleasant and unattractive as a woman can be. They can get away with it because they aren't facing much competition. But, what if they were facing a mountain of foreign competition? That would be more opportunities for you and more competition pressure on American women. You wouldn't be in a position of having to settle for tenth rate American merchandise. Millions of economically desperate women with traditional values would be waiting for you. You don't need to be an economist to see the advantages that would bring to American men.

If we can eliminate the entire welfare state - government schools, medicaid, and food stamps - then the best thing we can do next is encourage completely open borders. Let's flood the marketplace of women with higher quality competition, and reap the benefits.

CHAPTER 39:

Lessons from Warrior Culture

Hector

One of the most critical, defining works of masculinity is the Iliad, the story of the Trojan war. According to many analysts, including philosopher Robert Pirsig, author of *Zen and the Art of Motorcycle Maintenance*, the defining moment of the story is when Hector, the prince of Troy, goes out to fight against Achilles in single combat.

Achilles cannot be defeated. Hector has no chance. His defeat and death are certain. His wife knows this, and she begs him to stay. He himself knows it; he will fight his hardest, but he will die.

On the surface, it seems insane. What kind of idiot would go to a certain death?

But consider the alternative. What if Hector had decided to stay behind the walls of Troy, and refuse to fight? At that moment, he would have basically said that the principles of courage, honor, and fighting for your values, the principles that defined who he was, weren't real. He would have denied the very essence of himself. He wouldn't have died; he would have been erased. He might have "lived" to an old age. He might have found some way to be useful. But he wouldn't have been Hector. He wouldn't have embodied the principles that Hector chose to define himself with. Certain death was better than certain erasure, than certain annihilation of who he was.

Zen and the Art of Motorcycle Maintenance quotes H.D.F. Kitto's analysis of this situation:

"What moves the Greek warrior to deeds of heroism," Kitto comments, "is not a sense of duty as we understand it...duty towards others: it is rather duty towards himself. He strives after that which we translate 'virtue' but is in Greek areté, 'excellence'."

Hector understood that he had a responsibility to be his truest, greatest self, that he himself, not his commodities, was the measure of who he was, that his own actions defined what Hector meant, what Troy meant, and what masculinity meant.

I cannot imagine that this was the only personal decision that Hector ever had to make. Like most people, he probably had to make hundreds of defining decisions. Each of those decisions clearly identified who he was, and who he was not. He chose to be courageous instead of cowardly, disciplined instead of lazy, honest instead of fake.

Choosing to fight Achilles, the unstoppable force, was his last and most significant decision, where he chose his essense over his life. Being who he was mattered more than even being alive. It was far better to die than to have his fundamental self erased.

I believe that many men today, in America, are living in a state of erasure. We made decisions that caused us to sacrifice who we were. Instead of fighting for our reality, for who we really are, we let our fundamental nature get erased.

Many of us have faced moments where we've had to choose between the courage of being ourselves, and the cowardice of being what someone else wants us to be. It's almost never a life or death choice. We don't sacrifice who we are in order to stay alive. Instead, we sacrifice who we are for minor gains, for social approval, for small amounts of money, for low value sex.

We apologize to traffic cops and judges in order not to pay some minor amount of money. In that moment, we are saying that our integrity is worth a couple hundred dollars. We pretend to support the welfarism of third wave feminism for social approval or minor sexual gain. In that moment, we are saying that our political values are worth less than being 20th in line to have sex with some girl we don't even respect, or the social approval of morons.

Some of us are, in our hearts, inherently polygamist. Unlike gay men who openly declare their sexuality, we hide ours in the closet. When society told gay men their sexuality was wrong, gay men found inner pride, and told society to screw itself. They also worked heavily to influence entertainment and media, to gain value dominance.

But those of us who are inherently polygamist are usually not open or proud about it. Nor do we even bother to pursue it, outside of lazy secret affairs. In that, we are saying that our sexuality that is inborn with us is worth less than society's opinion. We abnegate ourselves preemptively.

By doing this in so many areas of our lives, we end up living in a half alive reality, anesthetizing ourselves with alcohol, drugs, and pointless entertainment. By denying all true aspects of ourselves, we end up becoming shadows of our true selves.

I've lost track of how many men have told me that they feel closer to their true sexuality when watching pornography than when having sex with actual women. What an absurdity! How can imaginary flat images possibly compete with physical reality?

Unless, of course, you have so denied every important part of who you are that even your sexuality has become numbed. Unless the only moments that your true self can surface is in the private trances created by pornography, where the social pressures you've given in to are no longer deforming your soul.

What if Hector had made all of his life decisions the other way, choosing cowardice, laziness, and dishonesty instead of courage, discipline, and integrity? He'd be someone else. The legendary Hector from history would not have existed. But the person he was meant to be would, I believe, still be there. It would still be a nagging idea in the back of his mind, a true self, truer than the person he'd resigned himself to becoming.

That's the situation many of us are in right now. For many of us, our true selves have never existed. We have simply never been. Our true selves have just been a thought in the back of our minds, so deeply buried, so unformed, that they're almost never present.

How do we become that person? I believe it's about choices. Every time you choose courage over cowardice, stand for what you believe in rather than pretending to believe something else for some trivial gain, you become more yourself.

Most of us, realistically, won't have to choose between our true selves and our lives. Most of the time, it will be choosing between our true selves and some paltry amount of money, some trivial amount of social approval, or some low value sex. Most of us choose the wrong thing out of panic, or when choosing short term gain instead of long term gain.

How do you reverse that? Practice. Practice saying exactly what you should say in different situations. Don't wait for the high pressure situation to happen. Practice in your head, out loud, or with a friend. Consider the situations in which you're likely to compromise who you are, and then plan out what you're going to say. If someone says, "I can't date anyone who believes _____", be ready to say, "That's okay, I don't like to surround myself with closed minded people. It was nice meeting you." If someone starts publicly bashing you for your opposition to the welfare state, be ready to stay calm, and use their fury to spread your message. Practice both sticking to your principles and maintaining masculine politeness.

Hector always knew that he would never sacrifice his true self for anything, even his life. He'd practiced that decision a million times before the moment of truth. At the moment of truth, he only had to pick the right words to express the decision he'd already made.

Be prepared to choose your true self over anything, and you will become the person you are meant to be.

The Bhagvad Gita

The Iliad is the most significant warrior epic in western culture. In Indian culture, the Mahabharata has a similar role. In this story, armies led by the five good brothers (the Pandavas) are about to face in epic battle the armies lead by their hundred evil cousins (the Kauravas).

The greatest warrior of the Pandavas is named Arjun. He is in a war chariot driven by the god Krishna. Unlike Hector, Arjun knows he is the superior fighter. He knows that he can wreak hell and destruction on his enemies. Like Hector, he would sacrifice his life before he sacrificed his courage, but his moral dilemma is a vastly different one, and a central dilemma of masculinity.

Arjun has come to the front of the battle lines, giving his armies great hope and inspiration. He looks upon the opposing army, ready to obliterate them.

Among the opposing army he sees his former teachers, whom he respects greatly. He sees hundreds of his kinmen. And his will to kill them vanishes. He says:

"Krishna! as I behold, come here to shed

Their common blood, yon concourse of our kin,

My members fail, my tongue dries in my mouth,

A shudder thrills my body, and my hair

Bristles with horror; from my weak hand slips

Gandiv, the goodly bow...what rich spoils

Could profit; what rule recompense; what span

Of life itself seem sweet, bought with such blood?

...grandsires, sires, and sons,

Brothers, and fathers-in-law, and sons-in-law,

Elders and friends! Shall I deal death on these

Even though they seek to slay us?"

This situation begins the most important sacred text in Hinduism, the Bhagavad Gita. In this text, the god Krishna answers Arjun's dilemma by exploring what it means to be a warrior, what it means to have responsibility to oneself, one's tribe, and one's principles, and most importantly, what it means to pursue right action even when unsure of the outcome.

Krishna says:

"How hath this weakness taken thee? Whence springs

The inglorious trouble, shameful to the brave,

Barring the path of virtue?"

As it was for the Greeks, virtue, again meaning something closer to "excellence", was a central principle in Krishna's response.

As he continues this intense discourse of enlightenment, Krishna says:

"If, knowing thy duty and thy task, thou bidd'st

Duty and task go by--that shall be sin!

And those to come shall speak thee infamy

From age to age; but infamy is worse

For men of noble blood to bear than death!"

If you know what you're supposed to do, and then choose not to do it out of fear, or sympathy, or empathy, or sentimentality, that is a sin against your own virtue. It is making yourself less; it is erasing your true essence; it is worse than death. Like Hector, Krishna understands that there are worse things than death or killing.

Krishna takes it further. He understands that actions matter, but who you are is defined by your thoughts. He advises Arjun not to seek external rewards, but rather to dedicate his mind to truth. The mind must be uncompromising. He says:

"Yet, the right act

Is less, far less, than the right-thinking mind.

Seek refuge in thy soul; have there thy heaven!

Scorn them that follow virtue for her gifts!

The mind of pure devotion--even here--

Casts equally aside good deeds and bad,

Passing above them. Unto pure devotion

Devote thyself: with perfect meditation

Comes perfect act, and the right-hearted rise--

More certainly because they seek no gain--

Forth from the bands of body, step by step,

To highest seats of bliss."

Through Krishna and Hector we see the fundamental core of true masculinity: willing to fight for your truth, your reality, your principles, no matter what the odds of success. Masculinity isn't about calculating odds of short term gain, and then deciding what to do. It's about making decisions based on integrity and principles.

Atticus Finch states this beautifully in *To Kill a Mockingbird*: "I wanted you to see what real courage is, instead of getting the idea that courage is a man with a gun in his hand. It's when you know you're licked before you begin but you begin anyway and you see it through no matter what. You rarely win, but sometimes you do."

We see the same in the masculine principle of sportsmanship. Athletes are expected to play their hearts out during a game. Afterwards, if they lose, they are expected to do so gracefully, shake their opponents hand, and remember that the pursuit of excellence embodied in athletics is deeper than who happens to win. We recognize the excellence embodied in the pursuit; a man who cannot see that, who loses his temper if he loses a game, is rightly seen as weak.

The same principle is discussed in Rudyard Kipling's poem "If", which he wrote as a description of masculinity for his own son. A man, he says, "can meet with Triumph and Disaster/And treat those two impostors just the same".

Even Hollywood can see this truth. In *Braveheart*, William Wallace's character embodies this masculine principle. He's fighting for freedom, but he also recognizes that he is overmatched. In his moment of supposed defeat, in the moment at which he is about to be executed, he remains true to the principle of freedom, even shouting out the word, "Freedom!" with his dying breath. It doesn't matter that he "loses". He stays true to his principles, his definition of excellence.

Those who want to weaken you as a man will first attack that fundamental principle. They will try to trick you into pursuing only the things that seem likely, rather than the tasks that are worthy of you. They will tell you that you are foolish for pursuing worthwhile goals, rather than the ones they deem pragmatic. They will tell you that it is somehow mature or pragmatic to pursue only the goals they want you to believe are likely to succeed.

Those people are afraid of you. They are afraid of what you might do if you tap into the masculine principle of pursuing what is worthy, regardless of the likelihood of victory. They know you might succeed. They know you might change the status quo that they depend on.

The principle of pursuing the right goals, not just the goals that others say are "pragmatic" enough, has been the core of masculinity for thousands of years. It has been what, in the past, allowed men to achieve cultural dominance. As many of us have forgotten or never learned that principle, we have lost that dominance. We've substituted the pursuit of insignificant, "practical", short term gains for any purpose of significance. The result is that we've completely lost value dominance.

Other social movements, while they have fooled men into fearful inaction, have pursued bold and seemingly impossible social goals successfully. The trans movement has successfully, legally argued that a person with a penis can be a woman, and a person with a vagina can be a man. A few years ago, anyone would have considered that goal ludicrous. But, by not letting others tell them what pragmatic goals are, they achieved the impossible.

Those who tell you that the welfare state is here to stay, that government schools are here to stay, that we are all condemned to complete economic disempowerment, that we've forever lost our economic right to say no, are just trying to trick you. They know those things are completely changeable. They know you can change them. They just don't want you to. They are trying to trick you into believing those goals are impossible, so you don't pursue them.

In my life, I've learned something important. I am not smart enough to know what the strategic move is. What might be politically strategic in one decade could be politically suicidal in another. But,

I've learned that I can pretty much always figure out what the right thing to do is.

Even when acting with integrity doesn't give material gain, you end up strengthening your own integrity - or at least not losing it. But when you act just for external gain, without integrity, you always lose your integrity, and only occasionally actually get external gain.

The businesses that pursue dollars instead of innovation and excellence usually end up with neither, but the businesses that pursue excellence and innovation often end up with money too. The men who sycophantically fawn over women, sacrificing their personal and political views, usually aren't very successful with women anyway. The men who refuse to kowtow to someone else's values, in addition to maintaining their own integrity, are often more successful with women.

But even if it was reversed, it wouldn't matter. No external gain can possibly match up to the value of maintaining your own integrity. In the Christian Bible, this is summed up perfectly: "For what shall it profit a man, if he shall gain the whole world, and lose his own soul?"

Your soul, your integrity, who you truly are, matter more than all the external gain. Being true to yourself matters more than money, social approval, or sex. If you lose yourself, all the other things cannot make up for it. But if you regain yourself, those other things just don't matter as much.

CHAPTER 40:

The Two Poles of the Masculine Experience: Adam and Jesus

The Christian Bible shows many great struggles of masculinity. We see Moses developing from a shy and uncertain boy to a powerful leader of men. We see the struggles of David, of the Israelite warriors, of many other strong leaders. We see men weakened by fear. We see men triumphant when they overcome fear.

Sometimes it's the same men who vacillate between courage and cowardice. Peter, out of fear of the Roman government, denied that he was a follower of Jesus. Later, he found his courage, and, when he was crucified, he requested to be crucified upside down, according to historical legend. He declared that he was unworthy to be crucified in the same way as his Lord. The same man who fearfully denied his leader later boldly told the Roman empire to go ahead with its punishment, and to make it worse.

But I believe that the most important lessons in masculinity come from a much broader view. The two most important men in the Bible are Adam and Jesus. These two men also represent, in my view, the fundamental struggle of masculinity.

Adam is weak and fearful. He's tricked by his wife into eating the fruit from the Tree of Knowledge. But he doesn't own up to his mistake. Instead, when God comes walking through the Garden of Eden, Adam hides and cowers.

"And they heard the voice of the Lord God walking in the garden in the cool of the day: and Adam and his wife hid themselves from the presence of the Lord God amongst the trees of the garden."

Jesus is the opposite. He fears nothing and no one. He opposes the religious authority and the political authority of the time. He's willing to die rather than renounce his view of reality. He proves this by dying, rather than renouncing his view of reality.

Like the other mythic figures mentioned, Jesus embodies the fundamental principle of masculinity. He works to do what he considers excellence, regardless of the likelihood of success. He doesn't worry about what's likely to work. In fact, at an initial glance, his methods fail spectacularly. He ends up being tortured to death.

But in the very moment of his supposed defeat, he achieves a legendary greatness that has lasted for millenia. The fundamentally masculine act of pursuing personal truths and personal excellence, while remaining indifferent to the consequences, has made him a legendary embodiment of masculinity.

If you've never read the bible, I recommend reading the Gospels. They aren't that long, and the character of Jesus is completely fearless and relentless. If you take out the supernatural elements of the Gospels, the story reads a lot more like the show *Firefly*. Interestingly, Thomas Jefferson did just that: he took out the supernatural parts of the bible, and instead used it as a template on how to behave. Given that Thomas Jefferson helped author the Declaration of Independence, one of the most famous examples of pulling out in history, it stands to reason that there are personal lessons for even secular people to learn from the Bible. I'm pretty much about as atheistic as it gets, but even I find inspiration in the Bible.

Jesus and Adam represent the two opposing poles in most men. Which man has never told a panic lie? Which man has never hidden a mistake? Which men has never been afraid, and backed down in front of more powerful opposition?

But most of us have had moments of fearlessness, or at least imagined them. We know what it looks like to refuse to kowtow to powerful opposition. We know it's scary. But we also know that you can only show strength and courage in the face of fear.

Consider those poles within yourself. There is a part of you that's weak, fearful, and hiding. No matter how many material possessions that part of you has, it will always feel weak and afraid. Adam had dominion over all living things, but it wasn't enough to make him strong.

That Adam part of us isn't going anywhere. It's part of me just as much as it's part of you.

But there's also that Jesus part of all of us, the part that is strong and powerful, no matter how few things it has. Jesus had very little in terms of material wealth or military might, but it didn't stop him from being fearless.

Most of the world will try to bring out that Adam part of you, the weak and afraid part. They will try to make you dependent on material things and social approval. They want you living in childish obedience and fearfulness.

Fight them with the Jesus part of your psyche, the part that is willing to defy any social order. In the Bible, Jesus is particularly skilled at debating with those who disagree with him. He's clever and bold.

If you're nonreligious like me, you've probably only seen Jesus pictured as a baby or dying on the cross. The religious establishment has obvious reasons to portray this, since those are basically the only two times that Jesus isn't actively opposing some establishment. The actual story, by the way, is not "Once there was a baby, and then he died." Not all of the gospels even mention his infancy. They focus primarily on his adult life, just as any normal biography would. That adult life is so anti-authoritarian that authorities tend to deemphasize it.

One of the most famous scenes in Jesus's life is when he storms into a synagogue, kicks over the tables of moneylenders and sellers of animals for sacrifice, and leaves those in charge too stunned to know what to do.

"And Jesus went into the temple of God, and cast out all them that sold and bought in the temple, and overthrew the tables of the moneychangers, and the seats of them that sold doves, And said unto them, It is written, My house shall be called the house of prayer; but ye have made it a den of thieves."

Given the extent to which theft has been normalized in American culture, that passage certainly hits close to home. My guess is you haven't seen that image in many stained glass windows.

That part of you, the part that's willing to defy, mock, and break the spoken and unspoken rules of a powerful establishment, is real. But just as they try to deemphasize the badass elements of Jesus's life, they will try to do the same with your psyche. They'll call that part impractical, nonexistent, immature, anachronistic, imaginary. But that part of you is real, far more real than the cowering, obedient sycophant they want you to be.

Only you can silence yourself. Only you can make yourself speak out.

Only you can turn yourself into the cowering, silent type. Only you can turn yourself into the bold, honest, powerful type.

Only you can sacrifice your own reality. Only you can fight for it.

When the Marquis de Sade was locked in prison for writing obscenity, he didn't just shut up. Even the Bastille was not enough to silence him. With four scrolls of parchment that a friend smuggled into his cell, he wrote the legendary 120 Days of Sodom, easily the most obscene book I've ever read. No one but the Marquis de Sade could silence the Marquis de Sade. It turned out he wasn't that interested in silencing himself.

Gandhi, the leader of one of the greatest mutinies against an established status quo in history, was willing to take his refusal to comply even further. He famously told his followers, "They may torture my body, break my bones, even kill me. Then they will have my dead body, but not my obedience."

This world belongs to you just as much as it belongs to anyone else. You, your mind, and your work belong to you more than they belong to anyone else. Your reality matters just as much as any alternative. Will you fight for it?

CPSIA information can be obtained
at www.ICGtesting.com
Printed in the USA
BVHW052206050622
638986BV00011B/190